I0805301

A Colonial Tragedy

A COLONIAL TRAGEDY

The Chinese Massacre at Batavia, 1740

Leonard Blussé

Leiden University Press

Cover design: Andre Klijsen
Cover illustration: 'Afbeelding van dat gedeelte van Batavia, alwaar eigentlyk de Schrikkelyke Slagting der Chinezen, na de Ontdekking van hun Verraad, geschied is, den 9. Octob: 1740' by printmaker Adolf van der Laan, collection Rijksmuseum, Amsterdam.
Lay-out: Crius Group, Hulshout
Printer: Scanlaser bv, Zaandam

Every effort has been made to obtain permission to use all copyrighted illustrations reproduced in this book. Nonetheless, whosoever believes to have rights to this material is advised to contact the publisher.

ISBN 9789087284770
e-ISBN 9789400605145 (e-PDF)
e-ISBN 9789400605411 (e-PUB)
https://doi.org/10.24415/9789087284770
NUR 680

© 2023 Leonard Blussé
Translated from the Dutch language
De Chinezenmoord
First published by Uitgeverij Balans, Amsterdam

Leiden University Press, Rapenburg 73, 2311 GJ Leiden

All rights reserved. Without limiting the rights under copyright reserved above, no part of this book may be reproduced, stored in or introduced into a retrieval system, or transmitted, in any form or by any means (electronic, mechanical, photocopying, recording or otherwise) without the written permission of both the publisher and the editors of the book.

Contact EU General Product Safety Regulation (GPSR): productsafety@lup.nl

Table of Contents

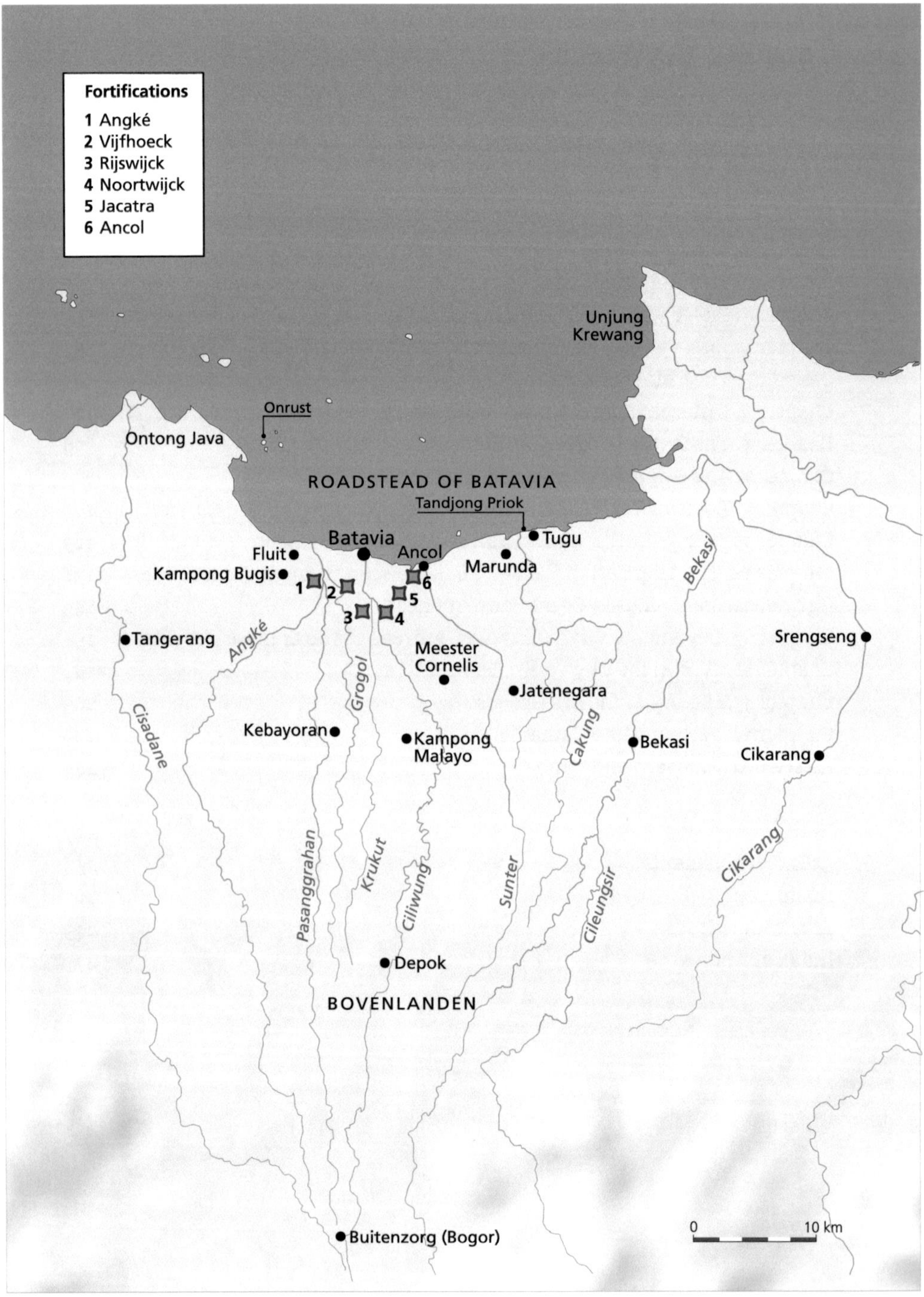

BATAVIA AND OMMELANDEN

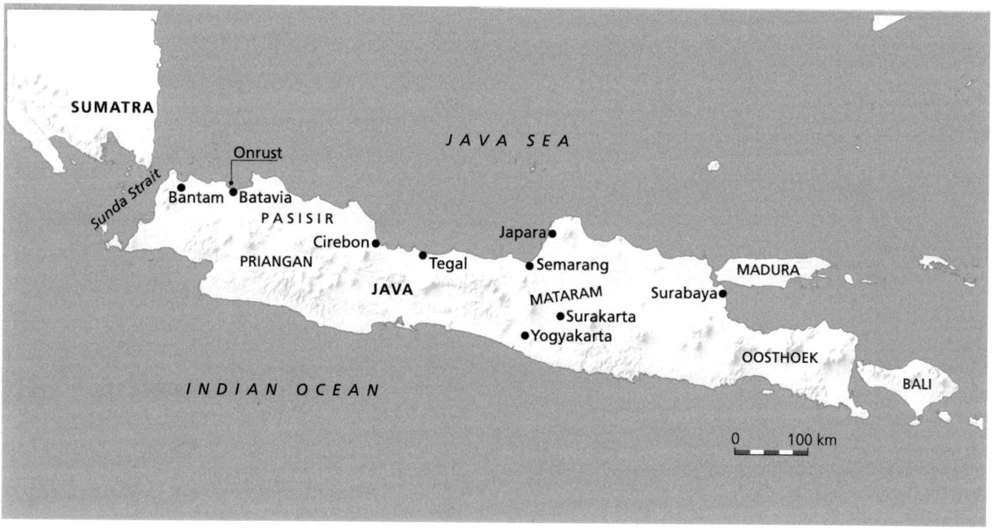
SUMATRA
JAVA SEA
Onrust
Sunda Strait
Bantam
Batavia
PASISIR
Cirebon
PRIANGAN
Tegal
Japara
Semarang
JAVA
MATARAM
Surakarta
Yogyakarta
Surabaya
MADURA
OOSTHOEK
BALI
INDIAN OCEAN
0
100 km

JAVA

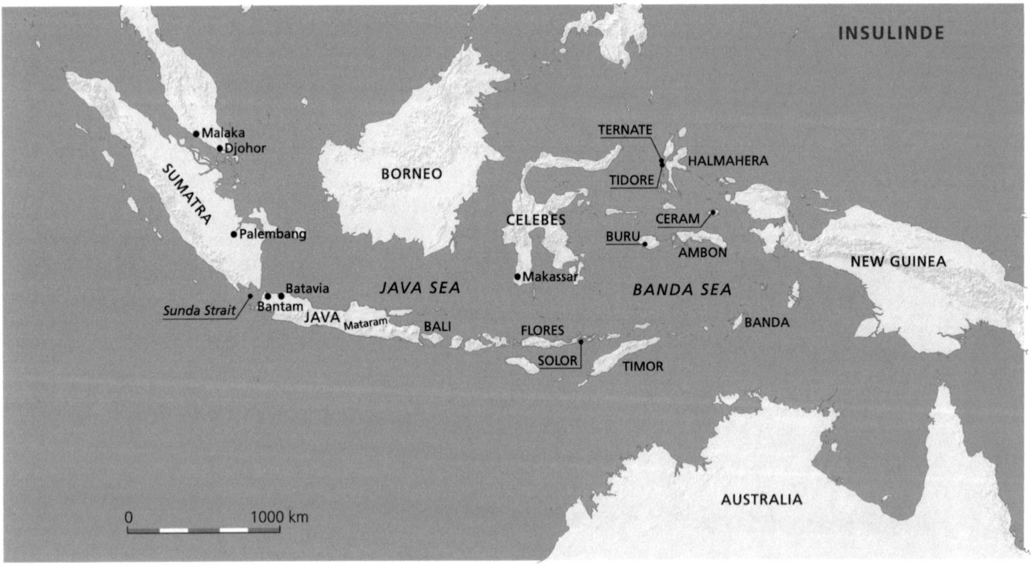

THE EAST INDIAN ARCHIPELAGO

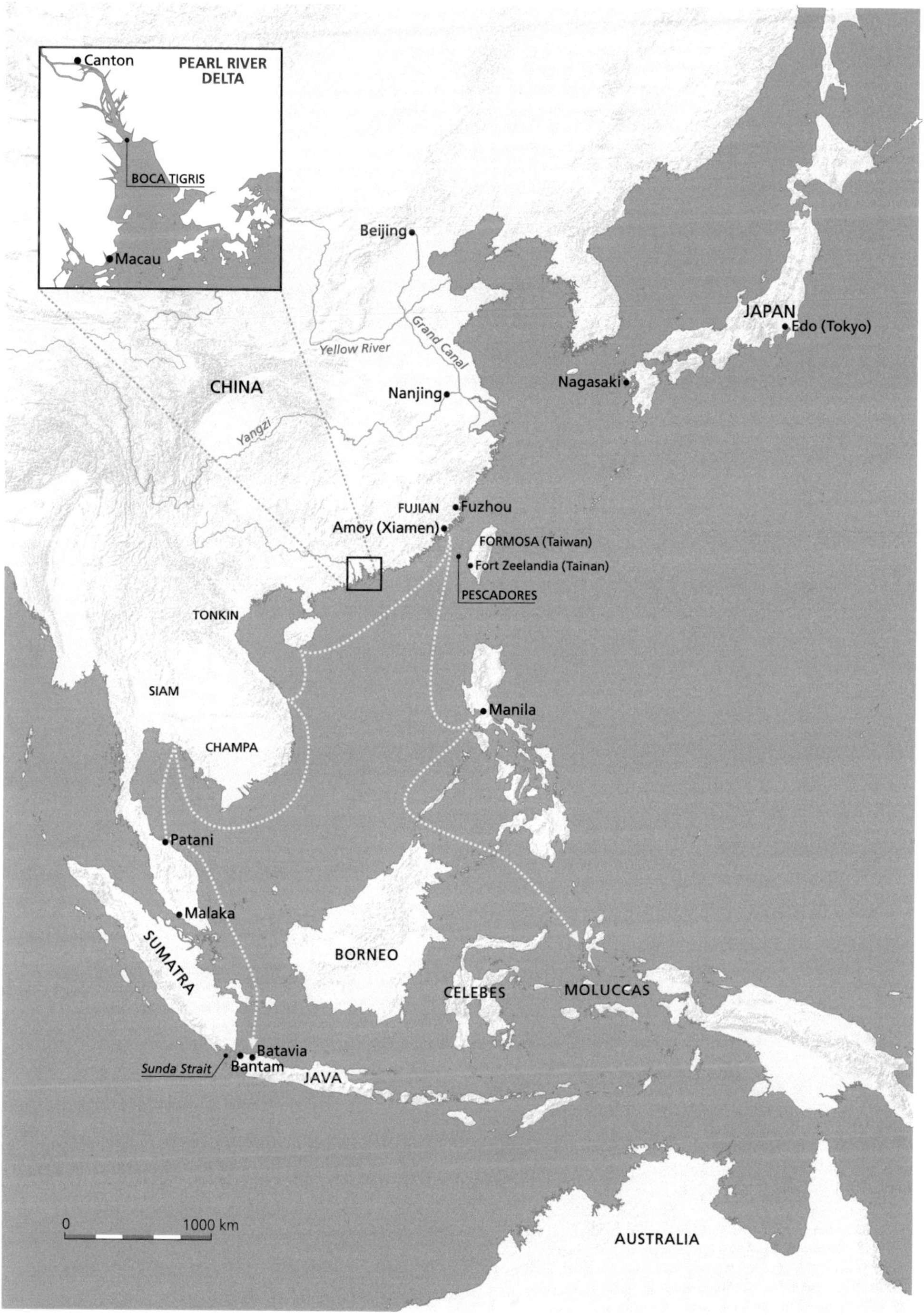

THE CHINA SEAS AND THE WESTERN AND EASTERN ROUTES

Foreword

> 'The world is a spectacle,
> each plays his part and gets his share.'
> —Joost van den Vondel.

In the early days of September 1741, the Gentlemen XVII, the directors of the United East India Company (VOC), held a board meeting in Amsterdam to await the arrival of the Christmas Fleet from Batavia. The previous month, several ships had already arrived with shocking rumors about a massive Chinese uprising in the hinterland of the Company's headquarters in Asia, which had provoked the massacre of all Batavia's Chinese between 9 and 14 October 1740. The waiting was for more reliable information.

On 7 September, the VOC ship, Nieuwerkerk, arrived with the councilor of the Indies, Elias de Haze, on board. To everyone's surprise he explained that Governor-General Adriaan Valckenier had banished him, along with two other councilors, Gustaaf Willem van Imhoff and Isaac van Schinne, for insubordination. As the other two gentlemen had been put on different ships, the wait was now for Van Imhoff and Van Schinne. When all three of them had finally arrived, they showed up at the Company's office in Amsterdam to explain themselves. After hearing them, the VOC board decided to disassociate itself from the expulsion order and restored the three councilors to their dignity. When informed of the dramatic events, the States General, the central government of the Dutch Republic in The Hague, immediately requested further clarification. On the basis of the information received, a commission of enquiry reached within one month the conclusion that serious crimes had been committed in Batavia and that those responsible should be prosecuted.

The Chinese rebellion and the ensuing 'Batavian fury,' as the massacre of the Chinese became known, caused a stir throughout the country. Newspapers and pamphlets were filled with sensational accounts of the 'infamous treachery of the rebellious Chinese brood' and its aftermath. In one of these pamphlets the anonymous author purported 'to have been told in a dream' what had actually happened. 'The river god of Batavia,' had revealed to him how a Chinese rebellion against the colonial regime had been nipped in the bud by the massacre in the city. In the face of this popular condemnation of the rebellious 'pernicious Chinese brood' that had received its well-deserved punishment, the Frisian poet, Willem van Haren, dared to stand up for the

Chinese. He believed that the city's Chinese inhabitants had been the victims of Dutch bloodlust.

> What Drama is this? What People are thus mistreated? ...
> It is not a Gaul, a Roman or an Indian,
> Who dares to strike his cruel hand at the helpless?
> Christians! they are, O Heavens! Batavians!
> Far madder than bulls whipped for battle and vengeance:
> They gave rein to their lust for Murder.[1]

No less than a hundred years passed by before the first critical study of the bloodbath in the city was published. In 1840, Batavian pastor W. R. van Hoëvell felt compelled to open 'a page [of colonial history] that must fill every Dutchman and Christian with sadness and shame.'[2] Based on original archival documents, Van Hoëvell made a precise reconstruction of the dramatic events of October 1740. In drawing his conclusions, however, he saw it as his task to exonerate the colonial regime. According to him, it was not the administration but one man who had emphatically failed: the killing had been executed under the sole authority of Governor-General Adriaan Valckenier. Everything was due to the man's pernicious character. Had he not 'behaved in a cowardly and petty manner when danger threatened and was he not callous and cruel when it was unnecessary'? For Van Hoëvell, the 'whodunit' was resolved.

Another hundred years later, the historian, J. Th. Vermeulen, obtained his doctorate in 1938 for a full-fledged academic study of the tragedy.[3] After research in the National Archive at the Hague, he concluded that it was impossible to lay all the blame at the feet of Valckenier.[4] He found no evidence that the governor-general had ordered the massacre. Contrary to Van Hoëvell, Vermeulen laid the blame on a 'government weakened by internal divisions, headed by an indecisive and listless man, incapable of leading in dire circumstances.' Vermeulen's study was partly translated into English in the early 1950s, and has since served as the source material for more or less historical studies, in which colorful views are presented along the well-trodden path of heroic Chinese resistance to colonial rule, deep-rooted racial hatred, genocide, and freedom struggles. Only in a few cases has an original approach been attempted.[5]

Now that almost another hundred years have passed since Vermeulen shed light on the 'Chinese troubles,' it is time for a revision. Fascinated by the events of October 1740, Van Hoëvell and Vermeulen paid little attention to the establishment of Batavia and the Ommelanden as colonial societies and the fundamental role played by the Chinese community in this historical process. Nor did they examine the aftermath of the affair. Although Van Hoëvell published a paraphrased translation of a unique, contemporary Chinese history of Batavia, he did little with it.[6] That is a pity, because the 'Chinese Annals of Batavia,' the *Kai Ba Lidai Shiji*, dating from 1793, give a unique view of the events. Instead of Valckenier, this Chinese source identifies his successor, Van Imhoff, as the instigator of the Chinese uprising, and therefore ultimately holds *him* responsible for the massacre in the city. The Chinese author says that the massacre was the unfortunate outcome of the rebellion which was caused by Van Imhoff's diabolical measures.

To reopen the case, let us start with two key questions: why were 'ten thousand Chinese' living in Batavia? And what role did they play in the colonial city and its hinterland? There are a handful of excellent studies on the social history of 'Old Batavia' in the VOC era, but nowadays, 'colonial history' is in such bad taste that hardly anyone wants to dwell on the colonization process as such. Nevertheless, the first part of this book will deal with the genesis of Batavia and its hinterland, a story that can only be understood against the broader background of the interaction between the Dutch and the surrounding indigenous polities of the Indonesian archipelago. After all, this Sino-Dutch colonial city was laid like a cuckoo's egg in the midst of Javanese society.

Was the massacre of the Chinese the result of the colonial administration's failed policies, of conflicting interests, or, as has been so often suggested, was it simply the inevitable product of long-dormant racial hatred? As we shall see, the latter is not very obvious, for in Batavia, the Dutch and Chinese coexisted in remarkable harmony for over a hundred years. Or did something happen in the years prior to the Chinese revolt that led to a breakdown in the mutual understanding of these communities?

The tragedy as a benchmark

The Batavian fury has all the elements of the tragedies that the Greeks used to depict human failings and the twists of fate on stage. *Tragoidia* is about 'la condition humaine,' the human flaw. Timeless themes such as ruthless struggles for power, with seemingly inevitable fatal twists, have set the tone for a dramatic tradition extending well over a thousand years from ancient Greece to Europe's renaissance and even after. Curiously, we will see that, in the Batavian case, the stage itself, that is, Mother Nature, also played her part as an actor in the background.

At the beginning of the seventeenth century, when theater was resurging all over Western Europe, the spectacular changes of regime in 'exotic' Asia captured the imagination of the Amsterdam theater audience and held up an 'East Indian' mirror to the spectators.[7] In his tragedy, *Zungchin*, the famous seventeen century's playwright, Joost van den Vondel, depicted how the last Ming emperor of China, 'a man possessed of intemperate avarice' and for this reason hated by his subjects, met his mortal fate.[8] One hundred years after Vondel, Onno Zwier van Haren (1713–1779), the brother of the above mentioned poet, Willem van Haren, wrote a tragedy in five acts, *Agon, sulthan of Bantam*, in which he showed how the VOC deviously deprived the old and devout Sultan Agon of Bantam of his throne.[9] Had Willem van Haren not already devoted a poetic lament to the Chinese massacre, Onno Zwier might have devoted a tragedy to it too.

The way Renaissance tragedy is set out, with the stage, the 'exposition' where the plot develops, the climax and finally the 'peripety' (turning point), has been a source of inspiration for me. The narrative has been divided into several acts in order to evoke the sequence of events which led to the catastrophic events in and around Batavia. It will be demonstrated how two protagonists, entrapped by the logic of the situation, brought about their own chaos. Colonial society became unmanageable and this resulted in a disaster that might have been averted by the actions of a competent leadership.

Anti-Chinese ethnic strife, persecution, and even massacres are, regrettably, a familiar occurrence in the history of Southeast Asia. The various massacres that took place in Manila in the seventeenth and eighteenth centuries, the Batavian massacre of 1740 and the 1965 mass killings in Indonesia are probably the most notorious. Although it is tempting to compare the other events with the present story, I have decided not to do so. As will be shown, the origins of the Batavian bloodbath were pretty much *sui generis*, even if they led to the same horrific outcome.

CHAPTER 1

Setting the Stage: Dutch trade and the Chinese Diaspora

Close to one million Europeans sailed to Asia as employees of the Dutch East India Company. With the sole rights to all commerce east of the Cape of Good Hope, the *Verenigde Oost-Indische Compagnie* (VOC), the world's first incorporated trading company, possessed during its nearly two hundred years of existence (1602–1799) an unassailable position within Dutch society. The Company's significant economic presence was evidenced by its ownership of large warehouses and shipyards in six prominent port cities: Amsterdam, Hoorn, Enkhuizen, Delft, Rotterdam, and Middelburg. This substantial infrastructure, along with its role as the largest and most stable employer in the country, solidified the Company's position as a major economic entity. With more than twenty thousand employees on its payroll at home and in Asia, the VOC provided not only the Netherlands but all of Europe with Asian products.[10]

The contribution of the Asian commerce to the Dutch gross national product was much greater than the 7 percent that is generally assumed, for the simple reason that the East India Company faced a formidable competitor: its own personnel. On board each ship returning from Asia, in addition to the so-called permitted trade of the Company servants, a fortune in private merchandise was smuggled in upon arrival, notwithstanding all kinds of strict rules to prevent this 'illegal' trade.[11] Each crew member, from skipper to sailor, was entitled to carry a precisely determined volume of private goods. But for a small tip, the inspectors, known as *garbuleurs*, were usually willing to look the other way.

Self-enrichment among Company servants in the East Indies occurred at all levels. This is not surprising, since the salaries paid by the Company were meager—no one could make a decent living on that. In his *East Indian Mirror*, ship's surgeon, Nicolaus de Graaff, noted that the ways and means of private commerce were 'motley and coarse beyond words.' 'Illegal, private trade could not be eradicated or forbidden in spite of the severe corporal punishments put upon it.'[12] Anyone who repatriated, did so with a chest full of porcelain, lacquerware, precious stones, or other curiosities.[13] Governor-General Van Imhoff, who we will meet below, saw no harm in this pilfering. Although a lot of the VOC's fortune ended up in the pockets of its employees, he thought everyone involved and even the Company itself, fared well enough.[14] Thus, not only the personnel in Asia but also the Company elite in Holland engaged in some kind of illegal trafficking. The Gentlemen XVII, the exceedingly wealthy directors living in their mansions along Amsterdam's canals, sold appointments underhand, all the way from merchant to skipper. It is no wonder that after the bankruptcy in 1799, it was said that the VOC had 'perished under corruption' (*Vergaan Onder Corruptie*). Of course, that was not the only reason why the Company came to an end.

In the first seventy years of its existence, the VOC managed to establish a comprehensive trade network in Asian waters, linking dozens of ports to its headquarters in Batavia on the island of Java. While its competitors had to export large quantities of precious metals to Asia because Europe had few attractive commodities to offer to Asia, the Dutch Company initially could purchase Asian products for export to Europe from the surplus profit gained from its spice monopolies within Asia itself.[15]

In the long run, however, the Company's supremacy did not last. Gradually, the VOC also became dependent on annual shipments of capital from Europe. In the second half of the eighteenth century, the British East India Company outstripped her Dutch sister by establishing a mighty power base in India. The renowned seventeenth-century jurist Hugo Grotius had already predicted this: 'The English seek their way as merchants, the Dutch as warriors, the English seek to profit, the Dutch seek to stabilize their affairs forever.'[16]

The VOC as a politically stable factor

It is not often that a Company can function in virtually unchanged institutional form for two hundred years. What explained the sustainability of the VOC in Asia? Apart from monopolies on spices and cinnamon, and enforced trade contracts on products for export such as tin, coffee, sugar, and pepper, the VOC possessed a secret weapon: its highly efficient logistical organizational structure in Asia. Under normal circumstances, all the trading posts of the Company were continuously supplied with trained personnel who were basically subject to the same legal principles and regulations. While promotions and succession issues were the Achilles' heel of any Asian kingdom or principality, the directorate in Holland, the Gentlemen XVII, determined who could fill the most important positions, while the High Government in Batavia decided on lower-level appointments. Thanks to this stable setup, the Company became entrenched within the changeable political world of the Indonesian archipelago, and thus the foundation for the Dutch colonial empire was gradually laid.

This is not to say that the VOC *ruled* the archipelago. Already in the 1930s, the Dutch historian, Jacob van Leur, criticized the then reigning triumphalist colonial historiography and put early modern European presence in Asia in proper perspective. In his view, the VOC was just another merchant in the midst of a bustling Asian trading world. He hardly discerned any innovative effect of the Dutch presence.[17] This view has also been expressed more recently by the German sociologist, André Gunder Frank. With his impressive study, *Reorient*, he sought to indicate how limited the Western influence on Asian traditional society actually was.[18] With their relativist views, these two historians (and many after them) wished to pave the way to an autonomous Asian historiography. But in their enthusiasm, they also overlooked some unique features of the early modern European trading companies.[19] As an extremely stable element, the Company was able to penetrate the trading world of the Indonesian Archipelago and entrench itself there permanently. Somewhat belatedly, the merchants of Coromandel compared the Dutch to snakes 'that everywhere they insert their head, they manage to get the whole body in as well, and that it is their nature to keep everything they have once obtained, and not to separate from it again.'[20] Nevertheless, the Dutch also had to adapt to the Asian environment and the political developments that took place there, as the genesis of their Batavian headquarters shows.

The Malay port principalities

With the spread of Islam in Southeast Asia in the fifteenth and sixteenth centuries, Malay port principalities sprouted up all along the straits and estuaries of the Indonesian archipelago. Not unlike the mercantile city states of Medieval Italy, they were often not much bigger than the settlement itself and a small area of surrounding countryside. For the Malay rulers, the number of subjects was more important than territorial size. The rajas, *pangeran* (princes) or sultans prided themselves on their ornately designed *surat emas* (golden letters), with which they maintained diplomatic relations among themselves, but they by no means shied away from the use of force when it suited them. At the time, except for the fertile volcanic core of Central Java, the island world of Southeast Asia was still sparsely populated. Therefore, raiding to kidnap people for slave labor was a widespread phenomenon in the area.

At the beginning of the sixteenth century, Sunda Kalapa, the renowned trade entrepot of the Hindu kingdom of Pajajaran in West Java, was overrun by its neighbor, the upcoming Muslim principality of Bantam.[21] Re-baptized Jayakarta (Great Victory), the port city was reduced to vassal status and lost its function as a venue for international trade. Located even closer to the Sunda Strait, the passage between the South China Sea and the Indian Ocean, Bantam grew henceforth into the ideal rendezvous for merchants from India and China who traded their own products there for the tropical products of the archipelago. Javanese skippers brought in spices from the Moluccas and traded them for Indian cotton and all sorts of Chinese products such as silk, porcelain, paper, and ironware. Such was the state of affairs when the first Dutch expedition to the Indies anchored at the roadstead of Bantam in 1595. In the years that followed, the VOC stuck to strategically located Bantam in order to coordinate its logistics in the Indonesian archipelago. This changed when in 1611, Jan Pieterszoon Coen was appointed director general of the Company's trade in Asia. Facing fierce competition with English and Chinese merchants while purchasing pepper and other tropical products at the local market, he was fully aware that Bantam's ruler, as a monopolist in the pepper trade, played the Europeans off against each other. Consequently, Coen began to look for another port in West Java where the Company would have more room to develop its activities.

Cuckoo's nest Batavia

It so happened that the ruler of quiet Jayakarta in the shadow of its mighty neighbor, Bantam, wished to breathe new life into his port. He gladly rented out a small plot of land at the mouth of the Ciliwong River where the Dutch merchants were allowed to build a warehouse. That innocent-looking new structure became a Trojan horse when in 1618, Coen, by then already governor-general, suddenly decided to transfer his base from Bantam to Jayakarta. Needless to say, a second warehouse now had to be added to the first. The unexpected move baffled not only Jayakarta's ruler, but also the English, not to mention the Sultan of Bantam, who saw the Company slip out of his grasp. This resulted in a protracted siege of the Jayakarta factory by all of the three parties, until Coen, with reinforcements brought in from the Moluccas, made short work of his opponents. On May 19, 1619, he overran the principality, set fire to the royal residence, and in the name of the States General of the Netherlands, declared the 'Kingdom of Jacatra' a conquered territory. If it had been up to Coen, he would have christened the city New Hoorn in honor of his birthplace, but by orders from Holland in 1621, the conquered territory was named Batavia after the valiant tribe of the Batavi of Roman times.[22]

Tropical Batavia may have gained a Dutch appearance with the canals, ramparts, and gates that were laid out, but in essence, it was more akin to the feudally governed Asian port principalities that neighbored it.[23] Nestled in the majestic Batavia Castle at the mouth of the Great River, the governor-general, assisted by the six-member Council of the Indies, ruled like a Malay sovereign in his own *kraton* (palace). The surviving diplomatic correspondence with the Asian rajas, *pangerans* (princes), and kings attest to how Batavia, 'Queen of the East,' gained its own prominent place in the Indonesian archipelago over time.[24] Yet, behind all the sycophancy of the surrounding Malay princes and the trade contracts signed with them, the military might of the VOC gradually came to claim its prominent place in the pecking order of the archipelago.

Batavia thus remained essentially a native port principality, albeit in Dutch disguise. The city's multicultural society was governed by the High Government comprising the governor-general and the Council of the Indies, assisted by Asian headmen ruling their own nations, the *shahbandars* (harbormasters), and bureaucratic institutions modeled on the Dutch example such as the *schepenbank* (aldermen's court), the Council of Justice, the bailiff, and the *landdrost* (rural magistrate) for police duties, a hospital, an orphanage, a *rasphuis* (jail), a school, a weigh house, notaries, estate managers (*boedelmeesters*), and the like.

Yet, there was an essential morphological difference between the walled city of Batavia and the indigenous port principalities. Whereas in the traditional Indonesian setup, various foreign merchant communities lived side by side, each in their own kampongs around the *kraton* of the ruler, within Batavia's city walls, ethnic groups lived all heaped together. Not until several decades after the town's foundation were the various allied ethnic communities settled in their own villages in the surrounding hinterland, the so-called *Ommelanden*. These Balinese, Ambonese, Bandanese, and Makassarese 'martial races' were given their own plots of land, where they remained available as auxiliaries to be deployed on call in case of military actions.[25] In the long term, extensive intermixing occurred, and the *Orang Betawi*, the so-called original indigenous population of the *Ommelanden*, gradually took shape.[26]

In search of a colonial middle class

Multi-ethnic Batavia counted few Dutch free burghers among its population, who, moreover, were given little room to develop their own enterprises, because the Company protected its privileges like a jealous deity. In such circumstances, the question posed was who were to become the middle class that the colonial town needed?

When he was appointed governor-general in 1617, Jan Pietersz. Coen received a memorable instruction from the company directors in the Netherlands: he was to recruit Chinese for the Company and make good use of *'these industrious, diligent, and unarmed people because, as far as we know, there is no fear that they will ever revolt or desire to make themselves masters of the country if good care is taken that only the most notable and ablest of our own nation serve in all administrative positions.'*[27] Lacking a sufficient supply of able Dutch free burghers, Coen therefore sought to entice Chinese residents from Bantam to come over and serve as the drivers of Batavia's local economy. Consequently, overseas Chinese settlers were given every opportunity to develop their own playing field in the new city, and they seized it with both hands. They came to fulfill essential middle-class tasks as shopkeepers, merchants, and contractors and practiced all kinds of crafts. In addition, they pioneered agriculture and horticulture as soon as this became possible in the immediate vicinity of the city. Meanwhile Coen and his successors successfully enticed Chinese shipping to Batavia in order to ensure a steady supply of labor from the Middle Kingdom. Thanks to their close bonds with the mother country, the Chinese community grew to become the largest and most important ethnic group in Batavia. Thus, a hybrid colonial city emerged in which Euro-Asian and Chinese characteristics intertwined.[28]

Early on, the Batavian High Government toyed with the idea of clearing the jungle around the city and planting market crops such as rice, sugar, and pepper. However, it took quite some time before the necessary, proverbial colonial 'law and order' was established in the city's hinterland. First, young Batavia had to gain its own position between the two powerful neighbors, Bantam in the west and the kingdom of Mataram to the east. As a matter of fact, just when the VOC was trying to gain a foothold in West Java, Sultan Agong, the ruler of populous Mataram in central Java, was expanding his power over the entire north coast of the island, subduing one port city after another. In 1628 and 1629, he twice tried to subdue Batavia but was successfully beaten off each time. 'Bands of poachers' from neighboring Bantam, however, continued to infest the hinterland for many years, making it impossible to reclaim the surrounding jungle for large-scale agricultural development.

In the seventeenth century, tropical Batavia was a pleasant place to be, not in the least because of the Great River that flowed straight through the city to the sea: 'The convenient water supply renders the city pure and clean and enables its people to bathe continually, for the Indians splash in the water without ceasing like ducks,' wrote a seventeenth-century visitor.[29] Reverend François Valentijn, author of an enormous study of the Dutch empire in Asia, wrote a hundred years later that the air was 'generally very fresh and healthy.' Even if during the dry season the heat was considerable, 'it was not so oppressive, as in summertime in Holland,' he asserted.[30] As we shall see, that pleasant situation would change dramatically in the 1730s.

All visitors to Batavia marveled at all the different Asian peoples living intra- and extramuros: Chinese, Bandanese, Balinese, Ambonese, and Malays, and the Christian Mardijkers (*orang merdeka*, free people), descendants of Portuguese settlers or manumitted slaves who formed a large segment of the free population.[31] For security's sake, Javanese were not allowed to live inside the walls of the city. At first sight, it was a truly pluralistic society, and in the context of the unequal relationships so characteristic of colonial society, Batavia remained, however, a melting pot where its citizens really only met in the marketplace.[32]

The Chinese Diaspora

The stereotypical image that the Dutch formed of the overseas Chinese in the early seventeenth century was clear: they were peaceful, hard workers, and there was little to worry about as long as they were kept under the thumb of a decent colonial administration. Thinking of the Chinese in this way, the almost rhetorical question arises: what would have become of the entire Dutch colonial project in the Indonesian Archipelago without the Chinese? The straightforward answer to this is: very little. Right from the outset until the end of colonial rule, Chinese played an indispensable role as intermediaries between the colonial and local economies. One might as well ask: what would have become of the Chinese without the Dutch colonial presence? Under a different political regime, the Chinese would undoubtedly have been able to adapt to the local situation as well.

Wherever Dutch merchants showed up in the Indonesian Archipelago, they found Chinese already settled there. After all, China boasted centuries-old trade relations with the Nanyang, the 'Southern Seas.' This does not necessarily mean that over the centuries, there had been a steady coming and going of Chinese trading junks between southern China and the tropics. The interventions of successive imperial dynasties in overseas trade resulted in fluctuating movements of shipping. Under the Yuan dynasty of the Mongols (1279–1367), there was intensive overseas commerce with Southeast and South Asia. But the emperors of the Ming dynasty (1368–1644)—with the exception of the first emperors, who sent large fleets overseas under the eunuch Zheng He (1403–1433)—were averse to adventurous subjects going overseas on their own account and thereby escaping supervision. The court in Beijing preferred that the 'overseas barbarians' from abroad come and deliver their own products—in the form of tribute gifts—to the port city of Canton (Guangzhou), which was designated for the reception of foreign tributaries. In 1435, the Ming emperor even banned Chinese shipping to foreign lands altogether under the motto: 'Not even a plank may leave the coastal waters.'[33]

During the Song and Yuan dynasties—that is, from the tenth through the fourteenth centuries—the southeastern province of Fujian, with its seafaring mercantile population, was among the most prosperous provinces in China, with the wealth of the port city of Zaitun (Quanzhou), according to Marco Polo, even overshadowing his native Venice. Owing to the maritime prohibition policy of the Ming emperors, however, China's coastal economy collapsed in the sixteenth century and faced a rise in piracy and plunder in which Fujianese and Japanese freebooters colluded. To put an end to this, all Chinese commerce with Japan was banned in 1549, but in order to accommodate the merchants of the coastal provinces, the imperial court opened the doors to tropical Southeast Asia in 1567. Fujianese trading junks were henceforth allowed to sail again to a variety of overseas destinations.

The *Dong-Xiyang kao* (A Treatise of the Eastern and Western Oceans) written in 1617 describes in detail how this expanding Chinese shipping network was organized, what its ports of destination were, what kind of goods were exported and imported, and how a sophisticated tax system ensured that the emperor could share liberally in the proceeds. The Eastern Ocean referred to the sea route that led from Amoy via Spanish-occupied Manila (1571) in the Philippines to the spice-producing Moluccas (Maluku) in today's Indonesia. That connection became extremely profitable when Spanish galleons started to cross the Pacific Ocean carrying from Mexico treasure chests full of rials, coined at the silver mines of Peru. With that silver money, the Spanish at Manila paid for Chinese goods for export such as silk, porcelain, and sugar for their American colonies. It is no wonder that tens of thousands of Chinese migrated to the Philippines to share in this extremely lucrative commerce.[34]

By the western ocean, the Chinese meant the coastal route along Vietnam, Cambodia, Siam (Thailand), the Malay Peninsula, and Sumatra, all the way to Bantam in West Java. Via this route, China was supplied with pepper, cloves, cinnamon, rare tropical woods, edible bird's nests, and all kinds of seafood that even brought about a change in flavor in southern Chinese cuisine.[35]

Dutch versus Chinese

When the first Dutch ships appeared on the roadstead of Bantam in 1595, they were welcomed by the Chinese merchants residing there. That first encounter would lead to a long history of both competition and cooperation. Both sides complemented each other well, as they displayed remarkable contrasts and similarities. First of all, there was the question of support, or the lack of it, by the home government. In the Chinese case, the great leap overseas into Southeast Asia was at most only tolerated by a distrustful imperial court in Beijing. How different the situation was on the Dutch side, where the VOC was provided with a monopoly on all navigation to Asia. Such government support was understandable given the enormous distances that the ships had to cover between Europe and Asia. On the other hand, the Chinese diaspora remained economically and socially connected with the mother country by kinship relations and received no protection or political backing from home.

And what about shipping? Dutch East Indiamen never made it back within two years, while Chinese junks used to return home within six months. The risky trading voyages via the Atlantic and Indian Oceans from Europe to the tropics and back called for a totally different type of investment and management than those from China. The Chinese junks or *wangkang* set sail every year in January, and, propelled by the northeast monsoon, they would arrive in the tropical regions within a couple of weeks. In early summer, they returned home again as the favorable southwest monsoon set in. Measuring 150 to 300 tons, the junks were typically half the size of the Dutch East Indiamen. In addition to a crew of usually eighty men, the junks carried on deck hundreds of hawkers and adventurers looking for work. A *nakhoda* (chief merchant) represented the business interests of the ship owners and the crew in foreign ports. All on board, the crew members and the passengers alike, engaged in peddling their master's or their own merchandise.[36] Every year, the inhabitants of Batavia eagerly awaited the arrival of Chinese goods such as ironwork (pans, needles, scissors), pottery for daily use, paper (umbrellas), and, last but not least, *picis*, the copper pennies with a hole in the middle that came in handy as change at the *pasar* (market).[37] On the way home, the junks carried all kinds of tropical products such as pepper, spices, sandalwood, edible bird's nests, and as much silver money as the Chinese merchants could collect.

In contrast to the Dutch, who were hardly inclined to emigrate and settle abroad, the Chinese roamed all over Southeast Asia in search of profit, sojourning and settling here and there for shorter or longer periods of time. While all Dutch sailors sailed to Asia in the service of the VOC, this was not the case for Chinese shipping. Chinese maritime trade and overseas migration were based on free enterprise, mutual cooperation, and, above all, the kinship ties that connected the Chinese family system. For the Chinese overseas, the junk trade was the artery through which new blood was brought in every spring.

While the Dutch company established its own trade factories from Nagasaki in the East to Yemen in the West, Chinatowns spontaneously sprang up all over Southeast Asia. Chinese men were allowed by their own authorities to stay away for one or two monsoons to transact their business, but women were forbidden to go abroad under any circumstances. This meant that the Chinese sojourner often had more than one partner: a wife at home who took care of the parents and kin, and, wherever he settled in the archipelago, a native *nyai* (concubine). Since the daily transactions on the local *pasar* in Southeast Asia (then as now) was generally in the hands of women, the Chinese newcomer had easy access to local markets thanks to his native wife.

Traditionally, overseas Chinese conformed to the conditions of the country where they settled for short or longer periods of time. In the local economies, they served as middlemen and moneychangers and were often entrusted with all sorts of administrative financial tasks such as levying tolls or taxes. This allowed them to build informal economic networks that extended to the farthest corners of Southeast Asia. Indigenous elites gladly incorporated Chinese helpers because, with their support, they could strengthen or expand their own power. As we shall see, the Dutch colonial administration in Batavia did the same.

Strikingly, both the Spaniards and the Dutch founded colonial headquarters based on significant Chinese populations: Manila in the Philippines in 1571 and Batavia in Java in 1619. Both cities were located at the crossroads of European and Chinese commercial networks; indeed, they owed their location to it. The similarities between Manila and Batavia were not accidental, because Coen unabashedly confessed that he considered Manila to be a model for Batavia.[38] Yet there was one striking difference between the two cities: outside the walled Spanish city of Manila, the Chinese lived in their own *parian*, a large China town, while at Batavia the Chinese were housed *within* the city walls. This made sense because, due to the town's precarious position between two hostile Javanese principalities, Bantam on one side and Mataram on the other, Batavia had to ensure the safety of its own Dutch and Chinese citizens.

Co-colonization

The close relationship between the formal colonization project of the Dutch East India Company and the informal Chinese diaspora constitutes a fascinating subject. In Java and Taiwan this type of co-operation has been characterized as 'co-colonization,' a type of collaboration in colonial plural societies, where unequal partners benefit from pursuing mutual interests, often at the expense of the indigenous people.[39] Not only in Batavia did the VOC call in the Chinese to help create a colony. They did likewise during the short-lived occupation of the island of Formosa (1624–1662). The establishment on Formosa (Taiwan) was originally intended to serve as a transit point for the

China–Japan trade, but soon after the construction of Zeelandia Castle at the entrance to Tayouan Bay in 1624, the colonial administration also established an export-oriented agricultural colony with the help of Chinese settlers. After ten years' time, the coastal strip around the castle had been pacified to such an extent that the first colonists could be welcomed from China to develop the virgin territory and begin the cultivation of rice and sugar cane for export purposes.[40] As we shall see, the same would happen at a later date in Batavia's hinterland, the *Ommelanden*. But if at the outset the collaboration in Taiwan and Java appeared to be a win–win situation between the partners in the urban context, this was not the case in the countryside. In Taiwan, a Chinese peasant revolt was suppressed with much bloodshed in 1652, and almost one hundred years later, in 1740, the same happened in Batavia. The question, then, is why Sino-Dutch relations seemed stable and harmonious in the city, but became strained and problematic in the countryside. In the Taiwanese case, the course of events leading up to the rebellion and the motives of the rebel leaders has been explained in a rather straightforward way: the popular unrest originated after a very bad harvest from a combination of problems connected with the collection of high taxes and unpaid debts in the agrarian sector. In Batavia, as we shall see, the situation was more complex.

Chinese pioneers and the building of Batavia

Let us briefly survey now how the cooperation between Dutch and Chinese took shape within and around Batavia's city walls. Governor-General Jan Pietersz. Coen made every effort to lure the approximately two thousand Chinese sojourning in Bantam because he desperately needed them as builders, fishermen, gardeners, and artisans. Within months, Bencon and Jancon, two prominent members, crossed over with their families. Owing to their different careers and personalities they complemented each other well in their function as stereotypical middlemen: Bencon as the responsible headman of the Chinese community and Jancon as its main contractor and matchmaker. When Coen said, 'There is no people in the world who can serve us better than the Chinese,' he must have been thinking of these two foremen.[41]

On October 11, 1619, only a few months after the founding of the city, Coen appointed Bencon (Su Mingguang) *kapitein* (captain or headman) of the Chinese—already a hundred in number—in order 'to maintain as well as possible good order and police among them.'[42] In the *Chinese Annals of Batavia*, he is praised as the founder of the country, who sported a large lantern with that proud inscription in front of the gate of his house in Mangga Dua. As his community's foreman, Bencon was entrusted with the administration of his compatriots, that is, to settle quarrels between them and hand out punishments for minor offenses. When this position of power soon led to complaints, he and Jancon received an official warning that they should not abuse their privileges. More serious offenders were handed over by the Chinese captain to the bailiff and the town's court of alderman, on which Bencon and Jancon also sat. The flagpole in front of the captain's house served a special function. On the first of each month, the flag was hoisted to mark the day on which the capital tax of 1½ rials that every Chinese resident of Batavia had to pay was collected. This tax exempted them from corvée work on the construction of Batavia Castle and the city walls. Nor did they have to serve in the town's militia. Since many Chinese sojourned only temporarily in Batavia, and received protection, legal support, and freedom of action during their stay, the capital tax levied on them might be considered a kind of 'tourist tax' avant la lettre.[43]

From his arrival from Bantam in 1621, Jancon distinguished himself as a labor contractor and builder: he carried out most of the public works in the city that took shape in the shadow of Batavia Castle.[44] While Bencon remained faithful to Chinese folk religion, Jancon had converted to Islam. In the 1630s, this enterprising man also invested in a sugar cane plantation just outside the city walls, but this venture proved unsuccessful because gangs from neighboring Bantam kept setting fire to the growing cane. Upon Jancon's sudden death in 1639, extensive debts emerged. The insolvency of his estate was due to his having had too much on his plate under the pressure of commissions by the colonial government. Problems between debtors and creditors caused by Jancon's bankruptcy led to the High Government's establishment of the institution of *boedelmeesters* (estate trustees), who henceforth were given the task of managing the estates of deceased Chinese.[45]

With their strong position in the town administration, the Chinese soon acquired their own institutional place in colonial society. They were assigned their own cemetery outside the Zuiderpoort. In addition to the capital tax, the Chinese were also charged taxes on gambling, Chinese *wayang* (Chinese opera performed in the streets), marriage ceremonies, and funerals. From the proceeds of these taxes, a Chinese hospital was established to take care of 'poor sick, impotent, and miserable persons who often lay perishing in the utmost misery of hunger, distress, stench and filth.'[46] The collection of these taxes, as well as the bulk of all other tolls levied in Batavia on the markets and the weigh house, came into the hands of Chinese bidders at the yearly tax auctions, who thus gained control of the urban market economy.

As Bencon's successor, a certain Lim Lacco (Lin Liuge) was appointed captain in 1636. He had also come over from Bantam, and like Jancon, was a

Muslim convert. Even after his move to Batavia, he had continued to maintain close relations with the ruler of Bantam with whom the VOC had been in constant enmity since the founding of the city. Thanks to his diplomatic services, many a dispute with the neighbors was resolved. When Lim Lacco died in early 1645, a well-defined procedure for the election of a new Chinese captain was finally drawn up. Since it was still early in the year, the High Government decided to postpone the appointment until the arrival of the Chinese junks, so that the *nakhodas* also could participate in the vote. On March 4, a list of twelve 'principal Chinese of this city' was drawn up from which a 'capable, experienced and agreeable person' could be selected for the honorable office of captain. By majority vote, a certain Bingam (Pan Mingyan) was elected, a Chinese merchant who had lived in Batavia for 23 years. This was a rather risky choice since over the years, he had made as much money as he had lost with daring business ventures. With the appointment of Captain Bingam, the first steps were taken to reclaim the city's hinterland, the so-called *Ommelanden*.[47] The new captain proposed to lower the capital tax to 'lure crowds of Chinese to Batavia' in the interest of promoting rice and sugar cane cultivation. In close cooperation with Director General François Caron, Bingam undertook the digging of canals to improve the infrastructure outside the city walls. Shortly before, as governor of Formosa, Caron had brought over numerous agricultural workers from China with whom he had initiated the sugar cultivation on that island.[48] In Batavia, Caron now was ready to perform the same trick, and soon he and Bingam became the biggest landowners outside the city walls.

This close personal cooperation between the Company elite and the Chinese aroused so much ire among the European free burghers that, bypassing the High Government, they sent a petition to the Gentlemen XVII in the Netherlands complaining about Caron and the privileged position of the Chinese.[49] As a result, Caron was recalled on the vague charge of illegal dealings. Following this, the Gentlemen XVII requested that the members of the High Government give their verdict upon the potential colonization of the Ommelanden, but this invitation was met with little enthusiasm.[50] In any case, the first serious attempts to establish sugar cane plantations and sugar mills around the city came to nothing because, despite the truce with Bantam, these were still repeatedly set on fire by wandering bands from the neighboring sultanate. Like Jancon, Bingam apparently fell victim to his own industriousness, for the estate trustees who executed his will in 1663 determined that his estate was insolvent, albeit because 'his resources had melted away in the great outlay of sugar fields in his possession.' The frequent arson attacks had finished him off.[51]

After Bingam's death, the High Government settled for a less flamboyant Chinese leader who could guarantee order and peace among his compatriots.

On account of his 'pious and honest conduct' and because he was 'loved among his own brethren,' a dignified elderly gentleman named Siqua was elected captain in 1663. He had lived in Batavia for forty years and, together with Bingam, he had served for many years on the city's board of aldermen. When Siqua died three years later, his young Balinese widow, Yan Erya, was appointed acting Captain of the Chinese. Apparently, the well-oiled cooperation with the Chinese was by now taken so much for granted by the colonial administration that a wise or enterprising headman was no longer sought after. Or was there a deliberate desire to weaken the important position of the Chinese?

The appointment of this Balinese woman, who served for twelve years as captain (1666–1678), must have been downright insulting to the Chinese in the town. One hundred years later, even the writer of the *Chinese Annals of Batavia* had a hard time explaining this sharp-witted lady's qualities: 'When Lady Yan Erguan, this Balinese lady, served as captain, every time she went to the *bicara* [assembly] hall she behaved like a man. She solved problems in the official hall clearly and quickly. She was so to say a strong man among the native women. But when the Company administered male affairs with a woman [...] yin and yang collapsed. This had great consequences for the majesty of the government as it ran counter to destiny and fortune.'[52]

An anonymous Chinese commentator on the *Chinese Annals* even believed that this interlude of female rule was a bad omen. His line of thought reflects well how the Chinese thought about their own situation in Batavia in later years: 'This Balinese lady had no wisdom and no agenda. Her customs were different from those of the Chinese. Is not it strange that she suddenly was put in charge of the Chinese? ... The *Shang Shu* says: When the hen rules the morning, what does that portend? It leaves us with a foreboding. The turning upside down of yin and yang dates from that period. Afterwards this was confirmed by the fighting and disasters between the Chinese and the Dutch.'[53]

CHAPTER 2

The Chinese puzzle

In early 1663, the Gentlemen XVII in Amsterdam appointed the retired governor of Taiwan, Pieter Anthonisz Overtwater, and the Amsterdam patrician, Pieter van Hoorn, to the Council of the Indies. Normally, such appointments took place in Batavia and were subsequently ratified by the Gentlemen XVII in the Netherlands, but in this case, both men were sent to the Indies with a special assignment. Because the Company was facing precarious times, both gentlemen were to assist the High Government in Batavia's urban administration so that the incumbent members of the Council could be assigned to other duties. The main crisis that had unfolded concerned the loss of Formosa. After a ten-month siege, the colony had fallen into the hands of the Chinese Ming loyalist, Zheng Chenggong, or Coxinga, as the warlord was generally known at the time.[54] Despite frantic efforts to keep aloof from Chinese politics, the VOC had become involved in the civil war that had been raging in mainland China for almost twenty years.

Loss of face

On April 25, 1644, the last Ming emperor took his own life when rebellious peasants occupied the palace in Beijing. Taking advantage of the general confusion, Dorgon, a Manchu prince with whom the Ming emperors had been at war for decades, herded his troops through the Shanhaiguan pass and, thus crossing the Great Wall, marched directly to the Chinese capital. After chasing the rebels out of the palace, he took possession of it and proclaimed the establishment of a new dynasty: the Qing (1644–1911). In the years that followed, the Manchu regime expanded its power over the entire Chinese territory, but in the coastal provinces, it encountered stubborn resistance from Coxinga. Relying on a powerful fleet, this Ming loyalist doggedly continued the struggle from his headquarters on the island of Amoy (today's Xiamen) in the coastal province of Fujian. Controlling China's coastal traffic and relying on a hefty income from the overseas trade, he was able to finance his resistance for years on end. In 1660, however, after a failed attack on the southern capital of Nanjing, Coxinga was forced into defense by the advancing Qing forces. Cornered, his gaze fell on the flourishing Dutch trading post on nearby Taiwan. In the spring of 1661, the warlord crossed over with an invading force of twenty thousand men and within days after his arrival, laid siege to the mighty Fortress Zeelandia, the Company's headquarters on the island. Eight months later, on February 1, 1662, the Chinese warlord forced the Dutch garrison to surrender. For nearly forty years, the fortress had served as an entrepot for the VOC's shipping traffic between China and Japan. The defeat of this strategic outpost was a blow to Dutch trading interests in the Far East, but even more so was a terrible loss of face in the eyes of the neighboring countries. It put the High Government of Batavia in a bind: should the Company send a fleet and wage a counterattack to recapture the island? Or should it join forces with the Qing regime to fight Coxinga—the Dutch at sea and the Manchu forces on land? This was not an easy choice. With its widespread trading network, the Company already had its hands full fighting elsewhere in Asia. In the Indonesian archipelago, war was being waged against the kingdom of Makassar over the spice monopoly, and in South India a large army force was battling the Portuguese. Since two prominent councilors of the Indies, Cornelis Speelman and Rijcklof van Goens, were in command on these battlegrounds, there was an urgent need for experienced administrators to fill the vacancies in the High Government of Batavia.

Two deputies

After consultation with the Gentlemen XVII, Pieter Anthonisz Overtwater, who had retired to his birthplace, Hoorn, declared himself willing to set sail again. The former director general, François Caron, who ten years earlier had been recalled on suspicion of engaging in private trade, was also invited to rejoin the Company, 'alongside or below' his fellow members of the Council of the Indies. That condition 'alongside or below' utterly disgusted the old Asia hand. He was willing to return to the East Indies, but only if fully restored to honor, that is, his former position of director general. This was unacceptable for the Gentlemen XVII, and a stalemate ensued. His pride injured, Caron backed out of the deal. He had something else up his sleeve. At the invitation of the French minister of state, Jean-Baptiste Colbert, he chose to return once more to Asia, but this time in the service of the French East India Company.

Now short of experienced candidates, the VOC management decided to choose someone from among Amsterdam's patriciate. The Amsterdam mayor, Cornelis Witsen, proposed a new candidate, the gunpowder manufacturer, Pieter van Hoorn, who happened to have family connections with the leadership of the Company through his wife, Sara Bessels. Her maternal grandfather, Cornelis Reijnst, had served as governor-general of the East Indies. After careful consideration, Van Hoorn was invited to join the Council of the Indies as an 'extraordinary member,' on the condition that he take his family with him and make a fifteen-year commitment to stay in the Indies. Although this candidate had never been to Asia, the Gentlemen XVII apparently felt that he could make a useful contribution to the High Government of Batavia as an administrator.

On Monday, April 16, 1663, the VOC ship *Alphen* set sail for Batavia carrying Pieter and Sara van Hoorn with their five children.[55] Two nieces accompanied them to help look after the children. Overtwater sailed out on the sister ship *Sparendam*. Thanks to favorable winds, the beginning of the voyage went smoothly. Within one week, the ships passed the Scilly Islands off southwest England, and on August 21, the refreshment station at the Cape of Good Hope came into sight. After a brief stop to stock up on fresh provisions and drinking water, sails were set again on September 9, and exactly two months later, the ships sailed into Strait Sunda, where the mighty Krakatoa volcano came into view. Fickle winds held up the ships for several more days before they could finally sail on to the Thousand Islands at the entrance to Batavia Bay.

First impressions of the city

When the *Alphen* anchored on the Batavian roadstead on November 16, 1663, Pieter van Hoorn witnessed from the afterdeck a wide, sunlit, intensely blue bay and as far as he could see, scattered islets with swaying coconut palms. Nearby, to the ship's port side lay the island of Onrust with its sawmills, shipyard, and ships undergoing refits. On the shore rose Batavia Castle and behind it, half hidden among the greenery, the silhouette of Batavia's city walls and church tower showed itself. As the last remnants of the morning haze lifted, behind densely wooded hills, the contours of the high Blue Mountains became visible in the distance. A little further down the roadstead, on the starboard side, the return fleet bound for Europe lay ready for departure. Closer to the shore on the inner reaches swung a forest of masts of the intra-Asian shipping fleet. Not a single Chinese junk was in sight; they would not show up until the new year, when the northeast monsoon set in.

Then, from far away, the cannons of the Castle could be heard in answer to the thunderous salute shots from the *Alphen*. A tangle of bobbing sampans soon encircled the *Alphen*. Chinese and Javanese peddlers loudly touted fresh tropical fruit and other foodstuffs in exchange for Dutch wares. The skipper sternly warned everybody not to gobble up these delicacies, for after so many months without healthy food, the stomach would not be able to handle an overdose of tropical fruit. Within an hour the *Labberlot*, Batavia Castle's official chaloupe, came rowing over to disembark the Van Hoorn family and bring them to the carpenter's yard, where they were to be quartered in the days to come.

The next day, Van Hoorn was ferried across the river to the Castle with its mighty white coral stone walls. Upon entering the large compound, he saw soldiers lined up and fully armed on the exercise square in front of the buildings where the governor-general's residence, the meeting hall, the secretariat, and the treasury of the High Government were located. A friendly *pennist* (clerk) of the secretariat thereupon showed him around the vast complex dominated at four corners by the strongholds of Diamond, Ruby, Sapphire, and Pearl. He even peeped into his future workplace, the council room, then passing by the director general's office, where a row of customers was waiting outside, he briefly visited the chart-room, and then proceeded to inspect the warehouses before finally descending into the cellars where gunpowder and weaponry were kept. He must have been mightily impressed.

One or two days later, after they had recovered a bit from the long journey, the entire Van Hoorn family would have gone into town to take a curious look around. Cut in two by the Great River, Batavia was surrounded on all sides by coral stone walls with no less than twenty-two strongholds. Across the bridge that connected the castle to the city, the family stepped into the Herenstraat. Before their eyes unfolded a typical Dutch townscape with houses of brick, canals and stone bridges. Around the municipal square stood the town hall, the *Kruiskerk* (Cross Church), and the weigh house. It all looked pretty familiar, but not a word of Dutch could be overheard in the streets—only Portuguese, Malay, Chinese, and a hodgepodge of other languages. Yet here and there, among the Chinese, Javanese, Malays, and Mardijkers (descendants of freed slaves), a sprinkling of Europeans could be spotted. In Porcelain Street, where they browsed in the Chinese shops, they may have met with a Dutch lady with a procession of slave girls carrying packages in her wake. Then, they were shown around the markets for poultry, fish, and vegetables and, right in front of the Chinese hospital, they even witnessed an open-air performance of Chinese wayang.

Invited to the home of a Dutch free burgher, Sara Bessels, who was quite used to having a household of a few servants and kitchen staff in Amsterdam, was amazed to learn that her hostess was waited upon by dozens of slaves. While in Amsterdam, there was never a shortage of domestic servants, in Batavia, the labor situation was completely different. Here, there were no free servants available; you had to buy your staff on the slave market. 'So many domestic servants, and what is more, all of them slaves!' the newcomers from Holland will have thought with some bewilderment.

A city full of slaves

Slavery was an integral part of the feudal society in Christian Europe until the Middle Ages. With the advent of the new era, serfdom gradually disappeared from the scene, only to return in the form of slavery on the other continents, to fulfill the urgent need for manpower in the colonial households, mines, and plantations. Discussions in recent years about the place of slavery in early modern Dutch history usually overlooks the fact that slavery arose from the specific nature of colonial society. In the mother country, slavery was unthinkable, so much so that enslaved people who reached the Netherlands became free in the eyes of the law as soon as they set foot ashore. Within Dutch East Indies society, which was based on the unequal relationship between European colonizers and the colonized indigenous peoples, slavery was accepted as a normal and even necessary phenomenon until the first protests could be overheard by the end of the eighteenth century. As Governor-General Jan Pietersz. Coen put it in 1623: 'There is nothing, I say again nothing, that will do the Company more service and profit than the purchase and collection of a large number of slaves.'[56]

When the Van Hoorn family arrived in Batavia, slaves made up more than half of the city's 25,000 inhabitants. At the time, they originated mainly from the Indian and Burmese coasts (Bengal, Malabar, Coromandel, and Arakan), but in later years, most were brought in from Celebes, Bali, Buton, and Sumbawa, islands within the Indonesian archipelago itself. Local princes from the latter three islands exported so many of their own people annually to Batavia that the High Government imposed a maximum of thirty slaves per ship. The Balinese rulers used the sales of their unfortunate subjects to pay for their own purchases in Batavia.[57] The Company generally did not engage in the slave trade itself but left it to European and Chinese citizens who brought enslaved people to Batavia to be auctioned off. The High Government even complained about 'the insatiable desire of our residents to provide themselves of slaves beyond necessity, as a result of which this colony is beset with too great a crowd of that rabble.' Slaves who earned extra income by doing manual labor for their masters regularly bought their own freedom for 80 to 100 *rijksdaalders*. As a matter of fact, the indigenous Christian Mardijkers community group of the town was partially made up by the offspring of manumitted slaves. Thus, Batavia's slave community in a sense produced its own free 'native' citizenry.

Slavery in all its facets was a widespread phenomenon in Southeast Asia. Serfdom, debt bondage, enslaved and kidnapped people or prisoners of war and all manner of feudal bondage were well-known features of social life. In the pre-colonial sultanate of Melaka, the Malay elite left land labor to slaves, and in the Moluccas, too, the *orang kaya* (wealthy merchants) used slaves to harvest spices and cloves long before the VOC formally introduced its own system of slavery on Banda. In Bantam, enslaved bodyguards protected the members of the court nobility from attacks. In his memoirs, the Swiss captain, Ripon, recounts with amazement the people of the island of Flores, who exported their own offspring on a large scale: 'Well-fed women who give birth to many children are highly valued and hardly have to work at all. They are treated like we feed our mares.'[58]

Nonetheless, slavery under the VOC regime differed considerably from the indigenous forms, because *lijfeigenschap* (serfdom), as it was termed, was declared subject to Roman law. The *Batavian Statutes* of 1642 defined the requirements that slaves and their owners had to comply with: slaves could only be sold by way of a notarial act and 'if anyone happens to beat his serf to death or otherwise kill him, he shall be bodily punished for this or even executed, as the occasion commands.'[59] Curious was the rule that only slaves who could express themselves properly in Dutch were allowed to wear a hat. Consequently, slave society also had its own rank and file and, as can be seen from the sources, proudly defended the families that they belonged to. But before the impression is given that all was not so bad, nothing could be further from the truth. Slavery remained a life bereft of freedom, and the fact that slaves regularly ran away and chose freedom in the Ommelanden, where they formed their own bands of outlaws, speaks volumes for their love of freedom and for the misery that they may have endured in the hands of their masters.

The bureaucrat at work

Pieter van Hoorn was allowed some time to take up his quarters, but on November 23, he assumed his position in the Council of the Indies. Having been sworn in and having promised that he would fulfil his duties 'in all fidelity, diligence and to the utmost of his ability,' he was immediately put in charge of the tolls and taxes department. The actual job of collecting taxes he could leave to the highest-bidding Chinese tax farmers. A few weeks later, other appointments followed, such as that of regent of the Company Hospital and Company representative of the Batavian church council. And as if that was not enough, he was also appointed president of the aldermen's court.

Unlike the other councilors, who had earned their spurs at remote trading posts, Van Hoorn remained based in Batavia and was assigned to the strictly bureaucratic work for which he had been hired. It comes as no surprise that he soon cast his eyes on a patch of virgin land outside the city walls to plant a garden of his own. He came at the right time, for only shortly before (1659), a truly lasting peace treaty had been concluded with nearby Bantam, so that now at long last, one could venture outside the walls in relative safety. The Company ceded land to anyone willing to cut down the trees of the jungle that here and there still reached close to the city walls. Even the soldiers of the garrison were put to use for this purpose: 'In fact, everyone could get as much land as he wanted to clear.'[60] For the removal of the timber and the draining of the now exposed swampy ground, canals were dug. In order to protect the newly reclaimed area, a belt of fortifications was constructed in a semicircle around the city at a distance of one hour's travel: Ancol near the coast on the east side, Anké on the west side, and Jakatra, Wilgenburg, and Rijswijk on the landward side. Pieter van Hoorn chose to plant his garden in the shadow of one of these forts, the redoubt Jakatra.

The Council of the Indies, to which Pieter van Hoorn was attached as an extraordinary member, met twice a week under the chairmanship of Governor-General Joan Maetsuycker. At these meetings, problems of all kinds were dealt with and disposed of by taking resolutions. While the High Government (consisting of the governor-general and Council of the Indies) had administrative and legislative duties, the administration of justice was the responsibility of the Council of Justice and, at the lower, urban level, the Aldermen's Court. Beyond participating in weekly meetings, council members held a variety of ancillary positions within the bureaucratic apparatus. Maetsuycker had already been in office for ten years before Van Hoorn's arrival. Trained in law at the University of Leuven, he had composed the *Batavian Statutes*, a code of decrees and ordinances that formed the basis for the Company's jurisdiction in Asia. He was a typical civil servant. During his 25-year reign, he surrounded himself with outstanding people and managed to keep a smooth atmosphere within the Council, something his successors could not always claim. With an artfully designed periscope, a contraption full of mirrors mounted on his desk, this curious man kept an eye on his secretarial staff working in the room next door. The amount of paperwork conducted by this platoon of 33 *pennisten* was breathtaking. Day in and day out, the scribes addressed the correspondence with all the factories in Asia and the VOC management in Holland and made manifold copies just in case another ship might get lost on the long, dangerous journey to Europe. The 2.5 kilometers of shelving in the VOC archives kept at Jakarta, The Hague, Colombo, and Cape Town still bear witness to that writing mania.[61]

Political developments

While Pieter van Hoorn was minding the store, he was gradually brought up to date on the political developments in the Company's widespread trading network. After two years of war, peace had been concluded with neighboring

Bantam in 1659. The empire of Mataram in Central Java had twice attempted to overwhelm Batavia, but the Company had been at peace with its ruler since 1647. This was thanks to the tactful actions of Councilor Rijckloff van Goens, who had visited the court of Mataram four years in a row, first as secretary to the envoy and then as envoy himself. With a handful of magic tricks, Van Goens had managed to gain the favor of Sultan Agung's successor, the *susuhunan*, Amangkurat I, who took a liking to Van Goens and addressed him amiably as *Si Panjang*, 'the Tall one.' But it was no easy job to maintain the fragile relationship with the Javanese court in Mataram on an even footing because of the intrigues and power struggles around the throne. As chief commander in the so-called Western Quarters, the coastal areas of India and Ceylon, the same Van Goens would show a very different face from the late 1650s onward, recording an impressive number of military victories over the Portuguese enemy. Owing to his successful army campaigns, no threat remained from the once-feared rival, the *Estado da India*, the Portuguese empire in Asia. At the end of his career with the VOC, the inexhaustible Van Goens also played a major role in giving Batavia a dominant political position over its neighbors in Java as we soon shall see.

Elusive China

Another major political issue was the relationship, or rather the lack of it with China, the mighty empire in the Far East with which the Company had been unable to establish steady trade relations. Insofar as commercial relations existed, it was via the Chinese junk trade between Southeastern China's coastal provinces and Batavia and not by the navigation of VOC ships to Chinese harbors. After the fall of Formosa, the relations with China became even more problematic. Every year since 1662, the High Government had sent a squadron under Commander Balthazar Bort to Chinese coastal waters to attack Coxinga's remaining outposts in the province of Fujian. Bort was instructed to make overtures to the Chinese viceroy of the Qing regime, Geng Jimao, who, based in the provincial capital Fuzhou, held a key position on the Chinese coast. This turncoat was tasked with the conquest of China's southern coastal provinces. In 1651, he had succeeded in taking the strategic port city of Canton (Guangzhou) after a nine-month siege. In retaliation for the tough resistance, he had all that city's men slaughtered, which earned him the euphemistic princely title of *Jing-nan wang*, the 'Pacifier of the South' (Singlamong in Dutch sources). In that same city, Singlamong had received the first VOC envoys, Pieter de Goyer and Jacob de Keyser, who came to submit a petition for the opening of free trade in 1655.[62] The Dutch envoys had theatrically emphasized that they had 'braved storms, traveled thousands of miles across the sea' to come and pay homage to the Son of Heaven. As a result perhaps, the Chinese court had allowed the Dutch envoys, to their dismay, an audience once every eight years, a privilege that was given to barbarian envoys from afar.

Since then, the emperor had transferred Singlamong to Fuzhou to take up the fight against Coxinga. And so it happened that the viceroy once more received the 'Red-Haired Barbarians' at his court. He knew what he was in for when Bort asked for freedom of trade in exchange for an alliance against Coxinga, or rather his son, for Coxinga himself had died shortly after the capture of Formosa. For three consecutive years, expeditions were sent to China under Bort's command without achieving the intended goal. Every time a battle was to be fought, Singlamong's troops withdrew and then left the hard work to the Dutch. One must fight pirates with pirates, the Viceroy must have thought. It is hardly surprising that the High Government of Batavia was terribly disappointed by the reaction of the 'ungrateful' Chinese. Given Bort's failed efforts, Governor-General Joan Maetsuycker felt that it made little sense to send another ambassy to Beijing. Enough money had been squandered on Chinese embassies. The Gentlemen XVII in Holland, however, were of a different opinion. They wanted to take one more chance, because recently letters had been trickling in from Dutch priests stationed in China, who believed that the Company had a better chance of success this time.

After careful consideration, Maetsuycker was therefore instructed to send a councilor of the Indies as an envoy to the Chinese court in 1666. When none of the council members showed any enthusiasm for the trip, since there was only 'very small hope of desired success,' Pieter van Hoorn raised his hand at the council meeting of June 1, 1666. Previously he had already remarked in passing that he was 'willing and ready' to go to China, but this time, he squarely put himself forward. It could not have been phrased more politely, and that was just as well, because his offer was not immediately accepted. Maetsuycker said that he wanted to sleep on it. The next day in the Council 'the ability and prestige' of Van Hoorn were once again scrutinized while he waited outside the door of the meeting room. Such caution was not really necessary, because he was unanimously elected by his colleagues, who probably sighed with relief that they could stay home themselves.

Van Hoorn had not just spontaneously applied for the mission. His fascination with China had been raised years earlier by a meeting with the Jesuit priest, Martinus Martini. This Italian missionary had returned to Europe from China in 1651 and came to Amsterdam to publish a survey map of China, the *Novus Atlas Sinensis*, with the famous cartographer, Joan Blaeu.[63] His visit caused a stir among the city's Catholics. *De Bello Tartarico*, Martini's account of the fall of the Ming dynasty, which he had personally witnessed at close quarters, even inspired the playwright, Joost van den Vondel, to write his tragedy *Zungchin or ondergang der Sineesche heerschappye* (Zungchin, or the demise of the Chinese dominion).

Two young Jesuits, Philippe Couplet of Mechelen and François de Rougemont of Maastricht, had also been so much moved by Martini's account that they chose to follow in his footsteps and enlist for the mission in China. En route to Lisbon, in late December 1654 they visited Amsterdam and became acquainted with several citizens interested in China, including Vondel, Blaeu, and Pieter van Hoorn. At the end of 1662, the same Father Couplet happened to meet with Commander Bort in Fuzhou. It turned out that he administered a local church with a congregation of one thousand Christians. On that occasion, he gave a letter to Maetsuycker asking him to convey greetings to his Amsterdam friends, Vondel, Blaeu, and Van Hoorn. Afterwards, Couplet must surely have learned with surprise that Pieter van Hoorn had meanwhile moved to Batavia.

Van Hoorn hoped to count on Couplet's help in Fuzhou. That wish did not come true, for shortly before the arrival of the Dutch envoy in China, the Roman Catholic mission fell into disfavor with the imperial court.[64] Years later, Van Hoorn wrote that during his year and a half stay in China, he had been unable to meet any 'popish clergy.' Although that may have been a disappointment, the diplomatic assignment allowed him to become acquainted with Chinese culture on a daily basis. Also involved in this adventure was his thirteen-year-old son, Joan, who accompanied him.

No fewer than five ships, carrying 486,038 guilders worth of merchandise, accompanied the envoy when he left Batavia on June 3, 1666. To this were added another 100,000 guilders in carefully selected gifts, such as blood coral necklaces (of which the Chinese were fond), spectacles, Leiden cloth, and weapons. The prize gifts were four thoroughbred horses from Persia as well as four dwarf oxen from Bengal to be presented to the young emperor. These rare animals were expected to cause quite a stir at the Manchu court.

But was all this enough to appease the imperial court in Beijing? Would the Dutch be allowed free trade? That was the vain hope. The answer is that free trade with foreigners simply did not fit the Chinese state ideology.[65] Visitors from surrounding countries were received as tribute-bearing vassals of the Son of Heaven, not as negotiators for favorable terms of trade. Pieter van Hoorn was instructed by his superiors to sell all the merchandise before engaging in the negotiations about the trip to Beijing, but he wisely left the haggling to his capable second-in-command, chief merchant, Constantijn Nobel. The latter had previously accompanied Commander Bort on his visits to the viceroy in Fuzhou and thus knew with whom he could do business.

Singlamong and the Chinese bureaucracy

The Manchus jealously maintained their position of power by building a 'diarchical' military authority structure: in all important military positions, a Manchu and a Chinese were placed next to each other in order to keep each other in balance. This rule also applied on the battlefield. In addition to the Manchu legions, Chinese troops fought under joint command. Thus, several hundred thousand Manchus were able to keep some three hundred million Chinese under their thumb. All this was not unknown to the Dutch, as evidenced by the statement that 'it is most surprising that within the whole of China only 40,000 Tartar [Manchu] horsemen are found, running night and day through almost the whole country, with hundreds of thousands of Chinese on horseback [...] and it is certain that the number of Tartars is so small that one counts some 10,000 Chinese against one Tartar.'[66] Yet, the organization of the civil service was left intact and consisted of Chinese mandarins who were selected by the empire's unique Confucian examination system that selected the country's most brilliant men for public office.

As viceroy, Singlamong held a position that did not actually fit into the traditional hierarchy of the Chinese mandarinate. In a sense, he was a product of the civil war that was raging. After twenty years of fighting, the Qing forces had not captured the entire coastal area. Narrow strips of land were still in the hands of Coxinga's army. According to evil tongues, the reason why Singlamong had not completed his mission was because he deliberately allowed resistance to continue so that he could maintain his position in Fuzhou. Although in 1666, the viceroy was still firmly in the saddle, he did have to share power with the governor-general (*totok* or *xunfu*) of Fujian and the provincial commander (*konbon* or *junmen*), two military officers appointed directly from Beijing. As Van Hoorn would find out, these two officials were rather haughty men who showed little sympathy for him.

Unlike his boorish military commanders, Singlamong was remarkably friendly. During the audience that he granted to Pieter and Joan van Hoorn, he allowed three granddaughters to appear and on that occasion, asked mischievously if a marriage had already been arranged for little Joan van Hoorn. Pieter van Hoorn was clearly impressed by this powerful man 'of middle stature, brown, dark, and shrewd of face, gentle of words, yet hasty and with great authority, correct and very orderly in his court and all his doings, understanding enough but in my estimation more arrogant than wise [...]. He is held to be the greatest merchant in China and like Coxinga he has stores throughout the empire.'[67]

Lengthy negotiations

After arriving in Fuzhou, Van Hoorn had to wait several months before permission came to leave for Beijing. At last, on November 18, the welcome news arrived. But before leaving for the capital, he wanted to make sure that the merchandise could be unloaded and sold as instructed. The Dutch ambassador therefore wrote a letter to the Chinese authorities emphasizing 'the necessity of sincerity and friendship for mutual understanding among the people of the world.' And in typical Dutch uncle fashion he continued, 'such friendship can best be confirmed by buying and selling so that it can grow steadily, like a tree.'[68]

The commercial undertone of this note understandably irked one of the provincial commanders. How was it possible that this Red-Haired Barbarian, who, let it be known, had been hospitably received as a tribute-bearing vassal, could utter such demands, desiring to trade his merchandise before he had properly revealed the purpose of his embassy to the court? This elicited the chastising comment: 'The envoy is a bit too eager to engage in commerce.' Had trade not been allowed at the proper time? 'He [the commander] was not an unreliable old bag.' He was well aware that the ambassador had come from a distant place, but 'if needs be, he would not hesitate to send him back empty handed without further ado.' In short, the general advised the Dutch envoy to behave as he was told by his hosts; otherwise, he might as well go home to Batavia!

On the road to Beijing

Van Hoorn's travel account has been characterized as 'sometimes fascinating, sometimes yawn-inducing, and impossible to summarize.' Therefore, let us deal only with the most salient details of the voyage. On January 20, the Van Hoorns, father and son, left in the Company of Constantijn Nobel and an entourage of twenty-four men. With a fleet of some thirty-eight vessels, they sailed upstream along the Min River. A little later, another ten barges joined them carrying officials and interpreters from the Ministry of Rites. All traffic with foreign visitors to the court was regulated by the ministry as part of the tributary protocol.

The convoy was towed up the Min River by toiling coolies until rapids made further progress impossible. Then, all the presents had to be unloaded so that the procession of visitors, the rare gift animals such as Persian horses, Bengal miniature oxen and a hundred coolies carrying the gifts could cross the Xianxia Pass between Fujian and Zhejiang provinces. The overland journey was a learning experience for both father and son. Pieter continued to marvel at how that immeasurably vast Chinese empire with its numerous land-based inhabitants was governed by a handful of Manchus. The hierarchical power relations between Manchus and Chinese may even have prompted him to think of a strange parallel. Did the Company not also deal with industrious Chinese? They were valued in Batavia as merchants, shopkeepers, gardeners, contractors, sugar millers, and so on, and obediently carried out their work as well. The analogy to the situation in China did not escape him.

After crossing Xianxia Mountain, on February 26, 1667, the whole procession embarked again on another river to descend to the lake district around the renowned city of Hangzhou, which, according to Van Hoorn, was known as 'the paradise of China.' There, a landscape awaited them 'everywhere with streams, brooks and canals intersected, partly dug with the spade, partly made by nature, almost in the same way as here in Holland.' Thus, the Van Hoorns had the rare opportunity to see in passing renowned cities such as Hangzhou, Shaoxing, and Suzhou with their beautiful architecture. Not until the city of Yangzhou, at the entrance to the Grand Imperial Canal, the main artery connecting the rice-producing Yangzi region with the capital in the north, did the Dutch embassy envoy join the normal tribute route from Canton to Beijing. Along this 1,800-kilometer canal, the Dutch travelers passed through dozens of locks in the wake of hundreds of barges carrying rice and other food to the capital. Van Hoorn was most impressed by the lock works of the canal: 'If European master builders were to contemplate the length of this canal, or the thickness and height of the dikes on either side, or the ornamentation of the locks made of pure hewn stone [...] they would be justified in marveling at the cleverness of the Chinese, and at their labor, which hardly any other people would know how to perform.'[69]

The reception at the palace

After six months of traveling by land and water 'past 37 cities, 335 villages and 34 pagodas,' the traveling party finally reached the capital on 20 June. Once landed, preparations for the audience at the palace proceeded quickly. Mandarins from the Ministry of Rites, *Li Bu*, decided that within a day and a night, the gifts should be prepared for inspection at the court. The entire night was spent unpacking the nineteen boxes. A large brass candelabrum and the carriage to be pulled by the small oxen were assembled. But once the carriage was ready, to everyone's consternation, it could not get through the door. In the afternoon, the chief regent, Oboi, showed up to inspect the rare animals. Not much later, the young emperor also appeared, 'a person of middle height, fairly white, and about sixteen [in reality thirteen] years old. He was not exquisitely dressed but wore a blue damask skirt, a little embroidered in front and on the shoulders and sported yellow boots.' The Son of Heaven 'smiling incessantly' could not take his eyes off the beautiful horses. That augured well.

In the days that followed, Van Hoorn handed over the gifts to the Ministry of Rites and presented Governor-General Maetsuycker's petition requesting the opening of free trade in Chinese ports. During deliberations with mandarins from that same ministry, the same questions were asked repeatedly: 'Where is Holland located, how far is it from China, who is the king, what is his name and who is the governor general? Are there any tigers and other fierce animals in Holland [...] even posing such trifling questions as what kind of tails the sheep and hares in our country had.' There was astonishment all around. The presence of little Joan van Hoorn, who did not leave his father's side, was also a source of wonder: what was that boy doing there? 'Had he come with the governor general's charge and knowledge?' Joan modestly replied that he 'possessed no capacity or position' but was merely allowed to accompany his father with the permission of the Batavian administration.

Prior to the audience, a dress rehearsal was held for the performance of the ceremonial *koutou*, the knocking of the ground with the head: 'Kneel down, bow your heads three times after the others, rise again, kneel down again, and bow your heads three times.' The court ceremony took place at dawn on June 25. Around midnight, the ambassador and his entourage were picked up and led to the imperial palace. There, to their surprise, they beheld five elephants with gilded towers on their backs. Four men walked in front of them cracking with whips. After passing through four large gates, the Dutch visitors were assigned a seat to the left of the throne. They watched as the highest mandarins knelt before the emperor three times and banged their heads against the ground nine times. Moments later, they were also instructed to perform this salute to the emperor.

At the conclusion of the ceremony, the Dutch envoy caught only a glimpse of the Son of Heaven. 'The emperor rose as if to come to us, but went behind the throne,' wrote a disappointed Pieter van Hoorn. In the days that followed the audience, he and his party were offered three formal farewell banquets. After the last, the Dutch envoy received the emperor's reply in a sealed envelope with the express instruction that the letter should not be opened before arriving in Batavia. That was a huge disillusionment for Van Hoorn. He had travelled to China with the idea that he could negotiate with the authorities there, but instead he had become entangled in a web of ceremonial acts.

A frustrated envoy

On September 5, the Dutch ambassador left Beijing and, freed of excess baggage, returned to Fuzhou on November 1, 1667, after only two months of travel. There, three ships sent from Batavia to bring the envoy home had been waiting for several months. An exhausted Van Hoorn noted that he had been on the road for '9 months and 12 days' without accomplishing anything. When he bade goodbye to Singlamong, his host told him that he had been fined because he and the *konbon* had allowed the Dutch ships to leave the previous year against regulations. The *konbon* had even been removed from his position, summoned to Beijing, and replaced. His replacement prevented attempts to sell the cargoes carried by the ships that came to collect Van Hoorn. Just before Van Hoorn left for Batavia on December 17, he learned that the young emperor had dismissed his guardians and had now taken power himself. All this made him even more discouraged. In Beijing, he had not been given the opportunity to further the Company's cause, and he had been prevented from selling the cargo of the ships that came to fetch him. How could he justify these failures upon coming home?

According to the 'Day Register of Batavia,' 'the three ships appeared on the roadstead of Batavia on January 9 and 10, 1668, with their cargoes of unsold goods valued at 343,130 guilders.'[70] Van Hoorn, who had fallen ill, was taken home without further ado and entrusted to the care of his wife. On the 26th, more than two weeks later—the exhausted envoy was still recuperating at home—a deputation from Batavia Castle boarded the ship *Victoria* to take delivery of the letters and presents from the Chinese court under the thundering salute of Batavia castle's cannon. Sent ashore, the imperial letters were placed on a carriage, while the imperial gifts were put in the hands of slaves dressed up in red garments. Then the procession got going with much pomp and circumstance: a Company of horsemen went in front, followed by a platoon of soldiers, the carriage with the letters, and the procession of gift bearers. A carriage with representatives from the High Government formed the rearguard. After a tour through the city, the parade arrived in front of Governor-General Maeysuycker's residence in Batavia Castle, where two lines of musketeers fired three charges. Under the cannon roar of fifteen more salutes, the Chinese epistles were presented, one from the emperor himself and three from officials of the Ministry of Rites. The following days were spent on the difficult translation of the documents into Dutch.

It soon became apparent that the ambassador had accomplished little or nothing, as Maetsuycker had expected right from the beginning. Among the correspondence were two letters from the dismissed *konbon* in which he explained once more how the whole ritual surrounding the tribute proceedings should be organized. He wrote that he had asked the emperor to allow the Dutch to send an embassy to Beijing once every eight years, as before, and to permit them to sail to Fuzhou to trade once every two years.

It was not until March 9 that a fully recovered Pieter van Hoorn was able to submit his report.[71] To his dismay, the account books in which he declared the expenses during the trip did not meet with the approval of the Council of the Indies. According to the Board, they were not drawn up with 'the most concise and clearest method'; nay, they were even 'intricate and obscure.' Affairs became even nastier when further investigation revealed that after the arrival of the ships in January, no less than sixty tubs with porcelain and a large quantity of tea had been smuggled into Van Hoorn's house. As a result, he was suspended. It was decided that Van Hoorn was to receive 'neither wages nor salary' until he was able to provide an explanation to the Council's satisfaction. For the time being, he was no longer welcome in the Council. To put an end to this unpleasant affair, the Council decided on July 13, 1668, to seize all goods that Van Hoorn had brought from China, assessed at 2,206 reals. The batch of tea valued at 607 rials was also forfeited. He was, however, allowed to keep the personal gifts that he had received at the imperial court. A few months later, tempers had calmed to such an extent that on November 27, 1668, Van Hoorn was re-appointed president of the Council of Aldermen. Two months later, he profusely apologized in a memorandum to Maetsuycker for all the misunderstandings that had arisen. Gravely ill as he was at the end of his voyage, he had not been able to properly take care of his luggage. The last word was, 'let bygones be bygones.'

What had Van Hoorn learned from the trip? Along the way, as befits every pilgrim, he had encountered a series of obstacles and challenges in the form of fast-flowing rivers, high mountains, and troublesome mandarins, to say nothing of severe culture shock. Entangled in the court ritual, he had not had a chance to negotiate the opening of free trade, and after returning home, the scorn of his colleagues had awaited him. The quest had, however, opened his eyes to the overwhelming impression of Chinese society. And the same counted for his son Joan. Traveling by ship via the intensively cultivated lowlands of China, where the industrious peasant population was governed by a small Manchu minority, the Van Hoorns could not have failed to gain inspiration about how to colonize and reclaim Batavia's Ommelanden with Chinese help.

CHAPTER 3

Pieter van Hoorn's Colonization Plans

Before the reclamation of the Ommelanden could proceed, it was necessary to have clear border agreements with the neighbors, Mataram to the east and Bantam to the west. These conditions were arranged in the long decade of 1670–1682, an extremely critical period during which the fortunes of the VOC were determined by clashes of arms not only in Asia but also in Europe. Back home in Europe, the fate of the Dutch Republic momentarily hung by a thread when the English navy, the army of the French king, Louis XIV, and the German troops of the bishop of Münster simultaneously attacked the Low Countries. In the Indonesian archipelago, Cornelis Speelman finally defeated the sultanate of Makassar on the island of Celebes, which had fiercely refused to accept the Company's spice monopoly in the Maluku archipelago. On Java, the Dutch were sucked deeper and deeper into the Javanese world by interventions in local political crises at the courts of Mataram and Bantam. The High Government could no longer afford to pursue a policy of restraint but felt forced into a more proactive approach.

The Company's colonial wars

If in the Indonesian archipelago the fire was extinguished in one place, only a spark was enough to rekindle it elsewhere. After Makassar was defeated, a large group of Makassarese warriors refused to acquiesce. They first made their way to Bantam, and although they initially received a warm welcome, the 'Roosters of the East' did not last long there. Jealousy over women led to discord between host and guests, and after two years, the Makassarese moved to Central Java, where they first roamed around as bandits before joining the Madurese prince Trunajaya, who had rebelled against the susuhunan (king) of Mataram.

After Trunajaya's father, Cakraningrat I, ruler of the island of Madura and vassal of the susuhunan of Mataram, had been murdered while on a visit to the court in Kartasura, the susuhunan, Amangkurat I, appointed the victim's brother as successor to the Madurese throne, i.e., Cakraningrat II. Consequently, a furious Trunajaya sought revenge against both the susuhunan and his uncle, whom he considered complicit in the murderous plot. The prince first managed to make himself master of all of Madura before he set his sights on Java. To his surprise, he even briefly found an ally in the crown prince of Mataram who wished to put an end to the cruel rule of his father. At the Mataram court, mutual friction, jealousy, conspiracies, and murders were the order of the day.

After fierce fighting, the port cities of central and eastern Java fell one after the other to Trunajaya's forces. Feeling cornered, Amangkurat I implored the High Government in Batavia for help. According to the treaty he had concluded with the Dutch in 1646, the Company was obliged to assist the susuhunan in the case of war. This was the moment when the High Government once more had to appeal to Cornelis Speelman, to solve the problem. At the end of December 1676, Speelman left for Central Java with a substantial army force. After a failed attempt to reconcile the warring parties, there was nothing left but to take sides.[3] Because he lacked sufficient troops to pursue Trunajaya into the Javanese interior, a region unknown to him, he decided to first occupy the capital of Madura behind his opponent's back. Speelman barely succeeded in this when he learned that the Madurese had already captured the capital Kartasura, but not before the *susuhunan* and the crown prince, reconciled again with his father, had escaped on an elephant. Exhausted, the old prince and his faithful elephant in Banyumas breathed their last, though not until the crown prince had received the heirlooms (*pusaka*) of the empire out of his father's hands.

Active interference

Because a huge war debt was anticipated, Speelman demanded from the new susuhunan, Amangkurat II, in exchange for more military aid, a reimbursement of expenses and the sole rights on the import of opium and textiles from India for all of Java, keeping the important port city of Semarang as collateral. This was agreed to, and thus the Company gained a firm foothold in Central Java. It so happened that meanwhile, Governor-General Joan Maetsuyker had passed away after a short illness and was succeeded by Rijckloff van Goens, who now called Speelman back to Batavia and appointed him director general.[72] After a grueling campaign, Trunajaya surrendered on Christmas Day 1679 on the promise of a pardon. When the penitent asked forgiveness for his rebellious behavior during an audience, the young susuhunan in answer stabbed him to death with his own *keris*. All this occurred to the indignation of the Dutch of course, but the monarch did not care about the terms of surrender with Trunajaya that had been made behind his back. As a result of all the fighting, the Company's position vis-à-vis Mataram had changed dramatically in only a few years. While Van Goens had visited the Mataram court as an envoy in the 1650s with his bag of magic tricks to please Amangkurat I, the late susuhunan's son, Amangkurat II, now had to address him in his capacity of Governor-General Van Goens as 'great uncle'!

At the treaty concluded between Amangkurat II and the representatives of the Company on February 28, 1677, the Company gained freedom from import and export duties as well as substantial compensation in money and goods for the expenses of the campaign.[73] The susuhunan agreed to supply fixed quantities of rice annually, and in the ports along the Pasisir (the north coast of Java), the Chinese shahbandars who levied the tolls by which the debts were to be paid off now came to stand directly under the jurisdiction of the Company, in order to prevent them from possibly evading the grip of Batavia. In addition to all this, a firm boundary arrangement between Batavia and Mataram was agreed upon: the eastern border of the Ommelanden was now extended to the Krawang River. When the Gentlemen XVII in the Netherlands read about this extension of territory, they shook their heads in dismay: 'How shall we conduct ourselves with regard to that large area of land, which the aforementioned sovereign [Amangkurat II] has ceded to us, is a matter which deserves great deliberation.'

The master plan

While his colleagues in the Council distinguished themselves with their fighting in Java, Pieter van Hoorn noted that little thought had been given to the future development of the Ommelanden. Was it not high time to draw up a plan for the reclamation of this virgin territory? He noted that the economic development of Batavia was visibly lagging behind that of Bantam. This was, he believed, because Batavia still lacked a developed hinterland where crops for export could be cultivated. Batavia's Ommelanden covered a vast coastal plain still overgrown by primeval forest. The hilly uplands in the back of it extended to the foot of the high volcanic mountain ridges to the south. The volcanoes Salak, Gede, and Pangrango irrigated this entire area with a multitude of criss-crossing rivers and rivulets that all ran more or less parallel northward from the mountains towards the sea. Although Pieter van Hoorn understood that a border arrangement with Bantam still had to be made, in his opinion, there was no harm in putting on paper what a future Batavian settlement should look like.

In a thoughtful essay, *Preparatory Considerations and Advice concerning the Dutch Colony in these Indian territories*, Van Hoorn stated that Batavia as a colonial settlement could only rival Bantam if the administration radically changed tack.[74] He urged that ample scope be given to private initiative. The Company was no longer just a merchant, but now had to deal with the territorial expansion into the Ommelanden. Founding a Dutch colonial settlement was by no means an easy task, because unlike the Portuguese, the prosperous Dutch were hardly willing to emigrate to foreign lands. This was all the more true for Asia, because the Company discouraged private initiative, announcing that it 'should not accommodate on its ships any families that wished to reside [in Batavia] to earn money outside of service of the Company.' In the 1650s, after François Caron had been recalled on account of his overenthusiastic collaboration with the Chinese Captain Bingam, the Gentlemen XVII had asked the members of the High Government to recommend how the Ommelanden should be settled. But at that time, none of the councilors saw a role for European agriculture around Batavia. They believed that even if European settlers were willing to put their foot to the spade, they would be unable to compete with the Chinese. As the then ruling governor-general, Carel Reyniersz put it: 'The Dutch are blunt and always come with empty hands, while the Chinese are astute, and always are able to shake this or that out of their sleeves.'[75] Now, some twenty years later, Pieter van Hoorn proffered his own views on the situation. The Latin term '*Colonia* or *Colonus*,' he wrote, originally meant agriculture and farming. This implied that people were needed to cultivate the land. This is how all colonies and overseas empires had been founded in the past. It should not be forgotten that in antiquity—he was thinking of the Greek colonies—trade and entrepreneurship together had contributed much to the success of overseas settlements. Therefore, he deemed it better to speak of a 'colony of agriculture and commerce.'

Van Hoorn distinguished two types of colonies: free and unfree settlements. The first one consisted of people who, owing to questions of faith, hunger, or danger of war, had left their country to start a new life elsewhere. Unfree colonies, however, were founded on foreign soil by law and under the administration of the mother country. Batavia and Ommelanden were good examples of this. In both cases, the creation of a colonial plantation was like the planting of trees. Therefore, he judged that it would take at least twenty years before a colony would begin to yield anything. A colony could, Van Hoorn believed, be better governed by a 'generous' power than by merchants who were only out for quick profits. Because of all the recent conquests, colonies were now a reality that the Company had to learn to live with. Ceylon, wrote Van Hoorn, had been conquered from the Portuguese by Rijckloff van Goens purely for its cinnamon monopoly. Only now had the government realized the great expense of maintaining the monopoly and administering the towns, forts, and fortifications on the island. Batavia, however, struck Pieter van Hoorn as a special case. The headquarters were indispensable for the management of all the Company's activities in Asia. He considered that the administration of this costly settlement with all its facilities for oceanic shipping could only be paid for if private entrepreneurs were given a free hand to develop their own agricultural enterprises in the hinterland. Founded as an entrepot port on a marshy spot by the sea, the Batavian colony now should climb up to 'the inner and higher parts of the landscape' because of the opportunities for the cultivation of market crops over there. In effect, Van Hoorn reasoned that the Company should abandon the old Portuguese (or Malay) example and should opt for the Spanish system of colonization. Instead of thinking in terms of a coastal trading enclave, one should open up to the idea of rural exploitation of the hinterland, as the Spaniards did in South America and the Philippines.

An unwelcome opinion

According to the 'General Instruction' of 1650, the entire prosperity of the East India Company rested on the trade monopoly that was granted at its founding.[76] Van Hoorn's plea to give private entrepreneurship was thus considered a snub in the direction of the Gentlemen XVII. An official reaction was inevitable. Coincidentally, shortly before Van Hoorn's Preparatory Considerations came into the hands of the Company directors, Van Goens had returned to the Netherlands from Ceylon to defend his costly expansion policy in India. A genuine hardliner, he pointed out to the Gentlemen XVII that Batavia's economy had recently declined because, according to him, the Company's trade monopolies were not well maintained. He attributed this to the policies of the aged Maetsuycker and his elderly Council of the Indies. Although he was himself not exactly a young man, he showed himself willing to accept the office of governor general for a few years provided that he was assisted by a younger, ambitious Council of the Indies. So it was decided: Van Goens was appointed director general to succeed Maetsuycker. Putting their money where their mouth was, the administrators sent a fast ship to Batavia with the instruction that the four oldest members of the Council of the Indies should retire with the further observation that these measures should not be seen as 'any slight or dishonor to the gentlemen.' When this became known in Batavia, it was up to young Joan van Hoorn, who by then had risen to the important position of secretary of the Council of the Indies, to report to the Gentlemen XVII that the resignation of his father and his colleagues Pit, Overtwater, and Pavilion had been accepted 'with reverent obedience, although not without our emotion.' In Batavia, it was clear to everybody that this dismissal of almost all of the councilors had fulfilled Rijckloff van Goens' wish to be rid of the old guard. Now he had a free hand to appoint his own pawns.

Sultan Ageng of Bantam

By 1680 there remained on Java only one formidable rival to challenge Batavia's progress: neighboring Bantam. Under the able administration of Sultan Ageng (r. 1650–82), this port principality flourished; English, Danish, French, and Portuguese ships delivered at its roadstead Indian textiles to be sold throughout the archipelago. Understandably, native merchants from across the archipelago preferred to moor at Bantam bypassing Batavia. Because Batavia simply could not match the low prices at which European competitors sold their merchandise, the city fell into an outright depression, while Bantam prospered.

It was up to Rijckloff van Goens, who had accepted the supreme command upon Joan Maetsuycker's death on January 24, 1678, to meet the challenge. Together with Cornelis Speelman as director general, he embarked on a new, tough course. Now that the power of Mataram had been curbed in the east, troublesome, principled Muslim Bantam should be dealt with. Yet it was clear that there was no way that the sultanate could be dealt with violently. The European competition would never let this happen. This meant that the Dutch had to wait patiently for a chance to interfere in Bantam's internal affairs. That opportunity soon presented itself, thanks once more to the characteristic weakness of the Javanese courts: internal bickering for power.

Sultan Ageng was a religious man who had no intention of bowing to his Christian neighbors. While in recent years the Company had its hands full with the turmoil in central Java, the ruler of Bantam had seen his opportunity to tighten his grip on the principality of Cheribon east of Batavia. Because his influence now extended via the Priangan mountain region behind Batavia to the areas east and west of the city's Ommelanden, he thought that he had Batavia in his grasp. Together with the devout Sheikh Yusuf from Makassar, he looked forward to a favorable opportunity to engage in holy combat with the 'infidel Dutch.' He transferred part of his administrative duties to his eldest son, Abdul Kahar, alias Sultan Hadji, and then retreated to a new, European-style palace at Tirtayasa east of Bantam. There, he waited for the right moment to strike: *Reculer pour mieux sauter*.

But the old tiger failed to strike at the right moment. As soon as the Madurese prince, Trunajaya, had been defeated and the Company troops were back in Batavia, Van Goens took the initiative by seeking rapprochement with the neighboring princes of Cheribon to ease them away from the grip of the Sultan Bantam and thus secure the eastern and southern borders of the Ommelanden. This political move Ageng quite rightly saw as a violation of his ancient rights and thus as a *casus belli*. His son, Sultan Hadji, however, did not agree with his father's bellicose plans. He did not want to risk a war with Batavia and thereby jeopardize the prosperity of his principality. While this struggle for power kept Bantam in discord, an old and now ailing Van Goens submitted his resignation and was succeeded by Cornelis Speelman, who continued to apply pressure on Batavia's neighbor.

By the spring of 1682, tensions between the old and young sultans had escalated to such an extent that a civil war broke out. When the forces of Sultan Ageng and Sheikh Yusuf surrounded Sultan Hadji's *kraton* (royal palace), the latter managed to smuggle out a message and appealed to the Company for aid: 'I request help in all haste; I have no persons whom I can trust, come to the customs checkpoint of my Castle! Please do not fail to do so, hurry!'[77] Captain François Tack, Johan van Hoorn's brother-in-law, was immediately dispatched to Bantam, and just in time succeeded in freeing the young sultan with a daring landing operation. Out of gratitude, the relieved Sultan Hadji, now turned into a pawn in Speelman's power politics, issued on August 22, 1682, an edict granting the VOC exclusive trading rights at Bantam, to the exclusion of all other parties. This meant that the English, Danes, and Portuguese, who had previously been denied access to Makassar, now also had to leave Bantam and thereby lost their last port in the Indonesian archipelago. And on top of that, the Dutch command that all Chinese merchants in Bantam move forthwith to Batavia dealt a death blow to the prosperity of the Islamic stronghold. With the elimination of Batavia's last rival on Java, the borders of the Ommelanden were now secured on both sides. Batavia's backyard finally lay open to be developed into an agricultural colony.

Mercator Sapiens

After his return from China, Pieter van Hoorn must have taken note with great satisfaction of the abundantly illustrated edition of his travel journal by Van Meurs, the same publisher who had previously published Johan Nieuhoff's travel account of the first Dutch embassy to China. Completely possessed by Chinese culture, Van Hoorn had immersed himself in the writings of Confucius. He believed that in the sage's moral teachings, virtue was 'more, and more clearly expressed and polished with words than has come to me from any

European author.' In 1675, he even published in verse form an anthology of Confucius's sayings with the edifying title *Some principal properties of the True Virtue, Prudence, Wisdom and Completeness, drawn from the Chinese Confucius*.[78] He dedicated this little book to his family with the edifying words: 'Receive my dear wife and children all fine things that I have brought you from China, and if you are able to make to use of this, it will be better than if I had provided you with great treasures from there.' It is the first (partial) translation of *The Analects* (*Lun yu*) of Confucius into Dutch and in any modern European language.

Liberated from all his official duties, the old gentleman moved to his beloved country retreat at Gunung Sari, where 'he spent most of his time there in quiet repose' until his death on January 18, 1682. A formidable funeral procession accompanied his coffin to the cemetery, led by the entire Company elite followed by a long procession of civilians, Chinese, and other native peoples, 'who were very many in number.' His tombstone with an enigmatic inscription is preserved in the cemetery of Tanah Abang in Jakarta:

Who forever strived to understand
the essence of all being
And possessed love's true
virtue in his mind has,
though covered by this stone,
risen far above the earth.
O father, may the Lord
fulfill your wishes for your children.

CHAPTER 4

Joan van Hoorn, Colonizer of the Ommelanden

By 1678, Joan van Hoorn, now twenty-three years old, had already risen to the position of first clerk of the General Secretariat. This year also represented a milestone for him in other respects. He suddenly became a wealthy man by his marriage to fourteen-year-old Anna Struijs, the only child of the exceedingly wealthy freeburgher, Abraham Struijs, who with his own ships traded with Portuguese Macau in China. Not long afterwards, Joan was promoted to the weighty position of Secretary to the High Government.

After all the sabre rattling with Bantam, Joan van Hoorn undertook two diplomatic missions to the sultanate. His first visit culminated in the conclusion of a 'perpetual alliance' on April 17, 1684, and a year later he again headed the embassy to congratulate the sultan on his investiture. A permanent boundary was demarcated at the Cisadane River in Tangerang, and Bantam renounced all claims to territories elsewhere in Java. In addition, the VOC acquired the trade monopoly in Bantam and the areas of South Sumatra subordinate to the sultanate. With the conclusion of the Mataram and Bantam treaties, the flanks of the territory around Batavia were finally secured.

Does this mean that only sixty years after the foundation of Batavia, the colonization process of the Ommelanden could begin? Indeed, not until 1683 did the real colonization start, with the creation of administrative institutions, the construction of roads and the planning and putting into operation of sugar cane plantations along the rivers. In short, the exploitation, the reclamation, and the optimization (*mise en valeur*) of the entire area could at long last begin. In order to make this possible, the Ommelanden had to be mapped. Moreover, the still unknown *Bovenlanden* (Highlands) were awaiting further exploration. This mountainous area—called *Preanger* or *Priangan*—was still terra incognita in Dutch eyes. Land exploration was a prerequisite for gradually imposing property rights and establishing authority in a responsible manner, and this required surveyors who could map the land by the use of trigonometry.[79] Although territorial agreements had been reached with Bantam and Mataram, and straight lines had been drawn on paper to the south coast of Java, it remained a challenge to work all this out in administrative terms because there was a large cultural divide in terms of how sovereignty was understood. The Dutch colonizers thought in terms of geographical areas over which they could exercise jurisdiction, but the Indonesian nobility thought in terms of the number of subjects. These were two totally different concepts of the exercise of power.

The contract signed with the susuhunan of Mataram, Amangkurat II, in 1677 provided for an eastern boundary of the Ommelanden along the Krawang River which theoretically ran from there across the mountains to the southern coast. Shortly thereafter, the sultans of Cheribon and the extensive adjacent territory they controlled were also made vassals of Batavia. This meant that although the traditional governance structure over the Javanese population of the entire Priangan area was taken over, it was left intact, for it was only with the help of the Javanese regents appointed by the susuhunan and their subordinate village heads that those areas could be governed to any degree.

As a matter of fact, the High Government of Batavia strove to intervene as little as possible in existing Javanese administrative practices. It preferred to exercise authority indirectly top down via the native regents and their subordinates all the way to the village heads of the scattered kampongs at the base. In 1684, the Company's emissary, Jacob Couper, summoned the Preanger regents to Cheribon and presented them with seven regulations stipulating that under the authority of the Company they would each continue to govern their own people according to their old laws and customs without interfering with the administration of their neighbors.[80] To what extent these Javanese regents were really willing to give up their traditional loyalty to the ruler of Mataram and conform to the wishes of the governor general in Batavia remained to be seen.

On the western frontier, according to the boundary arrangement with Bantam, an imaginary line was drawn that continued southward from the Cisadane River to Wijnkoop Bay (Pelabuhan Ratu). Thus, the Company's sovereignty was extended across the vast mountainous area of the Preanger all the way to the Indian Ocean. All of this was reflected in the pledge of May 14, 1686, which ordered the people of the chiefs of the Highlands and the Preanger to 'render subservience to no one (Javanese kings, princes or whoever it might be) but to the Company by the yielding of tribute and estimates or whatever.' To put an end to the incessant bickering among the local regents and village heads over 'such matters as the administration of the population, the defection of subjects from one head to another, or the possession of land,' the local headmen had to hand over name rolls of all the people, men, women, and children, including male and female slaves, under their authority.[81] Henceforth, Joan van Hoorn could set out to create the administrative arrangements for the finally more or less defined Ommelanden. While he put into practice the plans that his father had once put on paper, Chinese help turned out to be indispensable for introducing the sugar industry into the virgin territory.

What did the new frontier look like? Dozens of sugar cane plantations were established including sugar mills at strategic locations at the edge of the jungle and along the rivers (to facilitate transportation of the sugar to the coast). In terms of labor, these sugar mills required Chinese specialists to refine the sugar cane and water buffaloes to turn them, in addition to large numbers of *bujang*, Javanese seasonal field hands during the sugar campaigns. In this dynamic social and economic development, the Company also had to deal with the settlement of a variety of Indonesian peoples in the Ommelanden such as the Balinese, Ambonese, and Makassarese, who traditionally provided auxiliary troops for military campaigns. The colonial administration allocated to these allies vast tracts of jungle where they could establish their kampongs. Ironically, the highlands also became a safe haven for elusive groups of runaway slaves.

Europeans already possessed country estates in the vicinity of the city, but the real settlers of the Ommelanden were, apart from the omnipresent Javanese, the Chinese and the indigenous allies of the Company. As will be understood, it was not easy for the Company administration to create some sort of order and peace in its vast backyard, the open frontier of the Ommelanden, south of the city. Efforts were made to keep the various ethnic groups physically separated and living under their own chiefs, but it was not easy. Over the years, the differences between these ethnicities blurred, and so out of this melting pot emerged the *Orang Betawi*, as today's locals proudly call themselves.

Colonial order and governance

In order to meet the new challenges of territorial expansion, interventions in local administration were needed. As early as 1651, a district officer (*landdrost*) had been appointed outside the city walls, who, like the bailiff in the city with his six *kaffirs* (police officers) in the Ommelanden, maintained the rule of law. When in the 1660s the Bantamese raids in the immediate vicinity of Batavia came to an end and new land was up for grabs, this led to mutual squabbling between the European and Chinese *ingelanden* (landowners) and the native allies who saw an opportunity to establish new kampongs far and wide around the city. Obviously, the landdrost could no longer manage all those issues by himself and was in need of a college of advisors to help him settle local territorial disputes. Hence, on September 19, 1664, a board of *Heemraden* (dike reeves) was established. When the work of that governing body took a turn for the worse, Vincent van Moock was installed as the new landdrost assisted by ten to twelve horsemen in October 1669.[82] In support of his arduous task, he was given a residence 'at a suitable spot outside the city [...] in order to allow the inhabitants to possess and cultivate their lands and gardens with greater peace and tranquility, and to free them from the violence of thieves, robbers and the like.' This was the first step towards a formal police force for the Ommelanden. After the ratification of the treaty with Mataram in 1677, a second landdrost with eight kaffirs was appointed, so that the field of activity of these two police officers covered a larger area.

Nevertheless, the area outside the ring of forts around Batavia remained unsafe. Although roving bandits from Bantam were no longer on the loose, gangs of runaway slaves increasingly posed a problem, because it was virtually impossible to chase them in the jungle. It was evident that, given these security problems, the task of clearing the wastelands and surveying newly issued lands would take years to complete. It did not make things easier that, for want of proper land measurements, landowners were shamelessly expanding their property far beyond what they were entitled to.

Reorganization of the Heemraden

In the summer of 1679, the High Government again decided to put a stop to the land grabbing and, on October 13 of that year, established a reorganized board of Heemraden, this time chaired by the scrupulous Joan van Hoorn. An extensive injunction instructed the newly appointed *dijkgraaf* (dike warden) to draw up a precise map, 'observing all creeks, marshes, fields, hills, forests and the like,' and to see to it that proper roads and quays were constructed. A year later, Van Hoorn drew up a strict Regulation for the Board of Heemraden.[83] Based on the new list of property and inheritance legal documents concerning plots of land within and outside the city, a fund was now created for the construction and maintenance of roads, bridges, and the collection of fair taxes.

When he joined the Council of the Indies in 1682, Van Hoorn surrendered his duties on the Board of Heemraden. Yet, less than two years later, he reassumed his role as its president, because after his departure, funds had been tampered with and the administration threatened to fall into disarray. Over the subsequent three years of his presidency of the Heemraden, Van Hoorn had the land holdings in the Ommelanden measured once more. These measures began to resemble a centrally managed land registry, but it proved no easy task to keep pace with the rapid developments in the field. The higher altitude areas more than 2,000 *roeden* (about 7.5 kilometers) from the city were sold to the highest bidder for reclamation, and it is no coincidence that members of the High Government in particular saw this as an excellent opportunity to take possession of large tracts of land.

Meanwhile, in order to prevent 'poaching, looting, and further mischief' among the Ambonese, Balinese, and Makassarese allies, Van Hoorn distributed large tracts of land on which they could make a living under the governance by their own heads in their own kampongs. He even tried to rein in the roaming gangs of runaway slaves and tie them to the land in the same way. Special police forces under the leadership of the Ambonese lieutenant, Patinggi, began policing and capturing 'thugs and arsonists' by the collar. For ten years in a row, in their capacity as 'commissioners over the natives,' Van Hoorn and his successor, Isaac de Saint Martin, undertook to settle the various native populations in their own kampongs.

In 1689, Joan van Hoorn was appointed director general. During his long service in this office (1689–1704), his organizational talent came into full play. He reorganized the administration of the Company's commerce in Asia and, as his private papers show, proceeded to do so with the utmost conscientiousness. These were peak years when merchandise assembled from all over Asia yielded record profits for the VOC in Europe. At the same time, Van Hoorn by no means neglected his own interests and, in cooperation with his Chinese friends, he became the largest operator of sugar plantations in the Ommelanden.

Tragic folk heroes

Affairs regularly came to grief at the frontier. A striking example was the gang leader, Surapati, a runaway slave who, after previously appearing willing to surrender, was dissuaded from doing so by the clumsy actions of a police officer. After the death of his master, the first merchant of Castle Batavia, Pieter Cnoll, Surapati (then known by the slave name Ontong, 'Happiness') had made his way to the Ommelanden.[84] Taking advantage of the chaotic situation during and after the war with Bantam, Surapati formed his own gang of runaway slaves with whom he terrorized the upper Ommelanden of Batavia. The adventurous life of this Balinese Robin Hood, his flight to the court of Mataram, his escapes, and the kingdom he finally founded in East Java are the subject of no less than three Javanese traditional *babads* (chronicles).[85] An attempt to get hold of this rebel at the court of Mataram cost Captain François Tack his life. It would be many years before Joan van Hoorn had a chance to avenge his brother-in-law's murder.

Paradoxically, commissioner Isaac de Saint Martin, a great lover of Malay literature, got into an argument with Captain Jonker, the loyal Ambonese war hero who had assisted Speelman and Hurdt in their army expeditions and had personally captured Trunajaya. The bickering between the two men led to so much friction that Jonker even seemed to be plotting an insurrection. During an attempted arrest, this 'good and alert man, who had done the Honorable Company very great services,' in the words of François Valentijn, was killed. Not for nothing has Jonker attained mythic status in Moluccan lore as a victim of the untrustworthy colonial administration.

A critical note

Cornelis Chasteleijn, a landowner who earned his own place in colonial history as a paragon of Christian charity, was critical of the manner in which the colonization of the Ommelanden took place.[86] In his *Invallende Gedagten ende aenmerckinge over de Coloniën* (Passing Thoughts and Comments on Colonial Issues) published in 1705, his moral ideas, with references to 'generous powers that are more competent than merchants' to establish colonies, are actually closer to the ideas of Pieter van Hoorn than to the conduct of his son, Joan, who was unabashedly rushing to enrich himself.[87]

Chasteleijn opened his essay with the observation 'that it is a well-known fact, that colonies or settlements are born and must grow up through the influx of people, who form their soul.' He insisted that as long as the Company elite (to which, incidentally, he himself belonged) adhered to its maxim of regulating everything according to its own commercial advantages, nothing good could ever come of a properly governed people's plantation. From his own research into the history of the Ommelanden, he concluded that virtually no one in the entire area was descended from the original pre-1619 population of Jayakarta. He diagnosed that this frontier area could only be controlled up to a day's travel from the city. Developments in the higher, more distant Bovenlanden were an entirely different issue. There, the runaway slaves who had fled from Batavia, sought refuge and pulled off all sorts of 'mischief' such as arson, murder, and cattle theft without the justice system being able to do much about it. Indeed, when there was manslaughter in the uplands, the *landdrost* did not even think of visiting the scene of the crime himself, but requested that the corpse be brought to them.' In short,' wrote Chasteleijn, 'the government can put up as many placards with all kinds of ordinances as it likes, but it makes little difference because they will be torn off and forgotten anyway.' Large plots of land had been allotted to the various indigenous peoples, in addition to the vast sugar cane fields, and captains, lieutenants, and ensigns (as with the Chinese) had been appointed. But, according to Chasteleijn, the chiefs took advantage of those rights to extort their own people.

A cynical view of the situation, perhaps, but also a realistic one given the large number of complaints of insecurity in the hinterland. Local authority needed to be better enforced by putting all neighborhoods and villages under their own head men assisted by *tienmannen* (decemvirs), consisting of the best and most capable men, and administer justice according to local norms on specified days instead of putting all problems before the aldermen's court of Batavia. Just look at China, Chasteleijn argued, where the 'restless Chinese' remain subjugated by the Tartars [Manchus] with little power because they are allowed to live according to their own laws and customs and religion, except that the Manchus keep military affairs to themselves 'without leaving the Chinese to have any say.' With his reference to the importance of *adat* (customary practices) and the methods and techniques of the native and Chinese farmers conducive to the systematic development of the new colony, Chastelein's thoughts dovetailed nicely with Pieter van Hoorn's remarks on the subject.

Optimization

The virgin territory of the Ommelanden was ushered into a new era, that is to say, the *mise en valeur* of the newly acquired area into a producer of food and market crops. As already mentioned, Van Hoorn took advantage of his high position to expand his own land holdings. According to Valentijn, he owed much to the Chinese, 'who knew how to get almost everything done with him. Together with Chinese *mandors* (overseers), he kept expanding his land holdings. Some of these lands he leased to Chinese sugar millers and brickmakers.' This reclamation of the hinterland received a huge boost when China opened its borders in 1684, which in turn created a startling upsurge in trade with Batavia.

In his colonization report of November 30, 1707, Joan van Hoorn addressed the main 'Javanese (market) crops' that were cultivated in addition to rice: sugar, indigo, coffee, and pepper.[88] Pepper cultivation was traditionally in the hands of local people, but its purchase and transportation to the coast was handled by the Chinese. He concluded that the experiments in the cultivation of indigo had failed. The Javanese and Balinese *tani* (farmers) around Batavia felt more comfortable growing rice. The acreage of *sawah* (wet rice fields), was increasing rapidly, and this required a major irrigation works fed by the rivers and streams from the mountainous hinterland. In the long run, the tapping of all that water via ingenious networks of canals probably also contributed to the water shortage that the city of Batavia came to face during the dry monsoon.[89] The sugar industry, so important to the VOC, was entirely in the hands of the Chinese. They brought their unique expertise and technology from China with them. Around 1708, the sugar cane plantations already extended from Tangerang in the west to Bekasi in the east and Maraberis in the south. Sugar mills could be found all over the Ommelanden.

The Amsterdam mayor and VOC director, Nicolaas Witsen, liked to boast that he had 'prodded Joan van Hoorn to have coffee cultivated' in the Ommelanden.[90] Coffee was initially purchased by the VOC at Mocha in the Arabian Peninsula, and the first cargoes began reaching the Netherlands in the 1660s. After several years of experimentation in the Ommelanden, it was found that the coffee trees grew better and yielded more in the higher regions. Thus, coffee cultivation came into the hands of the Javanese regents of the Preanger, who saw to it that the local population started to plant trees. Each family was required to plant and maintain between five hundred and one thousand saplings. Shortsighted management eventually led to overproduction, resulting in lower prices and unrest among the Javanese population. Gradually, however, they recognized that growing coffee was a reasonably profitable occupation that did not even require that much care. All in all, thanks to Van Hoorn's intermediation, the cultivation of sugar cane and coffee trees became an outstanding success story for the Company.

Mother Nature makes herself heard

In the years around the turn of the century, the natural environment consequently underwent a shocking transformation, but not only as a result of human intervention. On the night of January 4–5, 1699, a volcanic eruption and an earthquake occurred, 'so heavy and strong, that no such thing is known to have ever happened or occurred here.' This natural disaster was colorfully described in the *Chinese Annals of Batavia*: 'At that time there occurred one catastrophe after another: fire clouds appeared, enormous floods reached the walls of the city, mountains collapsed and the earth split open. Sulfur flowed down. In the bay, dead fishes and clams floated around everywhere; all water creatures were poisoned! The earth tremors of Batavia continued for three days before peace was restored.'[91]

Owing to this heavy quake, river basins that irrigated the lowlands of the Ommelanden became disrupted for a long time. Perhaps the greatest victim was Batavia, for the Great River that flowed through the city and supplied the canals with fresh water lost much of its volume and velocity, with all its consequences. In the absence of river flow, banks formed at the mouth of the river that seriously hampered shipping traffic. During the dry monsoon, the city canals even ran dry. There was no alternative but to hire 'mud-Javanese' from Cheribon, poor devils who were supposed to remove the sludge.

An enigmatic person

Having attained the rank of director general, at first Joan van Hoorn had a difficult relationship with his immediate superior, Governor-General Willem van Outhoorn, an Indies-born and bred extrovert, who had no problem maneuvering three of his own brothers into the highest positions in the East Indies. Shortly after his first wife Anna had died in 1691, Van Hoorn elegantly smoothed out his strained relationship with Van Outhoorn by asking his daughter, Susanna Agneta, to marry him. 'Peeking into the inheritance,' that is, securing property and social position through marriage between equal families, was a well-known marriage tactic in the Dutch patriciate. This same strategic maneuvering was evident in the baptism of the four daughters from this marriage. Among the godparents, we see such pre-eminent Amsterdam surnames as Valckenier, Bessels, and Witsen. According to François Valentijn, no director general before or after Van Hoorn could match him as administrator of the Company's commerce. Not without irony, he noted that no one even dared to envy Van Hoorn because he allowed everyone to share in his wealth. It did bother some people, however, that they had to wait at the doorstep of the director general's office while this or that Chinese was let in first. That these were Chinese with whom Van Hoorn had his own business to do, one may only guess.

On June 18, 1701, Van Outhoorn's request that he be allowed to resign was granted by the Gentlemen XVII with the stipulation that Joan van Hoorn should succeed him. But the latter was reluctant to take over, fearing confrontation with, and perhaps even opposition from, some incumbent members of the Council of the Indies. He was particularly apprehensive of the always contrary, headstrong Christoffel van Swoll and the short-tempered Abraham van Riebeeck, who were both candidates to assume the position of director general from him. After he managed to negotiate that the Council should be expanded to include three sympathetic extraordinary council members—Hendrick Swaardecroon, Mattheus de Haan, and Willem de Roo—he was willing to accept the high position. It was precisely at that moment that Susanna van Outhoorn passed away on October 16, 1703, 'after nine months of ailing, illness, and vomiting blood.' Of the four daughters, only two were still alive at the time, and only the youngest, Petronella Willemina, would survive her father. When Joan van Hoorn accepted his appointment as governor-general in 1704 after three years of opposition, he indeed had to deal with short-tempered Abraham van Riebeeck as second-in-command, but he did not hesitate to clear up the atmosphere by now asking for the hand of Van Riebeeck's daughter, Johanna Maria. On November 16 of that year, the groom's fifty-third birthday, the marriage was consummated with much pomp and circumstance. From now on, everything was peaceful at the top of the government. Informed about the marriage half a year later, the Gentlemen XVII took exception to these marriage tactics, and agreed that they should put an end to this kind of collusion of interests at the top. They therefore decided that in the future, the governor-general and the director general should no longer have family ties.

Embroiled in another court dispute in Mataram

Shortly before Van Hoorn took office as governor-general, two envoys from Mataram visited Batavia, heralding an issue that would complicate most of his tenure as governor-general. The old susuhunan, Amangkurat II, had died in April 1703, but he had appointed his son, Sunan Mas, as his successor. The latter sent an envoy to Batavia to inform the High Government that, as the designated heir to the throne, he had succeeded his father—but without having sought permission from Batavia beforehand. It was widely known that Sunan Mas and his father had plotted the fatal ambush into which Joan van Hoorn's brother-in-law, Captain François Tack, had been lured on February 8, 1686, when he arrived at the court of Mataram to demand the extradition of the rebel leader, Surapati. This betrayal, of course, had created bad blood among the members the High Government and in particular with Van Hoorn, who had Tack's corpse interred in his parents' family tomb.

Coincidentally, a second pretender to the throne also sent an envoy to Batavia and requested that the High Government ratify his appointment. This was Pangeran Puger, who, as the brother of the deceased susuhunan, also laid claim to the throne of Mataram with the support of several important noblemen at court. Under pressure from Van Hoorn, the High Government decided to ignore the request of the self-proclaimed susuhunan, Amangkurat III, and give preference to Puger, who thereupon ascended to the throne under the name Pakubuwana (Nail of the World). During the four-year long Javanese war that ensued, Surapati was killed after a long manhunt, and Sunan Mas was captured and taken to Batavia in 1708. There, he was told that he had been sentenced to a life-long banishment to Ceylon. Peace was restored at a very high price: tens of thousands of Javanese had lost their lives in the internecine struggle, and between 1705 and 1708, the Company had wasted 2.3

million guilders on military expeditions. The sultan of Bantam was so upset by the VOC's interference in the succession to the throne of Mataram that, in order to ensure that his own son would not suffer the same fate, he requested a meeting with Van Hoorn. In order to speak to each other on equal terms, they agreed to meet on 'neutral territory': on a ship at sea.

Farewell to Batavia

When Van Hoorn asked to be allowed to resign for health reasons, the request was granted on condition that he return to Holland in 1709. He had not expected this, but there was little choice but to comply, although he feared that his constitution, after so many years in the tropics, was no longer up to the cold Dutch climate. This of course also meant that he had to relinquish all his extensive land holdings. Saying goodbye to Batavia was hard on him, but he was not the only one who lamented his fate: the Chinese of Batavia were also shocked to hear that their benefactor was returning to Holland. A group of prominent Chinese citizens expressed 'with deep reverence and humble submission that, having arrived from China at a young age, they had known "His Highness's" personality and accommodating disposition for thirty, yes, forty years.' Thanks to Van Hoorn's favorable assistance and administration 'they had often been saved and protected from an apparent downfall, so that they were again able to restore their crumbling business with peace of mind under His Highness righteous protection.'[92]

The suppliants therefore could not refrain from wishing Van Hoorn 'on the one hand happiness but on the other hand express with due humility that after his Highness's departure they would miss the fair benefits and protection of their trade that they had enjoyed from his Highness for so many years.' Therefore, for the sake of the Company, they begged Van Hoorn 'earnestly and very humbly to stay in town a few more years and furthermore to sustain and protect the suppliants in fairness.' Judging by the content of their request, the Chinese were not aware that Van Hoorn himself did not want to leave at all, but that he was ordered to do so by his superiors.

On November 6, 1709, the Van Hoorn couple, together with their little daughter Petronella, bid farewell to Batavia. At the request of the ailing governor-general, his Chinese physician, Thé Bitsia (Zhou Meidie), accompanied the family on the sea voyage to Europe.[93] The return fleet made a long stop at the Cape of Good Hope, where Johanna van Hoorn was able to acquaint herself with the native soil of her father, Abraham van Riebeeck, son of the founder of the Cape Colony, Jan van Riebeeck. The homecoming of the prodigal son after forty years' absence in the tropics caused quite a stir in Amsterdam. Within six months, however, Joan van Hoorn felt he could no longer bear the vicious Dutch winter. In early February 1711, he visited the Nieuwe Kerk to select a site for his grave and three weeks later breathed his last. On February 21, the coffin was interred at night by torch light as was not uncommon among the elite. And thereby the career of this remarkable man literally fizzled out like a damp squib.[94]

CHAPTER 5

The Chinese Surge

How did the Chinese experience the reclamation of the Ommelanden? Did forms of co-colonization continue beyond the city, or did mutual interests diverge from now on? Was enough room given to Chinese development? Dutch-Chinese society within the city walls might be characterized as a type of *convivencia*, that is, an urban situation in which various ethnic population groups coexist in relative harmony. Daily togetherness within the city walls required its own ambiance of mutual give and take at the *pasar*. However, as we shall see, it was questionable whether that atmosphere of interconnectedness could last beyond the city walls once enterprising Chinese began to roam out across the Ommelanden. Because well-structured Chinese archival sources such as those of the VOC are non-existent, it is almost impossible to follow the process from the Chinese point of view, although the Chinese sojourners and colonial settlers must also have had their own agenda. Nonetheless, from a variety of seemingly disconnected data—anecdotes from the *Chinese Annals of Batavia*, correspondence, eyewitness accounts, data from the VOC archives—a picture does emerge of independent Chinese entrepreneurs who, whether taking advantage of the Company's presence or not, pursued their own success and aimed at their own autonomy.

A new Chinese captain

After his appointment as governor-general in January 1678, Rijcklof van Goens received requests from many quarters in the Chinese community to appoint 'as in former times, a man and no longer a woman' as Captain of the Chinese. Van Goens himself understood that it was foolish to deny the Chinese community a more representative head. On June 14, the time had come. The choice fell on the venerable Tsoa Wanjock, a Chinese who had been living in Batavia for forty years and was considered by his compatriots to be 'the most agreeable, beloved and principled' among them. Given Tsoa's advanced age, he was provided with a lieutenant and an ensign to assist him in administrating the Chinese in town. Two weeks later, the new captain was sworn in in front of a 'great sway and concourse of Chinese residents, best dressed according to their manner, waving many vanes and silk bows of various colors accompanied by the playing of all kinds of Chinese instruments.'[95] Joan van Hoorn had the honor of announcing the appointment together with the Chinese merchant, Tenglauw. Despite all the decorum that was once again bestowed by the government on the position of Chinese captain, it was clear that Tsoa, given his age, could not be much more than an interim pope. Still, not until seven years later, had another successor to be sought. By then, as a result of the sweeping changes in the Ommelanden, the position of the Chinese in Batavia had completely changed. There was an urgent need for a captain who could address the major new challenges and who knew how to tackle them.

This was evident in the choice of Tsoa's successor, Captain Quee Conko, who was elected on August 3, 1685, presumably at the urging of his personal friend, Joan van Hoorn. He was a man of an entirely different caliber.[96] Quee Conko did not belong to the Batavian elite, but had come over from Bantam, where he made his mark as a foreman of the Chinese. The new captain was promised a second lieutenant to 'maintain more skillfully the affairs of the Chinese, whose numbers were already increasing.'

Batavia was witnessing an unprecedented influx of Chinese guest workers as a result of a political turnaround at the court in Beijing vis-à-vis overseas trade: Chinese merchants were suddenly allowed again to freely trade with the Nanyang. This about-face was possible because in 1683, the Manchu regime finally succeeded in bringing the entire coastal region directly under its control.[97] This final victory had been preceded by a revolt by the Chinese viceroys, who had initially played a crucial role in the Manchu conquest of China. One of them was Singlamong, the powerful viceroy who two decades earlier had received the envoy, Pieter van Hoorn, at Fuzhou. For a while, the 'Rebellion of the three feudal lords' (*san fan zhi luan*) posed a serious threat to the Manchu regime, but after it was quashed in 1681, all that remained to be extinguished was the last hotbed of Ming resistance: Taiwan, where Coxinga's descendants still ruled. The Manchu regime even sent two envoys to Batavia in 1680 to gauge the VOC's willingness to participate in the conquest of the island, but the members of the High Government, sadder and wiser after Admiral Bort's money-grabbing expeditions in the 1660s, were no longer interested. In the summer of 1683, Admiral Shi Lang led an invasion force of 300 ships with 20,000 men against Taiwan and brought the island under Chinese rule.

Volte-face in Beijing

Once Chinese territory was pacified on all sides, as well as enriched by Taiwan, the Kangxi emperor initiated a new policy not unlike Deng Xiaoping's successful economic reforms three hundred years later.[98] Now that the coast had been pacified, the maritime ban could be lifted, and private enterprise was given free rein in the southern coastal provinces. This led to a stunning revival of Chinese overseas shipping, and the effects were immediately felt in the ports of surrounding countries in the China Sea region. These included, to name but a few destinations, Spanish Manila in the Philippines, where Chinese silk, tea, and porcelain were paid for with silver Mexican dollars; the ports of Hoi An and Tonkin in Vietnam; Ayutthaya, the capital of Siam; Malacca and its environs in the Malay Peninsula; and finally, of course, Batavia on Java. All were prime destinations where Chinese exports could be bartered for tropical products such as sandalwood, pepper, cloves, edible bird's nests, and the like.

The VOC was directly affected by these developments in China, for wherever the Company was operational, the Asian world remained the all-determining factor for its policies. Precisely because their trade interests were so widespread, the interplay of the ever-changing political developments in Asia determined the day-to-day affairs of the Dutch trading Company. This was evidently also the case at the very center of the trade network: Batavia and the Ommelanden. The Batavian administration now suddenly had to deal with a large influx of Chinese, and this time not just peddlers and merchants, but also adventurers looking for new opportunities. Almost as soon as the news of the volte face by the imperial government become known in Batavia, the High Government sent another envoy to China in 1685 to gauge whether there might be new trading opportunities for the Company's ships. Like the earlier envoys, the ambassadors, Paets and De Keyser, came home empty-handed in 1687. That cleared the way for the High Government to cut the Gordian knot. Further attempts to search for a free port in China seemed futile.[99] Instead, Batavia henceforth chose to focus entirely on receiving the Chinese junks that arrived in Batavia in ever larger numbers, laden with cargo and immigrants.

In the eyes of the High Government—and this was confirmed by the Chinese officers—many 'adventurers' and 'fortune seekers' landed alongside those willing to work. On May 21, 1690, the Batavian Ordinance Book (*Plakaatboek*) mentions that the influx of 'all kinds of Chinese rascals' had become so great that even the Chinese captain urged the High Government to institute strict measures to quell the stream of immigrants.[100] He and the lieutenants could no longer control the influx. Many 'new guests' (*xinke*) brought almost no merchandise. They were looking for work, and if they could not find it, they pulled off 'many roguish tricks, thievery, cheating, and other improper behavior.' When the junks left in June, many *xinke* went into hiding in the jungle of the Ommelanden.

In response, the High Government stipulated that all Chinese who had arrived after 1683 had to present themselves and their families to the office of the Chinese captain to identify themselves and provide an explanation about their employment. Furthermore, newcomers wishing to settle were required to adopt the long hairstyle with a bun (*condé*) on the head, after the Ming Dynasty hair fashion that was still in vogue in Batavia. Shaving the forehead and wearing the hair in a braid (pigtails) as had been imposed by the Manchu government on all Chinese was strictly forbidden. This strategy, it was hoped, would make a clear distinction between the settled Chinese and the newcomers. Understandably, a newcomer who did not want to stand out first had to hide himself for some time so that the hair on his forehead could grow again. These attempts by the colonial administration 'to separate the wheat from the chaff' proved to be rather ineffective. In 1706, it was decreed that skippers should henceforth not carry more crew on their junks than necessary (eighty men on smaller and one hundred on larger junks), and strict regulations were imposed on visiting Chinese merchants to Batavia.[101] Throughout the city, more Chinese district masters (*wijkmeesters*) were appointed in addition to those already present. For each illegal straggler, the responsible *nakhodas* (chief merchants) of the junks were charged a hefty fine of 15 rixdollars.

Meanwhile, the Chinese government had also instituted strict rules to prevent the indiscriminate sailing of adventurers, although corrupt local officials regularly turned a blind eye to the practice. Many 'illegal' migrants had themselves been taken by fishing boats aboard Batavia-bound trading junks. The same shadowy ritual repeated itself just before their arrival at Batavia—little sampans awaited the arrival of junks around the Pulau Seribu, the Thousand Islands in the bay, and stealthily transported these newcomers to the mouths of the Maronde, Ancol, Ankee, and Tangerang rivers so that they could escape 'ocular inspection' in Batavia. An official notice of February 3, 1711, referred directly to this practice and ordered that all shorn Chinese (that is, those just arrived on Java's northeast coast, the Pasisir) must be rounded up in neighboring Cheribon or the Batavian hinterland and sent to Batavia. Not surprisingly, in the Ommelanden, where Batavia's Chinese officers seemed to have little say, groups of 'illegal' Chinese took refuge at the sugar mills or formed gangs in their vicinity.

One regulation was, however, strictly observed by the customs authorities in China. It was forbidden to transport Chinese women to countries overseas. The *Chinese Annals of Batavia* tell how, in 1699, the bride that a certain Wang Jie had brought over from China caused a stir among the astonished townspeople: a Chinese woman, elegantly dressed according to Chinese fashion was never before seen in Batavia! Governor General Van Outhoorn even invited her to the castle because he wanted to see what a real Chinese lady looked like. After the junk returned to Amoy, the local authorities learned of what had happened, and all the crew members who had been involved in the affair were sentenced to death.[102]

The Chinese according to François Valentijn

European authors around 1700 wrote with undisguised admiration about the Chinese in Batavia and the prominent position that they occupied in urban society. The omniscient François Valentijn is one of them. He had a high opinion of them, which is quite surprising because the prejudiced reverend often had something disreputable to say about almost every Asian whom he encountered:

> They are an unusually shrewd, polite, diligent and obliging people, who render great services to this city. They not only figure large in Batavia's tea, porcelain, silk and lacquer trade, but they also exercise themselves very diligently in many handicrafts [...] There is nothing one can think of that they do not undertake. If there were no Chinese here, Batavia would be quite moribund and deprived of many necessities [...] How many of these people there are in Batavia is not easy to say. Some presume that there are as many as a hundred thousand in and outside the city. True or not, it is certain that the houses of the Chinese in and especially outside the city are crammed with people, and that they also inhabit the best places everywhere in the city. [...] Mister [Joan] Van Hoorn greatly favored the Chinese and it is certain that it was not harmful but very beneficial to his Lordships and Masters [the Gentlemen XVII]. Since his [Van Hoorn's] time this has not diminished, but has rather sharply increased.[103]

Batavia in French eyes

No less interesting is the commentary of the French Huguenot, François Leguat, who in 1696, after adventurous wanderings, reached Batavia and feasted his eyes on the town.[104] He described in detail the manners and customs of the Chinese and noted that not a beggar was to be found among them. He attributed this to the guild associations, the special sense of community, and the sense of justice among the Chinese in the town. In his view, this stemmed from the 'political and moral ground rules' handed down to them in their ancient writings. In particular, they owed their public spirit to the teachings of Master Kong (Confucius) and this could, he reckoned, serve as a shining example to the Christian states of Europe.

Leguat apparently visited Batavia at a time when everything in this plural society appeared idyllic. That may have been an idealized view, but it is nevertheless striking how much this outsider was pleasantly surprised by Batavia's Chinese who honored their traditional way of life.

Joan van Hoorn's Chinese friend

An exemplary Chinese who indeed lived by the teachings of the Old Sage was Joan van Hoorn's great friend, Que Kiauko (Guo Qiaoge), who held the position of lieutenant between 1695 and his departure for China in 1702. Thanks to Chinese lore, we know that Que Kiauko and his younger brother, Que Hoenko (Guo Xunge), had lost their father at an early age. They grew up in the village of Fugong, in Zhangzhou prefecture, the birthplace of the majority of Batavia's Chinese. In the early 1680s, they decided to leave and seek their fortune in the Indonesian archipelago. As was common among Chinese, to adopt different given names or even pseudonyms for different stages and situations in life, the two Que brothers adopted new given names connected to their overseas adventure. Que Kiaoko means something like 'Que emigrant.' They received a warm welcome on Java because family members already held prominent positions as shahbandars (harbormasters) or as Chinese officers in the coastal towns. Their older brother, Quee Congko, was Captain of the Chinese in Batavia between 1685 and 1695, and Que Pauko served as a lieutenant from 1685 to 1692. Que Kiauko, after first earning his spurs as shahbandar in Semarang, was appointed lieutenant in Batavia under his brother in 1695. He was promptly succeeded in Semarang by his younger brother, Que Hoenko.[105]

These three Ques, whose entrepreneurial interests were presumably also firmly connected with the sugar industry, earned immortal fame among the Chinese of Batavia for their many good deeds on behalf of their own community. They committed themselves to laying out a new cemetery, which required the collection of a large sum of money, and they also raised funds for the construction of the Guanyin Temple, which was consecrated during Que Congko's captaincy. According to the *Chinese Annals of Batavia*, Buddhist priests were invited to take up residence in the temple and conduct the rites there, recite the sutras, and 'dust off the statues.' In the back of the temple, they worshipped an image of their ancestor, Que Lakko.[106] Furthermore, the surname, Que, was associated with the reorganization of the Chinese hospital and the orphanage, and they also helped establish a Chinese school open to all. The Chinese commentary on this event is too precious to pass up:

> It seems the Dutch erected this school for Chinese children because they knew that our flowery nation surpasses the surrounding countries in literature, because it possesses poetical discourses, literary compositions, civilized ceremonies and exalted music, on which the responsibilities of humans are founded, and from which the five cardinal virtues sprout. The Dutch books differ from Chinese works; by giving up their own doctrines and teaching those of China instead, the

> Western people showed that they were willing to conform to the wishes of the people, and showed tolerance and cordiality towards strangers.[107]

Captain Que Congko died around 1703 in Batavia. Que Kiaoko left for China a bit earlier as a man of means and decided to remain there. In Batavia, he left behind his wife and daughters, presumably under the watchful eye of his younger brother. His original goal had been to build a suitable grave for his deceased parents in Fugong, the village of his birth, but once he returned home, he dedicated himself to numerous good works, such as the construction of a new wharf and the hiring of two ferries that allowed everyone to cross the river for free. As local temple inscriptions mention, he and his brother and other prominent Batavian Chinese sponsored the restoration of two important temples in their home county. Just as the Dutch Company servants took care of their relatives back home, the Chinese transferred money to their *guxiang* (home district), but they also made donations to the temples of the gods to whom they owed their prosperity.

Joan van Hoorn constantly urged Que Kiaoko to return to Batavia. Van Hoorn's letters are lost, but those in which his Chinese friend explained that he could not return owing to his filial duties have survived. With appropriate reverence to Van Hoorn, they open with lines like: 'Heaven has provided you with extraordinary qualities, may the sun feed you with high virtues. The people of Batavia are grateful for your kindness, the Chinese envy your humanity, virtue and way of life.' Que Kiaoko wrote that he was surprised to learn that Van Hoorn was refusing to accept his appointment as governor-general. As a good Confucianist, he suspected that he did so out of courtesy to his father-in-law, Willem van Outhoorn. He therefore urged Van Hoorn to accept the appointment anyway for the sake of the city's residents, but he apologized in advance that he could not be present at the assumption of this office because his mother had not yet been buried in the appropriate place according to the rules of geomancy (*feng shui*) and because the mourning period had not ended. In a subsequent letter, Que Kiaoko wrote that even though he had already been in China for three years, his filial obligations to his deceased parents still prevented him from leaving. Yes, he had received many favors from the Company during the twenty years he had spent in Java, but family obligations took precedence. In yet another letter, he related that he had learned that his brother, the former Captain Que Congko, had died, and wrote that a cousin would leave for Batavia to pick up the coffin and bring it back to the village of his birth, so that the deceased could be interred in the family tomb.[108] When Que Kiaoko heard that Van Hoorn had gone back to Holland in 1709, he no longer had any reason to return to Batavia. He purchased some civil service titles in his native county and continued to serve as a mandarin in various civil service positions. Before he breathed his last, Que Kiaoko erected a huge tomb in his native village on which all his achievements are listed.[109] Exactly how Que Kiaoko amassed such a fortune during the twenty years that he spent in Java is not known, but his tenures as shahbandar of Semarang and lieutenant in Batavia, not to mention his close collaboration with Joan van Hoorn, must have laid the foundation for his wealth.

The sugar industry in the Ommelanden

What prompted so many Chinese migrants to move to the Ommelanden? They found work on and around the sugar cane plantations, which were laid out in wider and wider circles around the city.[110] The sugar cane industry was pre-eminently a Chinese enterprise. First and foremost, running a sugar cane plantation required experienced personnel, skill, capital, and good water-bearing soil before one could even think of installing a mill to press out the cane and refine the sugar. The plantation should be positioned close to a virgin forest for access to the necessary firewood. Likewise, it had to be adjacent to a river or canal so that the refined sugar could be transported downstream to Batavia. A team of water buffaloes to run the mill was a prerequisite for every sugar mill. Between May and July, the cane cuttings were planted in rows in the plowed land and watered and filled up with earth. About ten months later, the cane was ready to be harvested and squeezed between the millstones imported from China. The preparation and refining of the sugar through a crystallization process using giant iron cooking pans required specialized knowledge.

The Chinese sugar industry in the Ommelanden used the same production method that was in use in the home province of Fujian and therefore fundamentally differed from the African slave labor-based methods of the Atlantic region.[111] Expertise and experience, including tools, came directly from China. Thus, the sugar miller, and the men whom he employed to press the cane and refine the sugar were all Chinese. This included the loggers and the burly fellows who looked after the safety of the staff and the herds of water buffaloes in this frontier society. Every sugar plantation, and everything associated with it, in fact formed an ethnically Chinese core. Each mill had its own shrine dedicated to the site's patron god, the Tudi Gong, and the usual collection of gods from the Chinese pantheon. The permanent Chinese staff of the sugar mills comprised at the very least the millers themselves, cashiers who took care of the accounts and equipment, and overseers or *mandors*, who supervised the work on the plantations. Besides weeding and cleaning the beds, the seasonal peak of the so-called sugar campaign, cutting sugar cane and transporting it to the mills, was mostly performed by Javanese *bujang*, or hired workers, who were supplied annually by the regents of the nearby sultanate of Cheribon. These seasonal workers were loaned for a fee and were not allowed to take their wives and children with them. They were forced to return home after the harvest was brought in and had to surrender part of their income to the village chiefs. Wives and children were thus effectively used by the regents as guarantors. Likewise, the *bujang* were the victims of extortion from the Chinese sugar millers, from whom they had to buy their provisions. When during the 1730s these seasonal workers were less inclined to do this exhausting labor, they were increasingly replaced by illegal Chinese migrants who thus found a safe haven at the mills.

Life around the mills

The sugar mills and adjacent plantations were scattered across the landscape of the Ommelanden and moved from one place to another when the soil became exhausted and the surrounding forests were depleted. They were thus relatively autonomous 'Chinese republics' that became increasingly distant from the urban life in Batavia and its atmosphere of convivencia. Yet, they did maintain contact with each other, and there was a cluster of communication lines along which news and rumors were passed. In and around each sugar mill, there were people of all sorts, as the later Governor-General Jacob Mossel put it: 'The people who come to work there are not always of the best sort; there are many rogues and runaway slaves among them, but it is still better that they work there, and thus become accustomed to a useful life, than that they should murder and rob.'[112] Quite rightly, he saw sugar mills as social safety valves in frontier society.

A fine example of such a somewhat isolated sugar enterprise can be found in the surviving annual contract of a Chinese miller named Tan Inkong.[113] In 1708, when sugar cultivation was experiencing a veritable boom, he rented from a Cheribon regent for 170 silver rials a piece of land measuring 3,200 by 1,800 Rhineland feet to be planted with sugar cane and to be equipped with two or three sugar mills. In addition, he was given a strip of land 1,500 by 55 feet to grow rice for the staff, and he was allowed to take as much timber from the nearby forest as he needed for erecting the mills and for refining the sugar. The lessee was obliged to look after the food and payment of sixty workers. Some restrictions were imposed: no more Chinese were allowed on the leased land than the number reported to the administration in Batavia, and they were forbidden to move further into the countryside. The colonial government clearly was aware that Chinese 'vagrants' were a potential danger. Tan Inkong was obliged to deliver all the sugar produced to the Company's warehouses in Batavia at a price to be determined by the Company.

The Gentlemen XVII acquired such a sweet tooth that they ordered the construction of special ships, '*suiker fluyten*,' to carry sugar to the Netherlands and established special rules for packing refined sugar in boxes of 800 to 1,000 pounds. To keep costs down, these sugar flutes were manned by crews of no more than 45 sailors. Initially, sugar cultivation was encouraged by the colonial administration with special measures. The millers were paid well for their labor—4 rixdollars per picul (120 pounds). But as time went by, they were increasingly extorted by corrupt Chinese middlemen, who, inserting themselves between the mills and the Company, offered less than half the price. Upon becoming director general in 1705, Abraham van Riebeeck intervened immediately to put an end to these malpractices. He ordered an inventory of all the sugar mills and calculated the amount of sugar that the Company needed. Based on these data, he came up with a plan to fairly distribute the desired sugar production among the registered mills.

These measures were apparently insufficient, because three years later, two councilors of the Indies were forced to launch a new investigation 'on the occasion of the decline of several sugar millers.'[114] They had identified 130 mills in the Ommelanden, belonging to 79 Chinese, one Javanese regent, and four Europeans. The mills elsewhere in Java they left out of consideration. The investigators stated that sugar was 'the principal and most advantageous product of Batavia's agriculture,' because this sweetener found markets in Arabia, Persia, India, and Japan and moreover served as an excellent ballast for the ships returning to Europe. They were amazed at how much was involved in running the mills and warehouses, housing the staff, and caring for the water buffaloes. Some two hundred thousand stools (roots) of sugar cane were needed for planting, and the land had to be cleared before the digging and plowing could begin. Annual wages had to be paid to the scribe, the headman, the four Chinese supervisors of the plowmen and about twenty Javanese who had to keep the sugar cane gardens clean, a Chinese supervisor of the work with the grinding stones, and the buffalo guards. This is to say nothing of the purchase of four large cast-iron sugar pans, the frequent replacement of the buffaloes (those poor beasts were worked to death at the mills), sugar pots, lime and stone for repairing the mill, provisions for the staff of the mill, and the replacement of the iron parts of the mill. Then there were the salaries of the Javanese who transported the sugar to and from the mill with their vessels, the Javanese grinders, fire distillers, water carriers, sugar cane cutters, for four grinding months, the Chinese sugar distillers, the Chinese who took care of the oil and candles for lighting, and the Chinese dusting the sugar in the clay pots.

And what about additional costs such as the purchase of two hundred bundles of firewood, packing materials, lime to put into the sugar during the production process, land rent, a year's interest on the construction of the mill, and the delivered roots of sugar cane? The inspectors calculated that all this put together required an investment of 6,807 rixdollars. The estimated output of each mill was 800 piculs of powdered sugar and 800 piculs of black syrup. Simple arithmetic showed that at the purchase price of sugar imposed by the Company, the mills could not keep running. The operating costs overwhelmingly indicated that this amount was too low. As an underlying cause of the decline of the sugar industry, the inspectors therefore cited the low procurement price of three rixdollars per picul that the Company imposed on the sugar millers.

CHAPTER 6

Different Century, New Protagonists

On its centennial anniversary, in 1702, the United East India Company had reached the height of its power, or perhaps had already passed it, just as the Dutch Republic's Golden Age was drawing to an end. With branches spread all over Maritime Asia, from Mocha in the Middle East to Deshima in remote Japan, the VOC was the largest trading Company in the world. As a memento, the Gentlemen XVII cast a medal with the uplifting text, *In altera saecula pergo* (Into other centuries I proceed), stamped on the edge. The solemn commemoration of the centennial planned on March 20 was canceled at the eleventh hour when it became known that Stadholder-King William III of Orange had died in England owing to a fall from his horse. The whole country was in mourning. So, without any festivities, a new century dawned with formidable new challenges for the Dutch seaborne empire.

With characteristic foresight, Joan van Hoorn had indicated in his reports to the Gentlemen XVII the path that the Company should take in the new century.[115] Like his father, he wished to promote the expansion of private enterprise within the Company's affairs in Asia, but to no avail. There was no room for a change of the time-honored paradigm. Everything remained the same: the monopoly system, the unilaterally imposed purchase prices of spices, coffee, sugar, and cinnamon, and the intra-Asian shipping carried out by the Company's own vessels stubbornly continued as a straitjacket that impeded any kind of reform. Meanwhile, the economic situation of the VOC in Asia had changed so much that its trade between Asia and Europe could no longer be financed solely with the proceeds of the intra-Asian network. For the most part, the mutual trade between the Company's trade factories in Asia was already operating at a loss. The only profits were now derived from the sale of Asian goods on the European market. In addition, the Company was facing increasing competition from the English and French East India Companies, which were expanding their operations in the Indian subcontinent and focused mainly on the lucrative export of high-quality textiles to Europe.

During the reign of Stadholder-King William III of Orange (1688–1702), the heretofore somewhat tottering English East India Company (EIC) had been revived to such an extent that the VOC faced a formidable rival. While in the seventeenth century the Dutch Company was still dominant, in the eighteenth century, it soon had to acknowledge the superiority of the English Company that had adapted its operations much better to the changing times and market conditions. As long as it maintained a monopoly on shipping between India and England, the EIC had—contrary to the VOC—no problems with independent merchantmen engaged in the so-called country trade within Asia.

The Dutch also faced new challenges at the local level of Batavian society. In the previous century, there had been a remarkable symbiosis between the Company and the enterprising Chinese in the city, not least because Chinese junks controlled the shipping corridor with their mother country and because the Chinese sugar industry was booming. This harmonious cooperation reached its apogee under Joan van Hoorn's tenure as governor-general, but came under strain under the rule of his successors, first when VOC ships began sailing independently to Canton from the 1730s onwards, but even more so when the Dutch East Indian sugar enterprise began running into all sorts of problems. Ironically, it was Mattheus de Haan, the last but by then aged survivor of the young lions personally handpicked for the Council of the Indies by Van Hoorn, who, during his short tenure as governor-general (1725–29), not only managed to harm the Company's interests in sugar and coffee cultivation, but also fomented bad blood in the Dutch–Chinese relationship by subjecting the Chinese to some very disadvantageous policies. He initiated an era in which Van Hoorn's favorable policies were challenged, if not done away with altogether.

During this time of growing trouble, two young protagonists appeared on the scene in Batavia, first the Amsterdam patrician, Adriaan Valckenier in 1715, to be joined ten years later by his future rival, Gustaaf Willem, baron van Imhoff. Youthful and 'fresh off the boat,' as they were, they initially figured as rather innocent bystanders on the scene, but by making smart marriages of convenience, they maneuvered to position themselves for solid careers in the later 1720s, when this chapter draws to an end.

The last of the Valckeniers

In the spring of 1714, Amsterdam's Mayor Nicolaas Witsen was visited by nineteen-year-old Adriaan Valckenier, grandson of his former patron, the renowned Gillis Valckenier (1623–1680), who had played a crucial role in rescuing the VOC during and after the Third Anglo-Dutch War in the 1670s, when the Company fell into serious financial trouble. In those difficult times, Mayor Gillis Valckenier had managed to steer his city and the VOC into calmer waters. Together with his brilliant nephew, Johannes Hudde (1628–1705), he set up a rescue operation to bring the Company's affairs back into the black.[116] Gilles's son, Pieter Ranst Valckenier (1661–1705), succeeded his father as the administrator and director of the VOC but died young. His son, Adriaan, was only ten years old at the time. Until shortly before the turn of the century, several other Valckeniers had served the VOC in high positions. Adriaan's uncle, Cornelis Valckenier (1640–1700), made his career in Asia between 1660 and 1675, and after his return home, was twice appointed mayor of Amsterdam and had even served as godfather to one of Joan van Hoorn's daughters. Another uncle, the councilor of the Indies, Wouter Valckenier (1659–1710), repatriated in 1699. Within the VOC, the name, Valckenier, had a magical ring to it.[117]

Because young Adriaan dreamed of making a career in the East Indies as his uncles had, he knocked on the door of the old family friend, the Amsterdam city mayor, Nicolaas Witsen, who by now had reached the blessed age of 71. He knew that this VOC administrator possessed the privilege of sending one junior merchant to the East Indies every year, and even though he was aware that he could not be sent out in that rank until he had attained the age of twenty-one, Adriaan called in 'uncle' Witsen's assistance. Normally, a would-be junior merchant had to post a deposit of 2,000 guilders to a Company trustee for this privilege, but in this case, Witsen may have waived that fee for him.

Thus, in the fall of 1714, we see Adriaan Valckenier embarking on the *Linschoten*, an East Indiaman of 804 tons. Before the anchor was weighed, he read the muster-roll in front of the entire crew, as befitted a junior merchant, and collected the papers of all the sailors. Once at sea, it was his job to keep the ship's records. As a scion of a powerful Amsterdam regent family, Adriaan was treated with respect by Captain Arie van de Linde. Only one junior merchant sailed on every ship and thus, although still wet behind the ears, he could claim a certain status.

Just before his departure, Adriaan had received a letter of introduction from Witsen to his 'special friend' at the Cape of Good Hope, VOC merchant, Johannes Swellengrebel. That note served its aim, because upon the *Linschoten*'s arrival at the Cape in April of the following year, Swellengrebel rowed out to the ship to invite Adriaan to come ashore and move in with him while the ship was provisioned for the following stretch of the voyage. Years later, Swellengrebel would remember the young lodger as a sociable fellow. Soon the anchor was raised again, and the voyage from the Cape to the Indies also went off without a hitch. In Batavia, Adriaan was able to report that everyone on board had survived the trip, although there was some concern about the health of Captain Van de Linde, who actually died a few weeks later.[118]

Once disembarked in Batavia, Adriaan Valckenier discovered to his disappointment that there was no one waiting for him. The last Valckenier of any standing in the East Indies, great uncle Anthony, had embarked a short time before on November 28, 1713, to return to the homeland as commander of the return fleet. They had missed each other 'like ships that pass in the night.' Adriaan ended up as a simple bookkeeper in the granary and, as explained below, nothing changed during his first ten years in Batavia.

A View behind the scenes

Adriaan had no preferential treatment to expect from Governor-General Christopher van Swoll (1713–1718). Within the Council of the Indies, the incorruptible Van Swoll was perceived as a demanding administrator, to put it mildly. Having risen to the highest position in 1713, he immediately cracked down on private trade. In doing so, he made himself so hated, that in the eyes of all employees, he figured as 'a perfect Satan.' The Gentlemen XVII, on the other hand, did not want to hear a bad word about him, especially when Van Swoll's first return fleet delivered 10 million guilders more than ever before.[119] That year, the Company's shares rose 10 percent in one stroke. Van Swoll saw little interest in the further development of agricultural crops in the Ommelanden but focused his attention primarily on the Company's trade. He ended the promotion of coffee cultivation, the hobbyhorse of his predecessors, Van Hoorn and Van Riebeeck, and also thought little of the Chinese and their privileged position. He noted with considerable alarm that thousands of Chinese 'fortune seekers' were landing every year, with a large proportion of them disappearing into illegality. In 1717, Van Swoll also fell out with the tea merchants of the Chinese junks whom he suspected of price fixing. This forced him to unilaterally reduce the purchase price of tea from 60 to 40 guilders per picul. When, to everyone's dismay, not a single junk appeared on the roadstead the following year, the entire citizenry of Batavia, with the Chinese in the lead, was deprived of the annual supply of tea and other imports from China that made their lives so pleasant. Van Swoll was confronted with this setback just before he suddenly died in 1718. In truth, his intervention had had little to do with the non-appearance of the junks.

As it turned out, the Kangxi emperor had re-imposed an embargo on all Chinese shipping to the Nanyang (Southern Seas). It had come to the attention of the Son of Heaven that, scattered throughout the South China Sea region, overseas settlements such as Batavia and Manila had sprung up, where tens of thousands of 'Chinese desperadoes' were seeking refuge far beyond the reach of the long arm of his imperial rule. There, they created mixed offspring with 'barbarian wives and neglected the ancestral graves in their home country.' For the imperial court, this was an intolerable situation that had to be curbed. Overseas resident Chinese who showed repentance were allowed to return home from

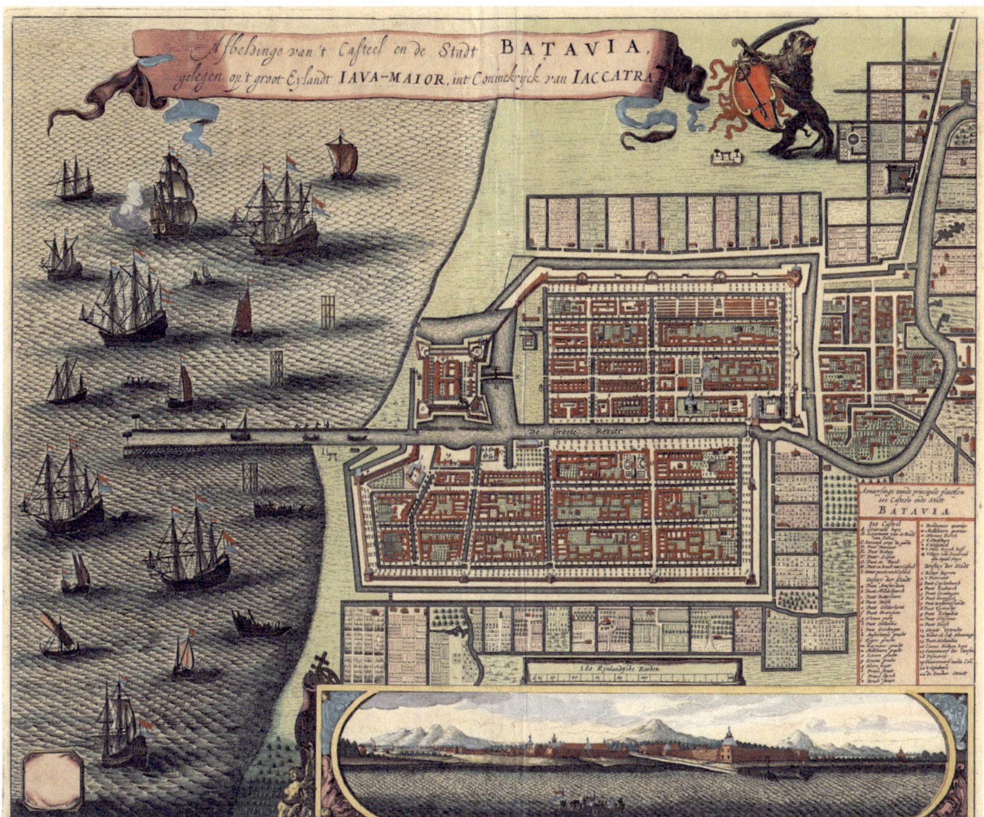

A general map of the castle and the city of Batavia, second half of the 17th century.
Bottom: a cartouche with a view of the city from the roadstead.

Jonque chinoise (dessin de M. Morel-Fatio).

Two illustrations of a junk.
This type of ship was generally half the size of the VOC return ships.

Street scene in Batavia with a *wayang* performance, a Chinese street opera, in the background. On the left and right are *kelontong*, street hawkers.

A shopping couple accompanied by their servants. On the left in the background is a stage where a Chinese *wayang* performance is taking place.

A Chinese captain in full regalia.

A Chinese peddler with three local women buying local fruit. The *xinke* (Chinese newcomers) gained access to the market through their local *njai* (concubines).

General map of Batavia and its surroundings (*Ommelanden*).

Chinese millstones used to crush sugar cane in the sugar mills and surrounding plantations. The mills were driven by water buffaloes.

The restored funerary monument of Que Kiaoko, who served as *Shahbandar* of Semarang and Lieutenant of Batavia.

The Town Hall of Batavia, the first stone of which was laid by Petronella van Hoorn in 1707. The building was completed in 1712.

Castle Batavia, at the mouth of the Great River, where the Governor-General resided.

abroad within two years; all others were banned for life. Almost simultaneously with this ban on Chinese shipping to Southeast Asia, the strict prohibitions on Western merchants wishing to bring their own ships to China were relaxed, making it possible for European ships to anchor upriver close to Canton without having to meet the traditional tribute obligations. This dramatic decision did not provide the free trade that the Dutch had sought for more than a century, but for the European merchants at large it was a first step in the right direction.

New prospects in China

The imperial embargo showed how dependent the VOC was on junks in the absence of its own shipping connection to China. Governor-General Hendrick Swaardecroon, Van Swoll's successor, did all that he could to restore relations with the Chinese *nakhodas* (captains) and laid out the red carpet for the visiting Chinese traders proclaiming that they should be treated 'with all gentleness and courtesy.' He raised the purchase price of tea again and relaxed Van Swoll's restrictions on the supply of Chinese migrant workers. To his immense satisfaction, Swaardecroon saw, notwithstanding the imperial embargo, some twenty-one junks (illegally) appear on the Batavia roadstead in 1723.

When the management in Holland was informed about the imperial embargo, the genie was out of the bottle. It dawned on the Gentlemen XVII that the Company's prosperity, and in particular their own personal interest in the lucrative tea trade, could no longer remain only in the hands of Chinese junk skippers. They also noted with concern that the Company had recently been bypassed left and right by English, French, and even Ostend shipping to Canton. In 1727, it was therefore decided, on a trial basis, to send one or two ships directly—that is, bypassing Batavia—to China to investigate the new trade opportunities. All this was agreed upon despite the loud protests from the High Government in Batavia, which believed that the Canton trade might be disadvantageous for its thriving Chinese junk trade.

Conspiracies, interventions, and setbacks

Hendrik Swaardecroon was one of three young lions with whom Joan van Hoorn had surrounded himself in the Council of the Indies before he was prepared to accept the governorship. Settled for good in Batavia after a career in India, Swaardecroon, like Van Hoorn, dabbled in agriculture and horticulture. Horse breeding was his favorite pastime. At his country estate, Kadoengan, he planted coffee trees and also conducted experiments with herbs and crops for medicinal use and the manufacture of dyes. Not surprisingly, like his predecessors, Van Hoorn and Van Riebeeck, he showed himself to be a great promoter of coffee and sugar cultivation during his administration, and faced the task of reviving those crops, which had been neglected by Van Swoll. Immediately after taking office, he had a survey made of the coffee trees and sugar cane under cultivation elsewhere in Java by Chinese millers or Javanese regents. It turned out that 57 sugar mills under Chinese management were already operating at Kudus, Pati, and Japara on Java's northeast coast. Although the yields of these sugar mills in these areas were still quite low due to the political unrest prevailing there, he believed that they would eventually be needed to meet the increasing demand for sugar. Yet, under no circumstances, he remarked, should these external producers be allowed to disadvantage the Chinese sugar industry in the Batavian Ommelanden, 'on which so much effort has been made over the past 30 years to animate our people to that culture.'[120] He trusted that with the combined proceeds of the mills in the Ommelanden and the outlying areas, the four flute ships that the Company had specially built to transport sugar to the Netherlands could be filled without any effort.

In late 1721, to everyone's horror, a conspiracy was discovered in Batavia. 'Native citizens, Javanese and slaves' were caught conspiring to overthrow the VOC regime and kill all the Europeans in the city. A wealthy freeburgher, Pieter Erberveld, and his Javanese crony, Kartadria, were identified as ringleaders.[121] Erberveld, son of a Company servant and a Siamese mother, owned land adjacent to that of Swaardecroon, with whom, as is often the case with neighbors, he picked a quarrel. Little by little, Swaardecroon had bought up 34 adjacent pieces of land and wanted to combine them into one contiguous plot. The only thing missing was a piece of land that Erberveld did not want to part with. It has been suggested that the whole conspiracy story was nothing of the sort, but a cunning move by the governor-general to get his neighbor out of the way.

Erberveld's confessions, admittedly on the rack, divulged a widely branched network of conspirators ready to stage a coup on New Year's Day. All of Batavia trembled with fear, especially since funny rumors had already been circulating in the previous months about arson, or what appeared to be arson, at the Company shipyard across the river from Batavia Castle. That the colonial administration felt like it was living on top of an unpredictable volcano is evident from the decision not to conduct any more in-depth investigations after the gruesome execution of Erberveld and Kartadria, for fear that this might spark an even greater Javanese rebellion.

Swaardecroon also came to face new challenges surrounding the succession to the throne in Kartasura, which resulted in the outbreak of the Second

Javanese War of Succession (1719–22). When Susuhunan Pakubuwana I died on February 1, 1719, the fat was in the fire. Besides the crown pretender, two other princes laid claim to the throne. It was up to Hendrik Swaardecroon to use a mix of diplomatic mediation and brute force over the next three years to settle the matter and help the crown prince finally ascend to the throne in 1722. And thus, with much loss of life, yet another VOC intervention settled the affairs at the Javanese court.

The Company also faced headwinds elsewhere. Again, in most cases, this was due to internal developments among the Asian business partners, over which Batavia could exert no influence: the largest market for Batavia's sugar in Asia, Persia, fell away in 1722 owing to an Afghan invasion that ended the Safavid dynasty, trade in Hindustan was hampered by entanglements at the Moghul court, the Mocha trade in coffee took a battering due to increasing European competition, and in Japan, a harsh political intervention by the Tokugawa government reduced the once profitable Dutch shipping to that empire to one or two ships a year.

Despite these gloomy developments, it hardly seemed to bother Batavian society. On the contrary, when Reverend Canter Visscher returned from India to the Company headquarters after an absence of six years, he found 'the city so considerably changed, that in many places it had become unrecognizable to me, for a great many new and beautiful houses had been added, also the splendor had increased so remarkably, that one almost seemed to come under a new people.'[122]

On July 8, 1725, Swaardecroon, who desired a peaceful retirement, was honorably discharged from service, and with a sigh of relief, he made way for Director General Mattheus de Haan. This was a most unfortunate choice by the Gentlemen XVII. De Haan had a meritorious career behind him—he was the last of Joan van Hoorn's energetic 'young lions'—but, by now he was rather washed out. He complained 'about his weak stature at the old age of 62 years,' which, he said, 'rather should earn him a quiet rest than many worries.' Although he appreciated the confidence placed in him, he still hoped for 'a speedy discharge from that weighty office,' so that he also could retire to his country estate and go out sailing on his yacht, *Merwede*. The Dordrecht native had clearly not forgotten the lovely rivers surrounding his birthplace. In the four years during which he and the equally 'memory lacking' director general, Anthony Huysman, were given the task of running the Company, they managed to undo much of Swaardecroon's good work. De Haan seems to have been eager to provide friends and acquaintances with jobs. Although he was 'not defective in intellect, nor ignorant in the Compagnie's affairs, he was such a procrastinator that thereby all excellence that was in him eclipsed.'[123]

De Haan acted in an almost servile manner to please the Gentlemen XVII. His tampering with the purchase price for coffee is a good example. It is fair to say that the directors in Holland also deserve blame for the fickle instructions which they sent. First, they wrote that Java should by no means enjoy a monopoly in coffee production. 'We consider it to be a dangerous consequence, that the Javanese by the supply of this fruit, would gather so much money and power, that they might begin to feel over-important.' They had learned that, thanks to the coffee cultivation, the Javanese regents in the Batavia Highlands and the Preanger were turning rich while they were sleeping.[124] Judging from the 50 guilders that they received per picul, it was feared that the many thousands of piculs would turn the Javanese noblemen into money bags, all the more so since they passed on only a small portion of that money to the farmers who planted the coffee on their orders. Yet, only a year later, the directors in Holland changed their minds and emphasized that Java should become the sole producer, mainly in the Bovenlanden and neighboring Cheribon. They concluded that this might, after all, also benefit Batavia.

Because considerable planting had taken place under Swaardecroon, during De Haan's administration, coffee trees started to provide ample yields. Patria announced that it could purchase as much as 4 million pounds of coffee annually but instructed that delivery from then on should proceed at half the 20 rixdollars purchase price that Swaardecroon had originally accorded with the Javanese regents and *umbul* (village heads). In the meantime, the purchase price had already dropped to nine rixdollars per picul, and De Haan thought that he could save another five. De Haan thus saved the Company hundreds of thousands of guilders, but this occurred 'at the cost of 210 million curses among the Javanese population!'[125] This indeed proved to be the case. Either peasants voted with their feet running off to Mataram territory, or they simply put the axe to the trees as a sign of protest. They did not wish to live on starvation wages. This juggling with the purchase price in order to maximize profits at the auctions in the Dutch Republic now also set the trend for coffee cultivation. In the following decades, the same wave movement occurred, from stimulating and expanding new plantations, to the forced curtailment of agricultural land, and the 'extirpation' of surplus crops.

A second start

Under the reigns of Van Swoll and Swaardecroon, Adriaan Valckenier's career had not progressed an inch, but in 1726, when De Haan took office, the now thirty-year-old Amsterdammer was suddenly promoted as if by magic to the rank of merchant and first bookkeeper at the 'Comptoir General,' and the same year he was also granted a seat on the alderman's bench. His marriage the previous year to Johanna Alida Tolling, the daughter of Councilor of the Indies Laurens Tolling, must have given Valckenier's career a big boost. In 1727, he was appointed bookkeeper general, and in 1730, he was elected to the Council of the Indies as an extraordinary member. At that stage in his career, he first crossed paths with his soon-to-be nemesis, Gustaaf Willem, baron van Imhoff, an ambitious young man who could boast support from the administrators in Amsterdam.

Fresh off the boat

Nineteen-year-old Gustaaf Willem van Imhoff signed on as a junior merchant on the VOC ship *Kockengen* in January 1725. He hailed from the East Frisian town of Leer, where his father, Wilhelm Heinrich van Imhoff, held the office of *landdrost* (sheriff). Through his mother, Isabella Sophia Boreel, he was related to Balthazar Boreel, director of the Amsterdam Chamber of the VOC. The Van Imhoffs descended from a distinguished merchant family from Nuremberg whose history dated back to the Middle Ages. The elevation to the peerage of the East Frisian branch had taken place only recently.

Gustaaf Willem wrote to his younger brother, Hieronymus Rudolph, many years later, that he himself had arrived in Batavia 'cherry fresh from Europe,' totally ignorant of all the things that a junior merchant should know in order to be promoted. Based on his own experience, he therefore gladly gave advice.[126] It made sense to find out on which ship and under which skipper Hieronymus could best sign on, because, he wrote, once on the high seas, some captains have so much self-conceit 'that they hardly seem the same persons anymore.' Next, the trick was to remain friends with the captain and the crew during the eight-month voyage. A decent life on board was only possible for a junior merchant if, in addition to the victuals provided by the Company, he also brought along a few barrels of wine and beer himself. These came in handy for generously sharing at the ship's officers' table: 'The pleasure which one derives from this during the voyage is much greater than the expenses required.'

From the day the young Gustaaf Willem set foot in Batavia, he had left nothing to chance, as evidenced by the battle plan he submitted to his brother:

> If you are not too ambitious, he wrote, the best thing you can do is become a member of the Council of Justice. You will then belong to the elite, your housing in Batavia Castle will be taken care of and the salary is also sufficient to lead a decent

> life. Unfortunately, you are not allowed to engage in any (ostentatious) side jobs, which means you can forget about getting rich quickly. The road to the big money ascends via the ranks of merchant and chief merchant to councilor of the Indies. Therefore it is convenient to take the inside track and head for an 'impeccable marriage' with a daughter of a high official. This is not easy, by the way; it is only reserved for the occasional 'white falcon.'

Gustaaf Willem van Imhoff did the trick himself by marrying nineteen-year-old Catharina Huysman (1709–1744), the only daughter of Director General Anthony Huysman, two years after arriving in Batavia. That marriage made him wealthy overnight and also ensured that his bed was made in the Company administration. Within a year, he was promoted to merchant and put in charge of the direction of the General Pay Office in Batavia Castle. That was no easy job for a recently arrived young man of twenty. He had to show himself to be proficient in clearing a large number of Asian currencies to keep the garrison, pay, and hospital books in order, not to mention the books of the deceased, including the connected inheritances. His intelligence and possibly even his Nüremberg merchant roots certainly served him well in this regard.

Tableau de la troupe

The Council of the Indies in which Valckenier and Van Imhoff, as extraordinary councilor and secretary of the Council, respectively, operated under the administration of Mattheus de Haan made an extremely weak impression. Because the governmental crisis that broke out under De Haan's successor at the beginning of the 1730s had its origins in this earlier period, a brief introduction to the various councilors makes sense, if only because it is owing to that crisis that Valckenier and Van Imhoff were eventually offered the opportunity to advance to the highest echelons.

Director General Anthony Huysman had earned his stripes in his good years as director of trade in Bengal, but he was now so worn out that he was said to be 'devoid of memory.' His right-hand man, Batavia Castle's first merchant, Adriaan Oostwalt, would later declare that Huysman had been 'mad and totally demented, yes he no longer even knew what he was talking about.' Petrus Vuyst (1691–1732), councilor of India and governor of Ceylon, was a young, arrogant jurist of wealthy Haarlem background, who arrived in Batavia in 1716 in the position of public prosecutor (attorney-fiscal). As early as 1721, this second cousin of Adriaan Valckenier joined the Council of the Indies as an extraordinary member. Between 1722 and 1724, he served as director of trade in Bengal, and returning to Batavia he again took a seat in the Council, this time as an ordinary member. In addition, he held the presidency of the Council of Aldermen in 1725. A year later, he was appointed governor of Ceylon, the highest within the Company's hierarchy after the governor-general and the director general. When he left for Ceylon, his level-headed fellow members of the Council watched this self-righteous fellow temporarily disappear behind the horizon, presumably with a sigh of relief—temporary indeed because in a letter to the Gentlemen XVII of October 31, 1728, De Haan mentions a secret letter from Vuyst in which the latter asked to be discharged. It was a curious letter 'riddled with such arrogant, injurious, and irreverent expressions that these could not be accepted from a governor and fellow councilor of India.' The next General Missive of March 29, 1729, shows that the High Government in Batavia was beginning to be genuinely concerned about the unrest among the Company servants in Ceylon who 'by such nauseous, confused, and dubious decisions and transfers [by Governor Vuyst] are kept in a perpetual alarm, anxiety, and uncertainty.' This was sufficient reason to 'go stirring in Colombo's messy barrel to elucidate the true state of affairs.'[127]

The third council member, Wijbrand Blom (1685–1737), often voiced long-winded and dissenting opinions on various matters during council meetings. He was continuously at odds with fellow council member, Diderik Durven, because the latter, as president of the Council of Justice, had refused to help him in his divorce case. On the contrary, Durven had stood up for Blom's spurned wife, Maria Haak, who was his own sister-in-law.

Cornelis Hasselaar (1676–1737) and his fellow councilman, Hendrik van Baerle (1685–1744), were spoiled scions of Amsterdam regent families. Devoid of any talent, Hasselaar had risen through the ranks thanks to his brother-in-law, Huysman, and his connections with the influential Amsterdam *bewindhebber* (VOC director), Lieve Geelvinck tot Castricum. He was called by colleagues 'a hollow vessel and a conceited dumbass' who was unable to even shoulder his share of work in preparing the annual regional reports that every councilor had to contribute to the General Missives. It was alleged that he was 'such a stupid beast that a man of sound judgment would not entrust him the care of his hencoop.'[128]

During De Haan's tenure, hardly any criticism could be heard inside the council with the exception of one stubborn voice. Only Mr. Diderik Durven (1676–1740), who also served as president of the Council of Justice, ventured dissenting opinions. In no uncertain terms, he addressed critical letters to the management in Holland. Within the Council, he occasionally deviated from the judgment of his colleagues on purely legal grounds, and this was held against him as disloyal behavior. The frank tone of his letters did not please the Gentlemen XVII either, and they let that be known in clear terms. Durven, an outsider from the city of Delft—one of the smallest chambers of the VOC—was a skilled jurist but not devoid of character flaws. He was known for his unadulterated use of language, 'calling a shoe a shoe, without ever using a foreign term [...] and handing out his orders which, in order to give them some force, were often laced with some particular and familiar curses.'

Standing as a rock in the troubled waters figured Michiel Westpalm (1684–1736), a man who got along well with all council members. Having put out to sea as a simple sailor, this good fellow would eventually make it to the rank of director general in the 1730s.

There was another person, by the way, who, although retired, continued to buzz around the heads of the council members like a hornet. After Swaardecroon had withdrawn to his estate at Kadoengan, he devoted himself with renewed zeal to his botanical interests. All his attention was now focused on silk cultivation, which he proposed to introduce alongside coffee cultivation. To De Haan's annoyance, he maintained a direct correspondence with the Gentlemen XVII about his experiments. De Haan's complaints about this were answered with the soothing observation that people who had dealt with weighty matters for years could not resist taking all kinds of initiatives, even if they tried to settle down in solitude and peace. So enthusiastic was the VOC-management about Swaardecroon's silk samples that he was rewarded for his efforts with a gift of 100 rixdollars. With undisguised relief, De Haan announced in his missive of December 8, 1728, that his tormentor had died on August 16 of that year. He looked forward to fewer quarrels in the Council, 'for which Swaardecroon had set a bad example.' Still, he was not to enjoy his wished-for respite for long, for only six months later, on June 1, 1729, De Haan also breathed his last. A new governor general had to be elected, and it was up to the members of the Council to elect one from their midst.

A sensational election

The members of the Council faced a difficult choice. Normally, they would have voted for the director general, but in this case, that was not possible. Huysman was no longer *compos mentis* and had already let it be known that he would cast his vote for his brother-in-law, Hasselaar. Since Hasselaar, the longest-serving member of the Council, also felt assured of the support of Blom and De Haan's two sons-in-law, a lot had to happen if the generalship was to elude him. To his amazement, that turned out to be the case after all. He had not counted on the extraordinary members of the Council, and that finished him off. When the votes were counted, Hasselaar was narrowly defeated by stubborn Diderik Durven, who, 'notwithstanding his advancing years, and weak physical condition as well as the miserable situation of many places in India,' was nevertheless prepared to assume the position of governor-general.[129]

The management in Holland noticed that the election had taken place in a rather unusual manner because the extraordinary members had joined the vote. Their suspicions were heightened when they learned of Cornelis Hasselaar's complaints. He claimed that, notwithstanding all his years of service on the Council, he had been unfairly passed over. A written interrogatory prepared by the Council with Durven's answers on the left side of the page and Hasselaar's on the right, incidentally, left no doubt that Durven was the better candidate.[130] Consequently, Hasselaar was asked to cease his protests and to accept the result. Although he did so in writing and was given the position of director general as a consolation prize, an embittered Hasselaar was in no way going to be a loyal colleague from now on. The Gentlemen XVII ratified Diderik Durven's appointment, all the more so because on June 10, 1729, they had transferred the governor of Coromandel, Dirk van Cloon, to Batavia as a 'political deputy' to keep an eye on the situation there and assist Governor-General De Haan where needed. After arriving in Batavia in 1631, Van Cloon had been installed in the Council of the Indies on March 23, and on 25 May, he accepted the presidency of the city's Aldermen Bench, thus immediately participating in the administration.

An unpleasant surprise awaited Durven when he took office. Both the administration and the bookkeeping accounts appeared to have been totally neglected. De Haan and Huysman had left behind an Augean stable of records. Even the resolutions passed by the Council of the Indies the previous year had not yet been summarized. Under a big pile of papers, Durven found a shocking report on all sorts of fraud surrounding the sugar mills and sugar warehouses and discovered the shady role that Chinese middlemen were playing in that sector.[131] It was clear that De Haan had deliberately spirited away those papers.

What shocked Durven the most, however, were the reports that had reached Batavia about the 'atrocities committed, unheard of atrocities, unchristian acts and unfair proceedings' committed by Governor Petrus Vuyst of Ceylon who, under the pretense of an imminent Portuguese attack on the island, conducted a veritable reign of terror, and with the help of a hastily created 'Blood Council,' had innocent people broken on the wheel, condemned, and executed. For a while, it seemed that Vuyst, like Swaardecroon seven years earlier, had managed to uncover a conspiracy against the administration, but in this case it turned out to be a fantasized plot. This is not the place to delve further into the tropical madness, the atrocities, and delusions of the insane Vuyst.[132] The councilor of the Indies, Versluys, whom Durven dispatched to Ceylon, met an obsessed man who declared himself to be 'a troubled soul in a troubled body.' Vuyst was taken into custody and transported to Batavia to account for his actions. The whole affair left deep wounds within colonial society and also cast a stain on the new governor-general, even though he had decisively intervened in a matter that had been festering since his predecessor's administration. After a long trial in which his relatives in Holland had tried to intervene in favor of the madman, the ex-governor of Ceylon was sentenced to death. The sentence was ratified by all the members of the Council of the Indies, with the exception of Adriaan Valckenier, who waived judgment for family reasons. On June 3, 1732, the insane Vuyst climbed the scaffold.[133]

CHAPTER 7

The Crisis of Governance

Governor-General Diderik Durven did not lack vision and intended to make a clean sweep in the administration thereby risking much opposition from his entourage. He was full of plans and felt supported by the secretary of the Council of India, Wouter Hendrix, a sharp-witted man. The new management team, to which Van Imhoff was added as second secretary, discovered that no less than 4,784,740 guilders were kept in the Castle treasury, while the High Government annually borrowed 2,524,926 rixdollars at an interest rate of 4.5 percent from private persons in Batavia. By using a substantial amount of the reserves to pay off the loans, the Company was immediately relieved of 505,500 guilders in 'cancerous' charges.[134] Whether the city's private money lenders were happy about this remains to be seen, since they were thus deprived of a very reliable investment. Durven was willing to give Swaardecroon's proposed silk cultivation a chance. He asked for experts from Holland and had Ceylonese girls come to Batavia to spin the threads. He was also interested in collecting vegetable dyes, and continued to encourage mining projects in which he had been involved previously. In the end, none of these ventures came to fruit, but at the very least they testified to a fresh entrepreneurial spirit. Furthermore, infrastructural repair jobs were tackled, including digging new canals for better drainage of the rivers around the city—in one case with disastrous results, as we shall see.

To clear the backlog of correspondence, Durven enlisted the help of chief merchant, Gustaaf Willem van Imhoff, 'for the purpose of cultivating him to the job of second secretary' because in the past, too often, inexperienced people had not been able to manage the complicated work of the General Secretariat. Wouter Hendrix, the first secretary, was thus freed to prepare and edit the General Missive—the all-important annual report of the High Government to the Gentlemen XVII on the state of affairs in Asia. On May 10, Hendrix also joined Adriaan Valckenier as an extraordinary councilor to the High Government. This was a major promotion for both of them. Durven also toyed with the idea of sending Hendrix as special commissioner to Malabar and Coromandel to inspect the situation in India and to appoint him, afterwards, governor of Ceylon to clear up the ongoing problems in that island's government. Valckenier he reserved for a variety of tasks in Batavia.

It all turned out differently because the new governor-general was not given the chance to properly attend to his job. Within the Council, Hasselaar and his faction continued to obstruct him, especially when disagreement arose between Durven and the president of the Council of Justice, Cornelis van Gaasbeek, over the appointment of the latter's nephew as the Company's representative (*resident*) on the island of Timor. The governor-general used his prerogatives and appointed someone else, a move with unpleasant consequences. In retaliation, Gaasbeek and his wife started a gossip campaign about Durven's private life and sent vicious letters to relatives in Amsterdam. This was the signal for anyone who held grievances against Durven to speak ill of him. 'We are reviled in the face of our inferiors and the tender point of our superior position is affected in a grievous manner,' Durven complained in a letter to the supreme authorities in Holland.[135]

Following the complaints about Durven, the Gentlemen XVII in Amsterdam formed a committee to investigate the situation in Batavia. First of all, the reverend, Hogerwaard, who had recently returned from the East Indies, was invited to testify. 'Invoking God's holy name,' he confirmed that Durven was 'of a very loose and unbecoming life.' He also revealed that at a very low purchase price, Durven had sold territory in the Ommelanden to his fellow members of the Council of the Indies, from the lease of which the Board of Heemraden used to receive a considerable income. He confirmed that 'the governor general conversed daily in his house with very bad and godforsaken people and had all kinds of sinister acts carried out by the latter.' These included a woman who 'had been engaged in a shadowy trade with four English ships on the Batavian roadstead' and curious characters such as 'a native youngster Jonker Sloot, a black whore child of a very bad behavior, a certain wench, Miss Smuijsser, addicted to strong drink, with whom the governor general sometimes shared a drop, as well as the widow Leydecker Reael, also a drunkard and Miss Petten (alias Mafje) who deployed scandalous language in her conversation.' Durven's greatest favorite, according to the pastor, was the councilor of the Indies, Wouter Hendrix, 'a man of great ability, but very wicked.' In addition, David Andreas Stier (the commissioner of the natives), 'a god forsaken rascal,' frequently called at Durven's residence.[136] After these accusations, it was every man for himself. Other ministers also bemoaned Durven's blasphemy and moral decay. Even the commanders of the homecoming fleets were questioned insinuatingly. We will never know the complete truth about Durven's passion for gambling, his carousing, and amorous escapades, because the Gentlemen XVII refused to reveal the contents of the letters and the names of the whistleblowers.

In Search of a Scapegoat

As a result of what had come to their attention, the Gentlemen XVII took action. In their letter of September 14, 1731, they reproached the governor-general and some other members of the Council for having expropriated land from the Heemraden at ridiculously low prices, supposedly to grow mulberry trees, but they had in fact planted other crops. This had to be reversed immediately. The directors had also been told that the sailors of the VOC fleet often were employed in Batavia for odd jobs at the garden houses and country estates of the members of the High Government. Moreover, they had found out that the minutes and protocols of the notaries had not been properly filed at Batavia's town hall. Given the nature of colonial society with all its comings and goings, such bureaucratic neglect could only result in administrative confusion. Even as far away as in the Dutch Republic, rumors swirled that citizens in Batavia were engaged in a lively trade in opium with English 'interlopers' in the roadstead. The Gentlemen XVII regretted that 'they had not been able to bring about heartfelt affection and unity among the members of the Government of the Indies' and registered 'a great decay in religion and justice [in Batavia] by which all doors are opened to the utmost license, extortion, corruption, fornication, and all manner of wickedness.'[137] It sounded like a vote of no confidence, and it was. A month later, the issue came to a head.

On October 9, the directors of the VOC issued a directive announcing, after careful consideration, their decision 'to discharge the present governor general Mr. Diderik Durven from his oath and to deprive him from the service and wages of the Company, including the director general Cornelis Hasselaar and the extraordinary councilors Hendrik van Baerle and Wouter Hendrix.' They had taken this action 'because of the great decline in trade and justice that they ascertained to their grievous regret everywhere in Asia but especially in Batavia and Ceylon. All this could only lead to 'the total ruin of the Company's business in the East Indies.' The Company had fallen into an unprecedented crisis of governance.

After returning to his hometown, Delft, Diderik Durven demanded reparations for the dishonor done to him.[138] When his protests to the directors of the Company were to no avail, he even challenged his resignation in an address to the States General. After years of litigation, his efforts seemed to yield an effect: in 1740, just as the Company's Charter was about to be renewed, the VOC management was asked to come forward with the real reasons for the governor-general's resignation, but before an explanation could be offered, Durven breathed his last, and so the matter fizzled out.

It was common knowledge that Durven had a loose lifestyle and liked to gamble, but we can only guess at the details, because the administrators kept their mouths shut. Wouter Hendrix, who knew Durven well, thought that it was not all that bad, especially if you compared him to his successor, Van Cloon, who 'was as hot as fire at the dice game and used to play until three or four in the morning.' To the surprise of many, the second secretary of the Council, Van Imhoff, got away unscathed. The administrators did note, however, that in addition to his appointment as second secretary, Durven's *anak mas* (favorite) also held the office of water fiscal. In this case, their judgment was less harsh. Van Imhoff was allowed to choose which position that he wished to give up.[139]

Although the almost entire top brass of the Batavia government was dismissed, it could hardly be deemed a sweeping measure by the Gentlemen XVII, for it was only a shot across the bow of the High Government. The Company directorate passed up the crucial opportunity to carry out a radical reform by sending, for example, a trusted replacement directly from Holland to the Indies. But ever since Hendrick Brouwer had been sent as governor-general to Batavia a hundred years earlier to steadfastly continue the course of Jan Pietersz. Coen, there had never been a governor-general delegated to Asia from the fatherland. In his scathing condemnation of the course of events, councilor Wouter Hendrix had nothing good to say about the Gentlemen XVII. They had, according to him, been asleep and had neglected their duties, so that now the Company 'was sinking behind the horizon in the late afternoon, gradually losing its luster.' Although one might expect the administrators in Holland 'to be men of reason,' they were 'completely ignorant of that,' he concluded.[140]

The Gentlemen XVII appointed Dirk van Cloon as Durven's successor. He was the trustee whom they had added to the Council of the Indies some years earlier. They also proffered the names of a few candidates with whom he could bring the Council of the Indies back to full strength. Patronage played a role in this: thanks to their Amsterdam connections, Valckenier and Van Imhoff in particular were able to benefit from this move. Their appointments as Ordinary and Extraordinary Councilors of the Indies respectively followed on May 28, 1733. For the sake of balanced treatment, they were charged with proportionate subsidiary duties. Valckenier became president of the Heemraden and Van Imhoff became president of the orphan masters. Thus, the balance was precariously maintained between these two self-conscious men, who, as everyone knew, simply could not stand each other.

Valckenier and Van Imhoff addressed each other as cousins. That family relationship went back several generations to the sisters, Rebecca (1600–1648) and Jacoba Carel (1607–1657). Nowadays, it is hard to imagine anyone knowing his or her ancestry so accurately, but in the Dutch patriciate, this was quite normal. A good family background was a passport for life, for kinship ties came in handy in the pursuit of a favorable appointment on the administrative circuit. The contrary could happen too. Families played nasty tricks on each other on account of old wounds. This was the case between the Valckenier and Boreel families, to which Gustaaf Willem van Imhoff belonged on his mother's side. The Boreels had not yet forgotten that the capricious Gillis Valckenier had played a trick on them by kicking them out of the city council in the *annus horribilis* of 1672, when the Dutch Republic was simultaneously attacked by France, Britain, and the bishop of Münster.[141]

Within Amsterdam's patriciate there were all kinds of oral agreements about the mutual allocation of administrative functions. These so-called 'contracts of correspondence' remained in force for generations on end, and if one of the parties did not keep to the agreement, this could lead to heated tempers and animosities that were not easily forgotten or erased. Apart from the tensions that had been created two generations back, the young, ambitious Van Imhoff and the ten years older, standoffish and vain Valckenier had now also conceived a *personal* reciprocal antipathy that would only grow in the years to come.

CHAPTER 8

The Slapping Hand of the Lord

While the political turmoil shook the Batavian elite, an even harsher blow struck everyone from high to low in 1732: 'God's slapping hand' meted out retribution for all evil in the city; at least that is how it was perceived. A colossal epidemic of tropical diseases broke out that would fester in the city for the next hundred years. In 1768, when the epidemic had already been raging for more than thirty years, the Scottish physician James Lind concluded that 'unhealthy Batavia has dragged more Europeans to their graves, than men have perished in the bloody wars of the Dutch in Asia.'[142] This was a shocking statement as Batavia, previously hailed as the 'healthiest place in the Indies,' had quite suddenly turned into 'the cemetery of the Orient.'

On December 22, 1733, Governor-General Van Cloon reported that 'dangerous diseases, which consist mostly in very malignant contagious fevers,' had not only recently dragged many people into the grave, but continued to do so indiscriminately. So many Company servants fell victim to the disastrous epidemic that he feared that soon the gates and parapets of the town and the castle could no longer be manned if it continued in this way—'which the Lord may mercifully forbid.'[143] The same danger threatened the crews in the roadstead. The ships of the Company would no longer be able to set sail if so many sailors dropped dead. A rather desperate Van Cloon hoped that the daily distribution of two *zoopjes* (drinks) 'to refresh the mates' would offer some relief to the morale of the soldiers of the garrison and sailors on the roadstead.

Further information reveals that the great mortality to which Van Cloon referred had already begun in the first months of 1732, when, by order of his predecessor, Durven, a short cut to the sea was dug from the Mokervaart, the canal connecting Batavia to the Tangerang River. This was intended to let excess river water drain from the Ommelanden into the sea during the rainy season and thus free Batavia from flooding. Seasonal flooding, *banjir*, had become a recurring phenomenon due to the widespread deforestation in the delta region. Within a couple of weeks, so many 'navvies' involved in the Mokervaart shortcut project fell prey to the mysterious fatal disease that work had to cease. This occurred at a place two hours' distant from town, but shortly afterwards, the epidemic struck Batavia itself. An outbreak of malignant malaria which, combined with already prevalent diseases such as all kinds of dysentery, created an inexhaustible pool of destruction.

Batavian fever

Malaria was known in the eighteenth century as 'Batavian fever' and also as the 'cake,' after the swelling of the spleen (splenomegaly) that was a symptom of it. Those who did not succumb within a week 'continued to languish for years.' Because the mysterious disease persisted, the Chinese community, with Captain Ni Hoekong as their representative, addressed the High Government in 1738 with an urgent request to undo the shortcut from the Mokervaart canal because they firmly believed that 'the infection predominating over there found its origin in the spadework at the shortcut.' The Chinese showed themselves even willing to finance the restoration of the Mokervaart to its former state, if need be.[144]

Reams have been written about the possible origins of the city's suddenly deteriorating health situation since the middle of the eighteenth century, beginning with an extensive report drawn up in 1753 (at the request of Governor-General Jacob Mossel) by the harbor master of Batavia, Johannes Paravicini. How critical the situation at the time still was may be understood from Mossel's lament that among the Company personnel 'almost all were half dead, and looked like ghosts.' The same applied to the Council of the Indies: 'Who does not know that most of the time the entire High Government dies out every ten years and one hardly finds a member who has sat there for ten years, even if nowadays often young councilors are elected. Because of such uncommon mortality everything goes out of order.'

In his report, Paravicini reviewed all possible explanations. He believed that the prevailing epidemics were due to a combination of 'evil vapors and stuffy air,' which in turn were the result of irregularities in the monsoon climate. It is not difficult to recognize in this the so-called miasma theory that was used to explain swamp fever or malaria (*mala aria* or bad air).

Only at the beginning of the twentieth century was it discovered that malaria is transmitted by mosquitoes of the genus Anopheles. The disease comes in many guises, in a debilitating but not immediately lethal form as had been prevalent in West Java for many years, the *Vivax malaria sundaicus*, but also in an extremely malignant variant, *Malaria falciparum*, from which the victim dies within a few hours of contracting the disease. In addition to malaria, chronically debilitated people also suffered from all kinds of infectious intestinal diseases such as the so-called recurrent rotting fevers (*remitterende rotkoortsen*). Countless people must have died from combinations of these illnesses.

Incidentally, according to the *Chinese Annals of Batavia*, there was another culprit besides the digging of the Mokervaart canal that had beckoned the mortal diseases: the salt pans surrounding the city.[145] Considering that these brackish ponds could serve as ideal breeding grounds for the malaria mosquitoes, this theory may not have been wide of the mark. It has also been suggested that the construction of fishponds on the west side of the city ensured that malaria took a permanent hold on Batavia.[146]

Wherever the flashpoint may have been, there was a much broader ecological problem. When Batavia was surrounded by jungle forests, the city was evenly supplied from the hinterland with clear water 'that made the city pure and clean,' according to all seventeenth-century authors. Over time, that natural balance had been completely disrupted by the clearing of the Ommelanden. First, the jungle in the immediate vicinity of the city was cut down to create gardens and *sawahs* for rice cultivation, but from the 1680s onward, the primeval forest was also felled around the rivers and streams on higher terrains to serve as fuel for the rapidly expanding sugar plantations. In 1716, according to the *Chinese Annals of Batavia*, the city first suffered a large *banjir* during the rainy season that flooded the city for six days. This recurred two years later, setting a trend for subsequent years.

Human hands were not solely responsible for the profound changes to the habitat of Batavia and Ommelanden. In 1699, an eruption of the Salak volcano caused massive landslides and made rivers burst their banks. Despite all the efforts to restore the lower reaches of the mountain streams, the original condition was never restored because in the rainy season, the river water came flowing down uninhibitedly through the Bovenlanden, which had been cleared of jungle. In the dry season, on the other hand, many rivers were reduced to small rivulets near Batavia. Nor should it be forgotten that in the lower Ommelanden, much of the water was collected for irrigation purposes in the *sawahs* for wet rice cultivation. Thus, the delta area in which Batavia was located became the victim of all these developments. Large quantities of silt and waste from the sugar mills located upstream were transported via rivers and canals to the city and deposited in the estuaries of the Grote Rivier, which became barely navigable as a result.

The clearing of the Ommelanden had permanently destroyed the local ecology. From the end of the seventeenth century, the coastal strip separating Batavia from the sea expanded visibly through silting up—an average of 13 meters per year! The city thus became surrounded on the seaward side by swampy marshland. Every year, legions of 'mud-Javanese' came to the city to deepen the canals and the mouth of the Great River, an extremely dirty job that in the end was of little use with the available tools.

Living with death

Just how fierce the pandemic was is evident from the calculations of the number of Company employees who died in the Batavia hospital, compared with the number of VOC personnel arriving from Holland. Between 1714 and 1718, when 23,816 personnel were brought in, some 2,814 patients died instantly, about 11 percent. Between 1734 and 1739, the numbers were 30,569 and 8,851, respectively, or 29 percent, more than a quarter of the number of the *orang baru* (newcomers). Of the 72,816 Europeans who arrived between 1714 and 1767, about 90 percent died in the Company's hospitals, a fateful sign of the horrible conditions that prevailed in and around Batavia.[147]

As if this were not enough, there was another factor at play that made life in the city and in the roadstead extremely tenuous. During the seventeenth century, the mortality on board the VOC ships on the outward voyage to the Indies was manageable, but in the eighteenth century, there was an explosive increase in deaths accounted for at sea. In their letter of August 18, 1729, the Gentlemen XVII mentioned that 'for some years now, an unusually high number of diseases and deaths have been reported on the Company's outbound ships, a phenomenon that, under the Lord's Blessing, has to be prevented by all human means as well as possible.'[148] It would be wrong to suspect that the ship's command did little about these conditions. By the standards of the time, the ship's surgeons of the VOC were properly trained. Surgeons were sent along on every ship, that is to say a chief surgeon, and a second and third as apprentices. Before each voyage, the Company provided an extensive medicine chest equipped with surgical instruments and medicines. Twice daily before and after the morning and evening prayers, the surgeon held consultations on deck after a ship's boy called out, 'Cripples and the blind, come let thee be bandaged! Up by the great mast, thou shall find the master surgeon!' There was undoubtedly an increasing mortality on board: 8.8 percent in 1729, 10.4 percent in 1733, and 11.8 percent in 1737. In the latter year, another 38.2 percent of the new arrivals in Batavia perished. Leaving aside the fact that in the eighteenth century the physical condition of enlisted personnel seems to have been much worse than in the preceding century, one suspects that spotted fever (typhus), in particular, caused most of the casualties on board. It would be a bit farfetched to suggest, as has been done, that the causes of the high mortality among Company personnel should not be sought in Asia but on the ships. The number of deaths on the ships should be added to the deaths in Batavia, and it should also be considered that the weakened sailors on arrival in Batavia were highly susceptible to the diseases prevalent there.

These terrible conditions must have led to a general demoralization of the city's inhabitants in the 1730s: contemporary sources speak constantly of melancholy and chagrin. Paravicini could not have expressed it more powerfully when he stated that in the not-so-distant past 'all the European sojourners, even if they lived a very irregular life, had a healthy fresh reddish color; nowadays most people look pale like ghosts, and are so lean and weak that they cannot support the slightest sickness that befalls them and inevitably have to bite the dust.' And what about Dirk van Cloon's letter to the Gentlemen XVII of December 22, 1733, in which he announced that he would call for a general day of fasting and supplication? 'We daily experience to our sorrow that dangerous diseases consisting of very malignant contagious fevers continue to rage in this city and its surroundings. They are dragging large crowds of people to their graves.'

The epidemic also affected the sizeable Chinese citizenry of Batavia and caused as much unrest there. Van Cloon, to the dismay of his fellow Christian citizens, even allowed the Chinese, in their own way, to perform an exorcism ritual of the evil devil that besieged the city. As Wouter Hendrix testified:

> Very tall bamboos were erected everywhere before the doors of this [Chinese] nation on which lanterns were hung with burning candles, which gave a hideous sight at night. Indeed, I could not believe it had I not seen the priests daily walking in and out of one house after another, accompanied by a great confluence of people and clamor of brass percussion instruments to chase away this evil devil at the expense of the purses of the good residents.[149]

This was not unlike the Chinese version of the Dutch Reformed Church's general day of fasting and supplication, and it was frankly just as ineffective, for the days of reflection and prayer accomplished nothing—nor would the countless days of fasting and supplication that were proclaimed by the authorities with dismal regularity throughout the eighteenth century.

How severely diseases continued to rage was reflected in the city's social life and economy: people went bankrupt, house prices fell, and the annual auction of the tax farms in December 1737 yielded considerably less. At one point, the High Government even apologized for the delayed reportage to the management in Holland. Most of the clerks of the secretariat were ill, as were the two chief merchants of the Castle. Extraordinary numbers of the inhabitants were 'immediately interred on a daily basis to the lamentable decay of this colony.' The annual supply of several thousand new Company servants from Europe was no longer sufficient to maintain a sizable, healthy workforce in Batavia. Only the well-to-do citizens and senior Company servants could nightly seek refuge in their garden houses in the much healthier Ommelanden outside the city, and the same was true for the Chinese and native allies living on the land. Batavia, once the jewel in the crown, had now become a burden to the VOC.

Muddling along

Under these circumstances, Van Cloon quickly backtracked from his original statement that he had 'submitted himself willingly to shoulder the important administration of affairs.' Less than a year later, he requested in no uncertain terms to be relieved of his thankless task: 'The general work is considerable and has increased to an extraordinary degree [...] in addition to many other hateful matters and challenges. All this is enough to deter any good man, who just wants to serve God, his masters, and all reasonable men to their pleasure, from the work under which he must sigh.' In short, he was sick and tired of the job. Nevertheless, during the three years that he was given to govern, the corpulent governor-general managed to diplomatically resolve two pressing worrisome matters with his neighbors, namely Banten and Mataram. He was assisted in this, as had been Durven, by the Council's able secretary, Gustaaf Willem van Imhoff, 'the *Lieroordsen Mof* [that 'kraut from Leer'] who as is well known governs India, while the governor general is too lazy to take care of anything,' as Wouter Hendrix snidely remarked.

First of all, Van Cloon sent Councilor of the Indies Wijbrand Blom to Bantam to mediate in the succession issue that had arisen in 1733 after the death of Sultan Zain al-Abidin of Bantam, the same monarch who had agreed with Joan van Hoorn in 1708 that his eldest son could claim primogeniture. That crown prince, however, had been stabbed in the street by an *amok maker* (deranged troublemaker) in 1723. The newly appointed crown prince (*pangeran ratu*), Zain al-Arifin, faced stiff opposition at court and enlisted the help of the Company. The High Government took this as a good opportunity to negotiate a new contract for the delivery of pepper supplies, which had been increasingly neglected in recent years. Blom accomplished nothing much, because he allowed himself to be taken in by Sharifa, the beautiful wife of the new sultan. Blom was notorious for his verbose reports, and once again his report proved 'of a very queasy, intricate, and in places almost unintelligible content.' It dawned upon his colleagues in the High Government that Blom had made a fool of himself at the crown ceremony in Bantam 'with a chaotic mix of haughtiness and vanity, more to the contempt than to the glorification of the principal [the crown prince] and to his own mockery as the ambassador.'

The High Government's subsequent observation in response to Blom's arrogant behavior is instructive for anyone who wants to understand something of the 'mindset' of the colonial administration of the VOC at the time and therefore worth quoting in full:

> And what must the native think when he sees that the Company, which on principle has always been accustomed to advocate its interests with gentleness and moderation and to live with the indigenous kings and rulers as with allies, in these days completely changes its tone and is made suspicious by such excessive ostentation by its own ministers, as if they want to swallow up the kingdoms one by one and regard the kings and rulers thereof not as allies but as vassals. This is truly incomprehensible![150]

This statement was strongly critical of Blom's behavior, but at the same time, it also reflected how cautious and tactful the Company had been in the Company of the neighboring princes. It was up to Van Imhoff to correct Blom's *faux pas* and to negotiate an advantageous contract for pepper deliveries. He carried out that task with verve, not in the least because he had forged a special bond with Sultana Sharifa in previous years.

The same diplomatic approach rang true in the negotiations regarding Mataram. There, the court had once again become entangled in intrigues, but thanks to the diplomatic efforts of the VOC envoy, Frederick Coyett, a palace revolution was averted by the timely apprehension of the wayward *rijksbestuurder* (first minister), who had seized power. This interference in local politics yielded the Company a favorable treaty with a grateful susuhunan, Pakubuwana II. Among other things, he promised that he would have all the coffee trees in his kingdom cut down, so that this cultivation could continue exclusively in the Company's territory in the hinterland of Batavia.

As under his predecessor, Durven, Van Cloon was in a constant struggle with the Council of Justice, whose 'lofty conduct exceeded all that one has previously had to endure from that college.' Even within the Council of the Indies itself, different factions continued to fight each other. A major blow for Van Cloon was therefore the death of Director General Westpalm, his fated successor. Van Cloon warmly remembered him as a comrade who lived 'in good friendship with the governor general and the other members.' These words must have sounded like a reproach in the ears of the members of the Council of the Indies, because squabbles promptly erupted again when, to the anger of Wijbrand Blom, Adriaan Oostwalt was appointed Westpalm's successor thanks to the support of the extraordinary members of the Council. In a new vote by ordinaries only, Blom emerged as the winner, but the following day, he renounced his appointment of his own accord. These laborious maneuvers could not prevent Oostwalt from also breathing his last a few months later, and with that, the Council was back to square one. Who would succeed Oostwalt now?

In view of all the disagreements in the Council, Van Cloon thought it wise to leave the appointment of the next director general to the Gentlemen XVII. Pending their decision—for which one would have to wait at least a year and a half—a two-man team consisting of Adriaan Valckenier and Johannes Thedens was temporarily charged with filling the vacancy. Six months later, on March 10, 1735, Van Cloon died after an illness of seven weeks, 'just after sunset, about one quarter after six o'clock, released from this worldly charge and taken into His Eternal rest and glory.'

CHAPTER 9

Adriaan Valckenier in the Lime Light

No one in colonial literature has had such bad press as Adriaan Valckenier. Especially the verbose river god who recounted what happened in the October days of 1740 in the pamphlet *The Dream of the Rebellion at Batavia* had nothing good to say about Valckenier. He called him a *Flagellum Chinezorum* (Scourge of the Chinese) and compared him to 'the high houses here, the top floor of which is the worst equipped with furniture, haughty, delusional and in some cases quite insolent [...] he thinks himself to be the smartest looking guy in town. According to the river god's dismissive commentary, Valckenier's reading extended no further than François Valentijn's *Oud en Nieuw Oost-Indien*, 'an author, who, apart from many good and true things, also dishes up much humbug and falsehoods.'[151] Valckenier was indeed so charmed by Valentijn's work that he wished to add to it a book of drawings by which the reader could take note of the beauty of Batavia and its environs. To this end, he had the German architect and surveyor, Johann Wolfgang Heydt, come over from Colombo in Ceylon and commissioned him to produce the illustrations for this 'coffee table book.' Valckenier was extremely proud of his country estate 'Zeelust' at Ancol. Heydt was therefore required to pay special attention to its 'extraordinarily beautiful garden furnished with statues, fountains and artificial rock formations.' Judging by the splendor of the depicted mansion in Heydt's picture book, it is not surprising that contemporaries considered Valckenier a vainglorious man.[152]

W. R. van Hoëvell, the first historian of the Batavia massacre, endorsed the negative characterization of Adriaan Valckenier. According to him, the governor-general was 'insisting on his powerful position, haughty and gruff, fierce and temperamental.' He also lacked 'the necessary strength of mind, firmness of will, and abilities to act with decisiveness and prudence under difficult circumstances.' Furthermore, he was 'cowardly and petty when danger threatened, and harsh and cruel where it was unnecessary. That is the harsh but true verdict which we pass on the governor.'[153]

What were these severe judgments based on? Was it Valckenier's behavior in general, or did they refer to his tormented actions during and after the lurid October days of 1740? Was it only then that Adriaan Valckenier showed his true nature? In the observation of J. Th. Vermeulen, who published his doctoral thesis on the Chinese massacre in 1938, 'Valckenier was a man 'of considerable intellect, of good character—which alone was enough to get ahead in the East Indies—but not very industrious and suffering from poor health.' In addition, he was 'suspicious, jealously guarding his authority, temperamental and impetuous, not very determined, lazy, eager to avoid difficulties and ready to choose the path of least resistance.'[154] This was altogether not a flattering portrait either. Psychologizing is a risky business, especially for a historian, but it does not take much imagination to understand that, defied as he was by his opponents in the Council of the Indies, at a certain point, Valckenier blew a fuse. This led him to take extreme measures that would later cost him dearly, but it was to his credit that he was prepared to take responsibility to the last, as we shall see.

Family life and further career

The turbulent reigns of Durven and Van Cloon by no means stood in the way of Adriaan Valckenier's chances for promotion. On the contrary, an entire cadre above him was ousted by the Gentlemen XVII, and at a time when colleagues were being wiped out by the epidemic in droves, he initially enjoyed, as he himself confessed, a steely health. The same was not true of his wives. On March 1, 1725, Valckenier married Johanna Alida Tolling, daughter of Laurens Tolling, president of both the Council of Justice and Council of the Indies. On April 10, 1728, Alida gave birth to a healthy baby who was baptized Susanna Catharina. However, the young mother died only one year later. On April 4, 1730, Valckenier remarried Susanna Christina Massis, the widow of his former boss, the receiver general, Adriaan van Biesum. From that second marriage, another year later, on June 10, 1731, Adriaan Isaak was born. Susanna was not long-lived either: she died on February 11, 1737. Once again, Adriaan Valckenier found himself a single parent, which is why he decided to send his two children to Amsterdam and entrusted them to the care of his brother, Pieter, and his unmarried sisters.

In the ten years that passed between 1725 and 1735, there is really not much to say about Valckenier, except that he steadily continued his climb up the ladder of the hierarchy. Still, it is useful to follow his promotions, especially if we compare them with those of his ambitious cousin, Gustaaf Willem van Imhoff. Initially working in different offices of the financial organization, the two were constantly at each other's heels. In 1727, Valckenier was appointed both alderman of the city and bookkeeper general. Van Imhoff had already been appointed chief of the general pay office a year earlier. In 1733, Valckenier and Van Imhoff were appointed ordinary and extraordinary councilors, respectively. The balance between the two was more or less maintained until the death of Director General Adriaan Oostwalt, when Valckenier and Thedens were given the temporary, combined appointment of director general pending a ruling by the Gentlemen XVII. Valckenier's promotion, even if temporary, was a blow for Van Imhoff. He contemplated revenge and seized his chance when a few months later, on March 1, 1735, Van Cloon also breathed his last.

Van Imhoff's nasty trick

Palace revolutions in Bantam and Mataram happened frequently as we have seen, but the same also happened in Batavia once in a while, albeit less bloody. On May 2, 1735, the Council of the Indies met to elect Van Cloon's successor. Although it seemed obvious that Adriaan Valckenier would be the first candidate for the vacant position in terms of experience and seniority, Van Imhoff, together with two accomplices, the extraordinary councilors, Van Schinne and De Haze, undercut this by voting for Abraham Patras, an absolute outsider. This elderly, upright Huguenot, born in Grenoble in 1671, was looking back at an honorable, long career in the service of the VOC. On his sixtieth birthday, he had been added to the Council of the Indies as an extraordinary member by the Gentlemen XVII, as a reward for his faithful service in India. To his own surprise, he was now suddenly put forward as a candidate for the governor generalship by the three Young Turks of the Council. After the votes were cast, Patras and Valckenier, each with three votes, emerged as the frontrunners, with the result that the vote was tied. This may have disappointed Valckenier, but he was not particularly upset. He argued that as an ordinary councilor, he was of higher rank than Patras and, moreover, that he as the offspring of an ancient Amsterdam patrician family, should have precedence. The latter argument made little impression on his colleagues. Therefore, Van Imhoff proposed to let fate decide by drawing straws. Fortune worked out in Patras' favor, and so this venerable gentleman was given the honor of being named governor-general at the age of 64. The consequences of this surprising election can be guessed. With great reluctance, Patras, who had not been expecting this at all, accepted the high office. He did attach a personal letter to the official notification of his election to the Gentlemen XVII, in which he earnestly requested the directors, in view of his advanced age, 'to be relieved of this heavy burden in a reputable manner.'

Since the position of director general was still open, Valckenier was appointed to that office. Informed of all this, the Gentlemen XVII in their letter of November 10, 1735, ratified the appointment of both gentlemen and additionally promoted the extraordinary members, Thedens, Coyett, and Van Imhoff, to the position of ordinary councilors. The directors in Holland clearly were unimpressed by the debilitating infighting in the High Government, for after wishing the councilors God's Blessing, they admonished them, as if they were a bunch of schoolboys, and conveyed their expectation that 'they unanimously would take up again the Company´s business with new energy.' They should maintain unity and avoid quarrels and discord and neither disregard nor go beyond the orders of their overlords and disgrace these with hateful writings 'such as, to our great displeasure, have been sent directly to our assembly, by some people who should be least entitled to do so.' If the authors of such dastardly letters did not cease complaining, the Gentlemen XVII informed that they would send the letters back to the Indies without mercy, where these epistles would end up in the hands of the people who were criticized by the letter writers. In a subsequent letter, sent almost a year later, the management once again expressed 'its utter astonishment' that it continued to receive all sorts of letters with accusations hurled back and forth by members of the Judicial Council and the Council of the Indies. This had to stop now once and for all.

Van Imhoff had effectively played a nasty trick on Valckenier, but he had been unable to prevent his rival from being promoted to second-in-command in the government, which meant he would have to tolerate his authority anyway. Fortunately, a way out suddenly opened up to avoid this embarrassing situation. It became known in Batavia that an uprising had broken out in Ceylon against the rule of Governor Diderik van Domburch. Since a series of successive governors, starting with Pieter Vuyst, had already caused enough unrest on that island, Governor-General Patras believed that a replacement for Van Domburch should be sought within the Council of the Indies. Van Imhoff immediately declared himself available, to the shock of Patras, who, like his predecessors, Durven and Van Cloon, relied heavily on Van Imhoff's command of the General Secretariat. In the end, he agreed to let him go.

The grey-haired governor now had to work closely with Director General Valckenier, the man who would have preferred to occupy his position. This actually proved no problem at all, as Adriaan Valckenier did his utmost to establish a harmonious cooperation. 'It is much better to be compliant and ready to concede than to dispute every point of competition,' he wrote confidentially to his brother-in-law in Amsterdam.[155] Thus, it so happened that Patras, who hoped for a quick discharge, soon regarded Valckenier as his ideal successor. Valckenier was allowed to give up all his subsidiary duties in order to devote himself entirely to the management of the trade. He could not count on much administrative support, because most of the clerks of the General Secretariat were ill from the pandemic. The two chief merchants of the Castle on whom he was supposed to rely were not available either. It mattered little to him. 'It therefore suits me very well that I am accustomed to work, nothing will be too hard for me if only God grants me good health,' he confided to a distant relative. But that was a pious wish; the pandemic continued to spread. There were as many as a thousand sick Company servants lying in the hospital.

As director general, Valckenier was responsible for the 'whole turnover' of the Company's commerce and shipping business. As far as shipping was concerned, the scarcity of sailors made it extremely difficult to maintain intra-Asian shipping connections with ports in the Indian Ocean and the China seas. Patients who seemed to be on the mend were transferred directly from the hospital to the ships ready to depart to the Western Quarters, with the hope that the sea air would further strengthen them. What manpower was left in Batavia was used only to load the ships. For navigation along the Javanese coast, the Company resorted as much as possible to native shipping. This meant that quite a few ships ended up anchored in the Batavian roadstead, where lying idle in the tropical climate, they quickly rotted away.

A new corridor in the China Trade

Meanwhile, the Gentlemen XVII had reconsidered their original idea of sending ships directly to China from Holland, thus bypassing Batavia. This turned out to be less practical than they originally thought. They therefore ordered the High Government in Batavia to send two or three ships to Canton every year. Instead of payment in silver, it still proved more advantageous for the Company to pay for tea in China with the pepper and other spices from the archipelago. Ships departing from Batavia also had the advantage of reaching Canton earlier than the ships of their European rivals, which sailed directly from Europe. Thus, the management in Holland hoped that the trade with China 'in these bad times and a general decline of commerce everywhere, here in the fatherland as well in the Indies, may be considered as the pillar of the Company's trade.'

Yet, in view of the prevailing high mortality rate, how could sufficient crew members be obtained in Batavia for the China trade, not to mention the supercargoes (chief merchants) specialized in the tea trade and experienced tea tasters who could negotiate favorable prices with the Chinese merchants? An old China hand named Henry Abbis, an Englishman who had sailed to China several times before, came forward. Despite initial objections—'we can do without English peeping Toms'—Valckenier hired him anyway. Abbis, incidentally, narrowly survived the first trip on the *Alblasserdam*. The ship went down in a typhoon en route to China, and only Abbis and a dozen sailors survived the disaster. The other China- and Japan-bound ships remained afloat in the same storm, albeit losing their masts. They eventually managed to limp to Macau. Typhoons, which usually strike the South China Sea between July and October were and still are notoriously hazardous for shipping.

On the route between Europe and Asia, the Company suffered an even greater loss. On May 21, 1737, as many as eight return ships (*retourschepen*, the largest ships that sailed between the Netherlands and Batavia) were lost when they were knocked off their anchors by a sudden northwestern gale in Table Bay at the Cape of Good Hope and ended up on the cliffs with a 'terrific loss of men and goods.' This again was seen as 'God's striking hand for which we must humble ourselves.'[156]

Governor-General at last

When Governor-General Abraham Patras passed away on May 3, 1737, the members of the Council of the Indies unanimously elected Adriaan Valckenier governor-general on the same day. In Van Imhoff's absence, everyone apparently now agreed that he was the right man in the right place. This meant that the vacant position of director general had to be filled. After a vigorous discussion about who could or could not vote, the eternal troublemaker, Wijbrand Blom, was elected. This problem solved itself when Blom died on November 4. Joan Paul Schaghen, runner-up to Blom in the spring election and a man with whom Valckenier was on good terms, was ready to replace him.

On all fronts, the Company's trade was suffering: the Company servants of the trade factories in Siam, China, Japan, Malacca, Malabar, Coromandel, and Surat were all complaining. In his first letter to the Gentlemen XVII, Valckenier foresaw new criticism from the fatherland and sighed 'that whatever efforts we shall make, and whatever means we may employ, these must prove fruitless, as long as the Lord does not provide us with His gracious blessing.' He just had to make do with what he had, which unfortunately, due to the epidemic, was not much. The shortage of staff had become so acute that only 525 sailors and 114 boys were available for the twenty-one ships and six smaller vessels for Asiatic navigation. Far fewer sailors and soldiers had come over from Europe than promised. In addition to the 21 ships sailing to the Eastern and Western Quarters in Asia, only a dozen return ships remained available for the traffic with Europe, and these had to be partly manned by Asian sailors. Valckenier noted that the High Government had taken all possible measures to alleviate 'the uncommonly long continuance of disease and mortality at Batavia.' The hospital facilities and care of the sick had greatly improved, and the garrison and sailors were provided an extra drink daily to support their morale. There was nothing more he could do.

Private correspondence

Up to this point, the 'inner soul' of Adriaan Valckenier remained hidden from us, but this suddenly changed as of October 20, 1738. Two letter books of incoming and outgoing letters have been preserved in which we can find all the personal mail that he received and sent between October 1738 and February 1739.[157] The months of November to February provided an opportunity to send letters to the homeland every year. The more than one hundred copies of the outgoing mail, combined with the letters that Valckenier had received shortly before, not only make us better acquainted with him, but they also show how in those days, long-distance friendships and family ties were maintained by the exchange of gifts. Valckenier received silk stockings, hats, books, delicacies, and wine from the Netherlands, and sent inn exchange from Batavia pots of *atjar* (pickled vegetables), tea, and all kinds of trinkets to family, friends, and patrons in the homeland. Johannes Swellengrebel, his host at the Cape on the outward journey in 1715, for instance, regularly sent refreshments such as the fruits of the field, bottles of gooseberries, dried artichokes, and so on.

In a letter to Egidius Tolling, father-in-law from his first marriage, who had returned to Holland, Valckenier wrote that the pandemic had claimed the life of his second wife as well. He himself was also hit by 'the tremendous attacks of malignant fevers raging here [...] which makes me long for the discharge of my present heavy service load.' In view of these circumstances he appealed to his childless brother, Pieter, and his sisters and brothers-in-law in Holland to take ten-year-old Susanna Catharina (Sanne Caatje) and seven-year-old Isaac Adriaan (Ary) under their care. Because his children had been born in Java, he had to apply for their citizenship in Amsterdam. For his daughter and son, Adriaan Valckenier deposited considerable sums of money in the coffers of the Amsterdam orphanage trustees, 145,921 and 62,430 guilders, respectively.

Indies children to the Netherlands

The governor-general took no half measures when he put his children under the care of Captain Guldenarm of the ship *Nieuwland*. They were chaperoned during the voyage by a couple named Banier, and several slaves were also sent along to care for them as far as the Cape of Good Hope. Two of them, Catjong of Sumbawa and Nassa of Mandar, sailed on to Holland where they obtained their freedom upon arrival. In addition, several crew members were hired, such as a steward and a gunner who happened to excel as a baker. As for food, nothing was left to chance: two cows, six calves, 38 pigs, 16 sheep, six deer, 20 geese, 500 fowls, and 200 ducks sailed on the ship. There was no end to it. During their stay at the Cape of Good Hope, the children were taken care of by Johannes Swellengrebel, and put up with a certain Jan de Wit.

Upon arrival in Holland, the two slaves were taken away from Sanne Caatje and Ary 'firstly because they were used to command them, and secondly because they would not learn the Dutch language in their presence.' As meanwhile Pieter Valckenier had died, his two sisters, Margaretha and Anna Catharina Valckenier, took the care of the children upon themselves. This sudden responsibility came as a shock to these old spinsters and led to an amusing correspondence, in which they reported on the curious behavior of the thoroughly spoiled young brats. 'We took in your children with tenderness [...]. They were in the first month so lively and little accustomed to be under discipline, that we feared to face a hard job of turning them into obedient children. Especially Sanne Catie was so self-important on account of Your Honour's high status that we often had to laugh about it, but we have already managed to make clear to her that this is not the way we behave in Holland and she accepts that. Little Ary is a bit wild, but of a very kind and flexible nature. Both children are very spirited.'[158] The manumitted slaves were shipped back to Batavia with 'proper outfit and gifts' such as a tobacco box for Catjong and a 'pair of golden ear crabs, each with a diamond' for Nassa to wear. An amusing correspondence unfolded around a 'delightful painting' which Valckenier had commissioned from Nicolaas Verkolje in Holland. The painter had created a collage of the entire family, using portraits of Valckenier and his late second wife and sketches of the children in his own studio. When Verkolje asked for 200 ducatons (630 guilders) for his work, Valckenier's representative in Holland thought that this was on the expensive side and preferred to first consult his patron in Batavia, as a result of which the painter probably had to wait at least two years to be paid.

In addition to enthusiastic letters from his sisters and other relatives about the two children, Valckenier naturally received generous letters of congratulations on his appointment from all quarters. Most letter writers did not hesitate to ask directly for a favor for an acquaintance or relative in the East Indies. Indeed, they apologized for it in advance. Contrary to the claims of his enemies, this correspondence shows that the governor-general was a not unsympathetic fellow in spite of his class consciousness. He wrote charming letters to his children, reminisced with friends, dreamed of a quiet life once he returned to Holland, and lay awake all night when he read that a fire had raged in the home of one of his sisters a year earlier!

Dreaming of Holland

One of Valckenier's correspondents was the *poète maudit*, Pieter van Gunst, a childhood friend with whom he used to go boating around the fishermen's island of Marken as a boy. While brother Philip van Gunst had advanced in life to become mayor of Amsterdam, Pieter had moved to the neighboring village of Nederhorst den Berg where he had married a wealthy woman and devoted his life to the muses. The collection of poems, *Echo of Batavian joys and hymns*, that Adriaan Valckenier received from Pieter van Gunst in 1738 elicited 'the unfeigned jealousy' from the governor-general, on whom 'the happiness and misfortune of whole countries and peoples depended.' 'Think of the man,' wrote Valckenier, 'who from daybreak until night, when he goes to bed, is constantly busy, nay, whose concerns for the general welfare prevent him from sleeping even at night. And judge then, whether such a one, in comparison with your undisturbed life outdoors, can have a quiet and contented and a happy life.' At the end of this letter, Valckenier wrote that he hoped 'that it will further please God to transfer me to the dear fatherland and grant me some more lifetime there.' He longed to be able to feel the difference 'between the lofty seat and the low couch, between a palatial palace and a peasant dwelling, and between a general's staff and a shepherd's staff.'[159] This comparison with the little hut on the heath, by the way, should be taken with a grain of salt, for where Valckenier intended to settle after returning home to the Netherlands is clear from further correspondence: an upscale house on the Herengracht or Keizersgracht in the city center and a country house on the Amstel.

On October 20, 1738, Adriaan wrote to his brother, Pieter, in Amsterdam that almost all the Christmas and spring ships had arrived safe and sound, carrying a large quantity of letters from the fatherland. He was now going to answer them 'with fresh courage and much pleasure.' He thanked Pieter for his cordial letter in response to the death of his much beloved wife and looked forward to receive more news of his children. Eleven days later, he wrote another letter to his brother and included a letter of resignation addressed to the Gentlemen XVII. He feared that after repeated attacks of severe fevers, he was no longer his old self. Gloomily, he added that without 'a proper supplementation of people and money from Holland, the East India Company might share the tale of 'neglected Brazil' and the other conquests of the West India Company whose downfall arose from the same (lack of support).' He asked Pieter to determine for himself an opportune moment to deliver his request for dismissal.

With the mail of the last arriving ships from Holland, however, Adriaan Valckenier learned that his brother had passed away. Still, he hoped that through his influential brother-in-law, Cornelis Baron Hop, he might still manage to submit his resignation. In retrospect, he need not have worried that much, for at the same time that he drew up his letter of resignation, the Gentlemen XVII in Amsterdam had already formally ratified Valckenier's election as governor-general with the note that in view of the dire health crisis in Batavia and his own symptoms of illness, he was allowed to resign if he chose to. This was an extraordinary gesture that had never before been granted to a governor-general.

Valckenier's strives for harmony

In Valckenier's correspondence, we can also find letters to his 'patrons,' that is, the prominent Amsterdam patriarchs who supported him, such as Mayor Van Bempden, 'my great patron and benefactor' (who, incidentally, had also just died), Walter Senserf, trustee of the Rotterdam VOC Chamber, Amsterdam Mayor Lieve Geelvinck, and Philip van der Ghiessen, director of the Levant trade. It would go too far to go deeply into the contents of those letters here. One thing is clear: in every letter, Adriaan Valckenier emphasized that he saw it as his task to restore harmony in the Council of the Indies 'by gentle means' after all the fuss of the preceding years. However, he was concerned that Van Imhoff (he carefully avoided mentioning his name) might spoil the mood again after his return from Ceylon. He said this quite clearly in a personal letter to Lieve Geelvinck. After all the problems surrounding Durven's tenure, he said it was his intention to restore peace in the High government. 'If someone in the Council was going to thwart him in the performance of his duties, he feared that he would not be able to please his praiseworthy superiors.'[160] For a good listener like Geelvinck, this hint to Van Imhoff must have been sufficient. In this context, a letter from Valckenier's cousin, G. H. Werndly, is very significant because it shows that people in Patria were also aware of the rivalry between Van Imhoff and Valckenier. Werndly had learned that Van Imhoff had already been granted leave to return to Batavia from Ceylon. He hoped that Van Imhoff would no longer continue to write insinuating letters to Holland, and that, having returned to the bosom of the High Government, he would be willing to assist Valckenier 'in sincere loyalty and friendship to bear the burden of the government.'

Other voices

Correspondence by other people also sheds light on the rivalry between Valckenier and Van Imhoff. For example, in a letter to his brother, Balthazar, in Amsterdam, the secunde (second-in-command) of the VOC factory in Malacca, Daniel Nolthenius, insinuated that Valckenier, in response to his rivalry with Van Imhoff, sought to broaden his power base by offering his friendship to him (Daniel) 'of his own accord and in respect of his patriotic friends.' Aware that there were, 'two strands' in the Council, Daniel Nolthenius wrote that one faction consisted of Valckenier and Director General Schaghen—who happened to be Daniel's great-nephew—and that the Van Imhoff faction counted among its members Pieter Pasques de Chavonnes, Van Schinne, and several more extraordinary members of the Council. Consequently, Daniel preferred to wait and see before committing his fate to the Valckenier faction.[161] His later letters to his brother are also interesting, if only because they give a good impression of all the scheming that was necessary to help him acquire the coveted appointment to extraordinary councilor of the Indies in Batavia.

Once that goal was achieved in November 1739, in his subsequent letters, Daniel Nolthenius not only reported on the tensions in the Council of the Indies but also took sides with Van Imhoff. In his letter of January 12, 1740, he wrote that in Batavia, Van Imhoff's return from Ceylon was eagerly awaited and that at that occasion 'many wonderful things are bound to happen.' He noted that Van Imhoff already had most of the votes in his pocket to become governor-general. According to him, the Gentlemen XVII should have recognized Valckenier's limited capacities so that Van Imhoff 'could be provided with the commander's staff.' All this did not bode well. It appears that Valckenier was increasingly under fire within the Council of the Indies by his sneaky rival Van Imhoff and his faction.

There was, however, a somewhat older, sadder, and wiser Company servant named Joan de Roode, who was willing to stand up for Valckenier, as evidenced by his confidential exchange of letters with his patron, the VOC director Jan Minne. De Roode proposed to 'enter into secret correspondence to revive the old friendship' with the intention of offering Minne a peek into the overseas scene. He promised 'to tell nothing but sincere and pure truths without injury to anyone's honor or dignity.'[162] De Roode was positive about Valckenier's reign despite the difficult times that the Company was facing. With the exception of a rebellion in Makassar, all was calm and at peace in the East Indies. To his relief, he could also declare that it looked like the mortality levels were falling, which made it possible to account for the damage suffered so far. Having been appointed auction master, de Roode noted that creditors and debtors in

Batavia had suffered heavy losses as a result of the continuous foreclosure sales: the value of most estate had fallen by three-quarters. On the other hand, by 1739, food prices had stabilized somewhat thanks to the excellent reign of Valckenier, 'whose generous and gentle government will still be spoken of fifty years from now' [...] 'No Company servant is nowadays transferred to another position for political reasons,' De Roode wrote, 'so that everyone can live a quiet and peaceful life under his fig tree and vine.' He suspected that the governor-general would probably retain his post for another two years because he possessed so much real estate that had to be disposed of first.

In a later letter dated April 30, 1740, De Roode mentioned again that everything was in desired harmony. As far as he was concerned, the governor-general could add a few more years to his office, 'for everyone here is afraid of an imminent change, the governments of Durven and Van Cloon still being fresh in everyone's memory.' With this remark he was referring to Van Imhoff's imminent return to Batavia and whatever might ensue.

De Roode had correctly assessed the situation. On December 12, 1739, Valckenier thanked the Gentlemen XVII for their kind offer that 'in the event of continued indisposition and diminution of forces' he himself could decide to resign and return to the Netherlands, retaining his dignity and pay with all the honors due him. In effect, he was now free to step down whenever he wished. He had amassed an enormous fortune; the way was open for him to buy a country house on the Amstel River or wherever he desired to do so. Soon, he hoped, to once again embrace his beloved children. After three generations of Valckeniers in India, he had reached the highest position. Was that not something to be proud of? Nonetheless, he declared that 'on account of his physical constitution he [wished to] bear the burden of the government of India at least for some time to come.' What drove Adriaan Valckenier to respond in this way? Did he want to make the most of the sale of his landed property, as De Roode suspected? Or did he think that the worst was behind him?[163]

In January 1740, the frigate *Ridderkerk* arrived in Batavia from Ceylon with news that Gustaaf Willem van Imhoff would soon follow, and that there was more important news to be expected. All sorts of rumors circulated that Valckenier's days were numbered. *Le roi est mort, vive le roi!* (The king is dead, long live the new king!) This talk spread through the city with lightning speed, and with Durven's resignation still fresh in their minds, many began to wonder if more heads were soon going to roll along with Valckenier's. Given the widely known enmity between the two gentlemen, it was wise from now on to be very careful. Every Company servant, from the highest to the lowest, was wondering whether he should remain loyal to the sitting governor-general or to take the gamble and side with the man of the future.

CHAPTER 10

Der Wille Zur Macht: Van Imhoff Goes to Ceylon

To insert in the ongoing narrative a full chapter about Van Imhoff's governorship of Ceylon may seem a bit of a rigmarole, but there is a reason for this short excursion. If Van Imhoff wanted to show his worth as an administrator, this was the right moment. Ceylon had seen a string of failing governors, each of whom had made a mess of his assignment. But there also was another reason why he jumped at the occasion to go his own way. He had reached a dead end in the Council of the Indies. The governorship of Ceylon was not only the highest position that he could attain for the time being, but the exalted office also represented a challenge. It provided a yardstick of his capacities. Unlike most of the Company's possessions in Asia, the colony of Ceylon was not merely a trading settlement with some rural property around it. It was a full size, sprawling colonial possession that at the time was considerably larger in area than the Company's territories in Java. The island was renowned for the cinnamon that was peeled by members of the Chalia caste from trees in the forests and on plantations. Because the Company had succeeded in bringing all of Ceylon's ports under its control, and was able to organize labor and control of the cinnamon production, a strict monopoly could be maintained. This, combined with pepper from Malabar and textiles from Coromandel, gave the VOC a rock-solid position on the world market. Yet in the sphere of administration, there was a fly in the ointment. The Company controlled the coastal regions of the island, but the king of Kandy reigned over the mountainous interior. The result was an ongoing tension between the two parties, with the Chalia caste of cinnamon peelers, who played an indispensable role in the spice's production, repeatedly being caught in the middle.

Administrative chaos

We saw above that in 1729, the High Government of Batavia sent Stephanus Versluys to Ceylon to replace the mentally ill Petrus Vuyst. This proved an unfortunate choice, for Versluys was no match for the temptations of power. By August 20, 1731, the High Government in Batavia decided to replace Versluys with his nephew, Wouter Hendrix, but the latter, while already on his way with his entire family and an entourage of one hundred personnel, was recalled to the Netherlands by the GentlemenXVII because he belonged to Diderik Durven's coterie. Not satisfied with the confusion that they had caused in the governmental circles of Batavia, the Gentlemen XVII now felt themselves compelled to interfere directly in the affairs of Ceylon as well. Bypassing the High Government of Batavia, they appointed Diderik van Domburgh, commander of the port of Galle in southern Ceylon, to succeed Versluys as governor of Ceylon. Because Van Domburgh first had to clear himself of a formal indictment of private trade practices that had been raised against him, he could not take office until October 5, 1733. But that was not the end of the administrative chaos, for Van Domburgh's government soon also left much to be desired. In 1735, hundreds of cinnamon peelers fled the Company's domains and sought refuge with the king of Kandy. A little later, a few districts around Colombo also revolted in response to land transactions by the governor that adversely affected them. Since Governor-General Patras had little faith that Van Domburgh would be able to restore order, he decided to replace him to 'rescue that government from the uncommon confusion into which it has so suddenly fallen.'

The savior

This was the moment Gustaaf Willem van Imhoff, then 31 years old, had been waiting for. For him, it was right up his alley to show that he, savior in a time of distress, was ready to take over the administration of Ceylon. Against the wishes of Patras, but with the support of the Council of the Indies (including Valckenier, who, after all, was eager to rid himself of his adversary), Van Imhoff received the desired appointment. On May 15, 1736, he and his wife were bid farewell at Batavia's roadstead by his colleagues. Only Valckenier failed to attend.

When the Van Imhoffs showed up in Colombo on July 23, they found a rudderless colony, as Diderik van Domburgh had died two weeks before. Everything was in turmoil, the peeling of the cinnamon had virtually come to a halt and the insurgents had ambushed and disarmed twenty VOC soldiers at a remote post and deported them to the king of Kandy. Van Imhoff somewhat theatrically let it be known that he wanted to think carefully for 24 hours before appearing in the Colombo Castle Council. On July 31, he announced that he was sent to restore order and do justice to the wronged. This ukase had a calming effect, but before everything was back to normal, he had thirty insurgents arrested and exiled to Batavia. A year later, he looked back with satisfaction on the effect of his resolute intervention and noted that 'the remaining rabble, seeing that the Company was serious about this [...] kept quiet, calm, and obedient in the three provinces that were once so troubled, for which God Almighty should be thanked.' In their private life, Van Imhoff and his wife had to deal with yet another setback just six months after their arrival. In the previous eight years, they had already lost three children, but on March 20, 1735, another child was born, Jacob Willem Balthazar van Imhoff. This little son, however, died one year later and was buried in Colombo, where his beautiful gravestone can still be seen in the Wolvendaal church.

For Van Imhoff, improving the strained relations with the royal house of Kandy was a top priority. He noted that the king and his advisors were deeply dissatisfied with the way in which the Company administration imposed its will, namely by keeping the island's ports closed to the court. This had prevented Kandy from maintaining its own trade connections with the Indian coast for 29 years, and the kingdom missed no opportunity to show its displeasure to the envoy that the VOC governor in Colombo sent every year to the king. It was the envoy's job, on behalf of the Company, to pay due homage to the monarch and strengthen mutual relations by offering all kinds of exotic gifts: Persian horses, fine glassware, mirrors, or an occasional exotic animal such as a lion, a pair of greyhounds, or a cassowary—whatever might favor the Asian monarch's wishes.

But what did Van Imhoff aim for? He desired royal approval to peel cinnamon in the king's forests, and free passage for elephant transports from southern Ceylon through Kandian territory to Jaffna in the north of the island. In order to attain those goals, Van Imhoff sent an envoy to Kandy, with 'an offer that could not be refused.' In exchange for a permanent contract, he offered that the court would be allowed to annually freight three ships with Ceylonese products for trade with the Indian coast. The envoy was received benevolently by the old king, but court officials from his entourage continued to raise objections against the disproportionately heavy burdens that the Company imposed on the population and once again sought compensation for the financial losses caused by the closure of the ports. In short, despite the pleasantries exchanged, there remained so much discontentment at the court that an irresolvable stalemate remained between the two parties.

Now that his shrewd plan had not worked out and further negotiations also did not lead to a firm contract by which a proper long-term cooperation could be arranged, Van Imhoff suddenly adopted an irreconcilable attitude. If there was no way to negotiate, then the Company, he believed, should bare its teeth. He sent his 'Considerations' both to Batavia and to the Gentlemen XVII and explained that the tug of war with the court of Kandy had accomplished nothing and would lead nowhere. Therefore, he proposed to show with a steel fist the Company's dominion over the island. In response to this impulsive proposal, the sedate Governor-General Patras wrote: 'The way of friendship, and good intelligence with the Kandian king is far preferable to all violence, which is always mixed with much hazard and danger, both with respect to the precariousness and uncertainty of victory, and the weighty and costly conservation of the conquest itself.'[164] These were wise words, and the management in Holland readily concurred.

Family feuds and personal hatred

The Company controlled the coast, the king of Kandy the interior. The result was an ongoing tension between the two parties, with the Chalia caste of cinnamon peelers, who played an indispensable role in the spice's production, repeatedly being caught in the middle. Van Imhoff had prevented Valckenier from being elected Van Cloon's successor, but when he learned that the Gentlemen XVII had formally ratified Valckenier's appointment as director general, he restrained his emotions and wrote a letter of congratulations. Nevertheless, he also spouted some venom in that epistle, by expressing hope that Valckenier had recovered from the illness that had prevented him from bidding him farewell on his departure for Ceylon. He presumed, he wrote, that he must have had a very good reason for his absence at that farewell. He added somewhat ironically: 'was it not a gesture of private courtesy but also part of Valckenier's official duty to bid farewell to a fellow councilor?' Piqued by Valckenier's absence at his departure, Van Imhoff had not sought to stay in contact, but he did not want to fail to congratulate his cousin on his appointment. Little did he know that Valckenier had already been unanimously elected governor-general a month earlier. When that news reached him, Van Imhoff dutifully wrote a second congratulatory letter on February 12, 1738, and condoled Valckenier on the death of his wife. In response, Valckenier wrote that he gladly accepted Van Imhoff's proposal to conclude the friendship 'erasing all previous various differences so as not to show that I would retain a spiteful temper against my equals much less against my own kin.' Whether the truce would last remained to be seen.

The governor in action

During Van Imhoff's four years as governor of Ceylon, he implemented useful reforms in the judiciary and education and radically revamped the *tombo* (land register) system that the VOC had inherited from the Portuguese colonial administration. There can be no doubt that he proved himself a progressive and zealous administrator in every respect. To personally acquaint himself with the local situation, he made four inspection trips around the island.[165] In 1739, he traveled along the coasts of Malabar and Coromandel together with the local commander, Julius Valentijn Steyn van Gollenesse. On that occasion, the two of them hoped, *en passant*, to deal with the Angrean pirates who were making the coastal waters unsafe, but to his frustration, they failed to do so, miserably. The commander of the VOC fleet allowed the pirates who were locked up in a bay to escape.

With the exception of this hunt for pirates, what Van Imhoff's expeditions had in common was that they were perfectly prepared and executed. The carefully crafted travel reports that he prepared 'on horseback, on foot or by palanquin [sedan chair]' attest to his tireless work ethic. He stood up for the locals everywhere and was always ready to consider complaints such as excessive workloads, extortion, or excessive taxes. He recorded everything in detail, and where possible he took immediate action. In 1738, Van Imhoff believed that he had completed his assignment in Ceylon. In a letter to the supreme management, he meekly asked to be relieved of his post without indicating where his further ambitions lay. Should he return to Batavia as a member of the Council of the Indies, where the two highest ranks were already occupied by other men? The mere prospect of having to serve under the hated Valckenier did not appeal to him at all. When he sent a letter to his cousin, Jacob Boreel, in response to the latter's congratulations on his appointment to the governorship of Ceylon, he was not yet entirely sure what to do in the future. This letter, dated 15 December 1738, ushered in a 'secret correspondence' between the cousins that gradually came to cast light on Van Imhoff's ambitions.[166] He asked Boreel, public prosecutor of the Amsterdam admiralty, if he would be willing to act henceforth as his representative in Amsterdam. He intended to 'detach himself somewhat from these tropical regions.' Ideally, he would like to become a citizen of Amsterdam, but that could not be done without the help of his cousin. Should citizenship fall into his lap, perhaps he could one day become alderman of the city 'and then see what else might turn out [...] but those plans are castles in the air! Let us speak more seriously and abandon these wild concepts for the time being. For now, I shall request my resignation in order, if it pleases God, to return to Batavia.'

A year passed by before the governor of Ceylon received word of his deliverance from the Gentlemen XVII. Incidentally, the High Government had already granted his request to resign and travel to Batavia. Thus, Van Imhoff was able to rejoin the Council of the Indies on March 12, 1740. For the time being, he had to abandon his plans to buy a landed estate in Holland, and now focused on the highest that could be achieved in the Indies, the office of governor-general. Now 36 years of age, he was beginning to grow impatient with 'that gentleman in front of him.' He grumbled that he had been part of the High Government for ten years but still in the same subordinate position, although he fondly remembered that he was welcomed by his fellow councilors council at the time 'with such applause as had never been shown to the wisest and ablest men [...]. Were Terentius still alive, he would surely say, *Huic mandes, si quid recte curatum velis'* [If you want something done, entrust it to this man].[167] Ambitious Van Imhoff was eager to replace the person who stood in his way.

CHAPTER 11

'The Ship Is Half Sunken': Batavia seen through Chinese eyes

> When I arrived [in Java], I was a young man who did not know anyone there. So, I wished to be hired by people for work. One day I reached the mountains carrying a knife to protect myself and I passed a dense forest where I saw the bones of dead people scattered out. I could not stay there for even one day! Afterwards I went to Semarang and thereupon to Batavia. I made a living ploughing my tongue [teaching]. There were often people who invited me to marry their daughter. But I stuck to what my father had said: 'You must remember that you can leave home because of poverty, but you cannot indulge in another pleasure place and forget your hometown and your duty.'[168]

Thus begins the main text of *The Concise Account of Batavia* (Gelaba jilue), a Chinese travelog written in 1741 by the Fujianese scholar, Cheng Xunwo, after his stay in Java between 1729 and 1736. Who was this author? The *Gazette of the Prefecture of Zhangzhou* (Zhangzhou fuzhi) of 1878 hails Cheng Xunwo (1700–1747) as a paragon of filial devotion to his parents.

> Cheng Xunwo was a man from Zhangpu in Fujian province. He was still a young lad when both his parents died leaving behind huge debts. At the age of 20, he left for Batavia to try his luck. When he had earned enough money, he returned home to pay off all the debts. The left-over money he donated to an older cousin who wished to marry. The people in his hometown were so moved by this gesture that they then sought out a bride for Cheng.[169]

The *Concise Account* represents a very detailed period piece of Batavia in the 1730s. It offers a fine description of the city as seen through Chinese eyes. The author starts out by describing the canals, the houses, the most prominent buildings, and the markets, and points out where the Chinese and Europeans lived within the city walls. Outside the gates, he feasts his eyes on the beautiful country estates to which the Company elite made their way on Sundays. Cheng was clearly impressed by all the pomp and circumstance of the Batavian elite.

'They leave the city in gold-trimmed carriages or sail in decorated boats with musicians on board. In their gardens you will find peacocks, talking parrots, flowers of all colors, coconut trees reaching to the sky, and *nangka* [jackfruit] trees loaded with huge fruits. Those are the right places to drink to one's heart's content and create poetry!'

Nonetheless, Cheng did not feel comfortable in Java. He could not settle in among the rough barbarians:

> Swords, halberds, spears, and firearms scare those who travel abroad. All the towns I have passed through are surrounded by moats and walls and are very strictly controlled and severely checked. On clear and sunny days, the guardsmen [at the gate] carry firearms but when it rains they hold a spear. They change watch every two hours [...] If passers-by want to enter or leave the gate, armed soldiers stand there lined up like trees. Even though it is not cold, we Chinese wishing to live in peace and tranquility, cannot help but shiver at such a sight. When the law is handled too strictly, one should not run counter to its sharp edges. When we enter a [foreign] country, we should investigate what will do or not. How can we afford not to know the laws one by one.

After a detailed description of the authority structure of the Company and how appointments are made based on merit, Cheng Xunwo discusses what he considers the (in his eyes) peculiar religious and burial customs of the Dutch, and reflects how they in turn look down on Chinese rituals: 'When they see how Chinese worship images of gods made of clay and burn paper money, they almost die of laughter.'

Following up on some comments about the tax farm system and the weights and measures used in commercial dealings, Cheng Xunwo goes on to describe in detail all the terrible punishments that are meted out in Batavia throughout the year.

> There exist no mercy or pardon. But however narrow the meshes of the net of the law may be, the penalty for adultery and robbery is invariably death. Robbers and thieves must be punished in different ways. Burglars are punished with the 'stick of the general' (*jiangjunzhu*), whereby an iron stick is pierced from below beneath the spine. Thus they let them die without food or drink. Or they are tied to a wooden bench and beaten to death with an iron rod. In case of theft, they hang the stolen goods around the thief's neck, pull down his underwear and lash him with split rattan until the blood gushes out and the flesh is bared, and then send him into exile after having branded him with a glowing stamp.

The bottom line is that not morality but the lash of justice prevails in Batavia: 'As those in charge do not set a good example, the ordinary people feel no shame. As a result, although their penal laws preserve order in the residential neighborhoods adjacent to main roads, they do not extend further to the more distant places.'

Cheng Xunwo also criticizes the behavior of the Chinese captain:

> The Chinese captain does not behave properly. Formerly the governor general and the Chinese captain shared the right to decide on the life and death of the Chinese. Nowadays the captain only possesses the rights to levy taxes of the weigh-house and of the coming and going of the Chinese junks, but has to share the income with the governor general. In the beginning the captain was elected on his own merits and worked closely together with the law officers, but today he acquires his position thanks to bribery and carries out whatever the governor general orders him to do. Is this not a disgrace to his own people?

At the end of his report, Cheng Xunwo summarizes the general situation at Batavia as follows:

> Since the Dutch observe how the Chinese are daily increasing in number, they have begun to despise and exploit them. They levy taxes on logging, sugar mills, arrack distilleries, stores and eateries, wayang performances, what not, yes even on marriages and funerals. Poor Chinese can no longer make ends meet, some run off with other people's goods, others trade in contraband. Those who see other people's wealth seek a living in crime and abandon themselves with debauched behavior. This will come to no good.

This premonition, Cheng Xunwo recounts, made him write a letter to a friend who had stayed behind in Batavia. He had urgently advised him to return home quickly: 'In Batavia hangs an extremely poisoned atmosphere. The ship is half sunken. This is perhaps because Heaven hates that Chinese live in Batavia! Oh, my friend come back soon!'

Judging by the somber tone of this account, not only was the privileged position of the Chinese in Batavian society at issue, there was also something else going on. Within the Chinese community the status of the Chinese captain appears to have been seriously compromised.

Cases of extortion

In the *Dream of the Rebellion at Batavia*, the river god points to some examples of Dutch rapacity which reveal how Governor General Mattheus de Haan and his Director General Huysman manipulated the Chinese.[170] The latter had set his sights on a pasar (market square), where Chinese and native people were selling their goods. He had the stalls removed and proclaimed that the square was to be auctioned off to the highest bidder. Then a group of twenty to thirty wealthy Chinese was forced to make the ridiculously high bid of 100,000 rix-dollars for the rights to the pasar. Because the revenues of the market turned out to be very modest, many of the investors promptly became insolvent, and this enabled the governor-general and his second-in-command to seize their goods and belongings at a low price.

A second example involved the manipulation of the all-important Chinese fish market in town and affected not only the livelihood of the Chinese community but also that of Company sailors. The story revolved around a spotted salted fish called *carwant* that was offered by Chinese fishermen at affordable prices as everyday food for the urban population and ships' crews.[171] Intervening in these operations, De Haan gave an overseer of the fish market total control of the sales. When that fellow promptly raised the price by 200 percent, this had dire consequences for the common folk who could no longer afford to purchase their daily food, and the skippers of the fleet who no longer had the means to supply their crews with provisions.

No less an evil was the new annual tax of 24 guilders imposed on the Chinese street vendors, or *kelontongs*, who set up stalls along the roads outside the town to provide the weary traveler with all kinds of edibles, drinks, tobacco, and a rest bench. Those who could not pay up that amount, 'were left with no choice but to go begging, die of hunger, or go out stealing.'

Irregularities in the sugar industry

Affairs also went awry in the sugar industry, which continued to remain one of the pillars of the local economy, even as the global export market underwent drastic transformations. Persia dropped out as an all-important export market when the Safavid dynasty was overthrown by an Afghan invasion. Fortunately, the port city of Surat in northwest India partially replaced it. There also remained a steady demand in Japan for Batavian sugar, which was quite convenient because sugar loads could serve as ballast for the ships sailing to Nagasaki. Exports to Europe, however, declined steeply because the

West Indian sugar plantations, much closer to Low Countries than Java, could deliver the commodity at a lower price.

Between 1719 and 1733, the Captain of the Chinese of Batavia, Que Bauqua (Guo Maoguan), worked hand in glove with a wealthy entrepreneur, Ni Locko, a rising star within Chinese society, as he headed a family that in due course would replace the Que dynasty in Batavia. Ni Locko served as boedelmeester (estate master) in 1715 and 1716, and then again in 1726 and 1727, and on July 8, 1729, he was elevated together with Ong Eengsaij to the position of lieutenant. Until his death in 1733, the wealthy Ni Locko owned in addition to several sugar mills, an arrack distillery and a freight junk for coastal trade along the Javanese coast. This patriarch headed a family of five sons, who all served in public office during the 1730s as captain, lieutenants, or estate managers. He laid the foundation for a large family fortune that would go up in flames in 1740.

That Ni Locko and Que Bauqua had been colluding with Director General Anthony Huysman came to light when, after the death of Governor-General De Haan, an alternative version of the report on the sugar industry was found amongst his papers, that had been drawn up by councilors, Joan Everhard van den Schuer (the son-in-law of De Haan) and Rogier Thomas van Heijningen in 1729.[172] In response to complaints about corruption in and around the sugar industry, these two gentlemen had launched an investigation into the state of affairs. It turned out that Huysman, contrary to earlier agreements, had lowered the purchase price of sugar to 3.5 rixdollars per picul for first-quality (*cabessa*) and 3 rixdollars for second-quality (*bariga*) sugar, but that Captain Que Bauqua and Ni Locko were still charging the old, higher prices. This discovery put the two reporters on the trail of sinister practices. The two foremen of the Chinese community appeared to be forcing impoverished sugar millers to hand over their produce to them at ridiculously low prices. The investigators also managed to figure out how these destitute millers had fallen into the clutches of Ni Locko and his cronies. As their land had been stripped of nutrients by the constant planting of sugarcane, the yields had sharply declined. In addition to this, the firewood needed for the sugar boilers had to be obtained from increasingly remote forests. Hiring seasonal workers from Cheribon also became increasingly difficult because the Javanese *bujang* on the sugar plantations who used to be supplied in large numbers by their regents, now preferred to plant coffee trees on their own land and felt little interest in leaving hearth and home to hire themselves out for a small pay to the Chinese sugar millers in the Ommelanden. Most likely, they were increasingly replaced by illegal Chinese immigrants. Almost half of all sugar mills had fallen into disrepair. Only ninety mills remained in operation, twenty-three were idle, and another twenty-three had disappeared altogether. Their staff had run away—where to, nobody knew.

In his critical retrospective, Wouter Hendrix also went into detail about all the abuses in the sugar industry. He attributed the decline in production to mismanagement as much as to the scheming activities of Ni Locko and his cronies.[173] According to Hendrix, the Gentlemen XVII in the Netherlands, who were so far away from the Indies, 'could not by any means in the world obtain sufficient knowledge or information to unwind that tangled information.' After all, it was the duty of the High Government to keep an eye on this, but it had failed to do so. He believed that the sugar industry of the Ommelanden, which only twenty years earlier was 'the principal and most profitable product of Batavian agriculture' had fallen into such disrepair that it could no longer meet the annual needs of the Company. The remaining fifty-one millers could produce only 27,850 piculs of powdered sugar, while the yield in 1710 was still 65,460. Inspections revealed that seventeen men who who did not even own a mill were registered as suppliers of sugar. Similarly, eleven men in the *kongsi* of Ni Locko and two other Chinese, whose mills no longer functioned, mysteriously still delivered sugar to the warehouses of the Company. In order to restore production, it was decided that henceforth no miller should deliver more than 300 piculs of sugar on an individual basis, a measure that in turn led to unnecessary problems with transportation, because the middlemen had previously combined those deliveries.

Five years later there appeared to be other problems with sugar production because Dutch demand had sharply declined. The High Government nevertheless felt obliged to purchase the sugar because the livelihood and businesses of many Chinese sugar millers and of their money lenders were at stake. Taking note of a new report that had been submitted to them by the chief merchants of Batavia Castle on September 13, 1737, the Gentlemen XVII even acknowledged that they sympathized with the problems in the sugar industry 'which provided work for so many Chinese in the Ommelanden and acted as a kind of safety valve to absorb the pressure of excess labor supply.' Suddenly, overproduction had to be accounted for because as many as a hundred mills had been recently added on Java's northeast coast. Owing to the resulting surplus, the syrup had to be preserved so long that it had to be boiled again, which detrimentally impacted the taste.[174] Moreover, due to competition with the plantations from the Pasisir, the sugar culture in the Ommelanden lost its luster to the detriment of the entire Chinese urban community and their relatives in China. For how, under these deteriorating conditions, could Chinese sugar mill workers continue to transfer part of their earnings to China to support their families? The privileged life of the Chinese in Batavia and their sugar enterprises in the Ommelanden came under severe pressure in the 1730s.

Increasing tensions outside Batavia

In the meantime, the Company's relationship with the Chinese elsewhere on Java also underwent change. Chinese had been visiting Java for centuries, but mainly as peddlers and in relatively small numbers. By this time, the nature of their presence was different. Under the umbrella of the Company's slowly expanding power over the island, many Chinese moved from Batavia elsewhere in Java further developing their own informal networks. Or, to put it more succinctly, they created a shadow world of their own, the beginnings of an 'informal empire' in which the Chinese took advantage of the protection afforded to them by the High Government of Batavia.[175] These developments were partly of the Company's own making.

Whenever military assistance was provided to the princes of Mataram to restore order in the Javanese empire, the 'grateful' susuhunan had to pay compensation in cash or in kind. These emoluments were mainly gained from the proceeds of the toll gates established by the so-called coastal regents (*strandregenten*) along the Pasisir. And obviously, those tolls and ports were put in the hands of Chinese shahbandars and other tax collectors. After the conclusion of Govert Cnoll's campaign in 1706, it was contractually agreed with susuhunan Pakubuwana that these tax collectors would be subject to the jurisdiction of the Company. The same Cnoll had earlier been alarmed by the sharp increase in the number of Chinese in this region and their growing wealth.[176] Through the network of tolls spread along the Pasisir, a semiautonomous Chinese trade network developed that remained connected to the local economies of China's southern coastal provinces via Batavia. Thus, the more or less intertwined trade networks of the VOC and the Chinese both cooperated and competed with each other.[177] Joan van Hoorn had left behind an exploitation model of market crops in the Ommelanden that was in fact ethnically determined. The Company leadership and the Chinese officers of Batavia grew into managers of the sugar culture, while the entirely differently organized coffee culture fell under the control of the Javanese regents. This may also explain why there was relatively little social cohesion or sympathy between the Chinese and native inhabitants in the Ommelanden.

Along the Pasisir, Java's northeastern coast, the situation was more complicated. After his death in 1726, Susuhunan Amangkurat IV was succeeded by his son, Pakubuwana II. Under the administration of this new monarch and two influential *patih* (court administrators), Islam and the central position of the court within Javanese society were revitalized. An additional problem was that the monarch, at the insistence of his patih, tightened his grip on the beach regents and tried to detach them with their Chinese clientele from the Company. The Kartasura court even took control of the appointments of the Chinese shahbandars and tollgate tenants and thus gained access to the collected revenues. All this meant that the High Government lost grip on the tentacles of the expanding Chinese presence all over Java. This aroused irritation, not least because the spread of Chinese fortune seekers was inevitably accompanied by an influx of 'undesirable elements.' In addition to the demand for the specific know-how for the refining process, the sugar mills always needed Chinese loggers and transporters. Thus, the mills naturally became the receptacles of unemployed illegal immigrants seeking work and refuge. In addition, the greater the distance between the Chinese sugar mills and Batavia and the Ommelanden, the more remote they became from the colonial administration and the Chinese officers in town.

Consequently, from the beginning of the eighteenth century, there was a widespread expansion of an informal Chinese trade network along the Pasisir.[178] It was not a uniform presence, because in addition to *totok* Chinese (those living according to Chinese manners and customs) one also encountered *peranakan*, Javanese- and Malay-speaking Chinese who were more or less integrated into Javanese society. Because of their role in the financial circuit as moneylenders and toll collectors, the leaders of the most important Chinese clans in the region forged close relations with the Javanese beach regents. In cooperation with these Javanese noblemen—the regents provided the field labor—they operated profitable sugar enterprises. When this led to overproduction, the High Government refused to accept all that sugar, and this, of course, also increased tensions.

It is impossible to obtain a completely reliable overview of the Chinese who levied tolls in the susuhunan's lands. Joan van Hoorn's report on Java's northeastern coast is probably the most thorough study of the situation at the beginning of the eighteenth century.[179] What it basically boiled down to was that the Chinese, 'a laborious people and vigilant traffickers,' as he described them, could do their own thing under the Company's umbrella. Army commander, Govert Cnoll, confirmed that he found Chinese all along the coast who had become entrenched in local commerce. In almost every coastal settlement, there was a Chinese who not only acted as shahbandar but who also levied tolls on the local pasar and often leased the best lands. Partly in response to this, Chinese who settled along Java's Pasisir were required to first register with the VOC authorities in Semarang.[180]

This Chinese presence occasionally led to quarrels with the Javanese population. That happened for instance when the susuhunan farmed out the toll gates along the road from Semarang to his court to Chinese henchmen. When in the 1730s complaints arose about Javanese 'riffraff' murdering Chinese rice buyers, a commission of inquiry determined that there were more than one thousand Chinese tenants, rice, and opium merchants and hawkers earning a living in the coastal region. The commission members ventured to doubt whether their safety really could be guaranteed. After all, the daily practice of the Batavia Ommelanden proved that there too it was very difficult to protect the Chinese pioneers operating in remote areas.[181]

The junk trade and the immigration problem

The decision made by the Gentlemen XVII in 1728 to follow the example of their European competitors and henceforth send VOC ships to China was not without consequences for the Chinese of Batavia. It soon became apparent that tea and porcelain could be purchased more advantageously in Canton than in Batavia. Although initially, ships were sent *directly* from the Netherlands to China, it was felt, that it was more profitable to send the ships *via* Batavia to China with cargoes of tin, sandalwood, spices pepper, and large sums of silver to pay for the tea. From Canton, these ships would sail with their cargoes of tea, silk, and porcelain directly back to the Netherlands without making a stopover at Batavia.[182]

Not surprisingly, this unilateral action of the Gentlemen XVII created bad blood among the members of the High Government in Batavia: would the direct trade link not adversely affect the Chinese junk trade to Batavia and the merchants who had an interest in it? Opinions were divided. Governor-General Diderik Durven thought that the consequences would not be so bad. Yes, the junk trade brought much prosperity to the city but, in his opinion, it also had its drawbacks. He pointed out that every year the junks diverted large quantities of silver money from Batavia to China to the detriment of the money circulation in the archipelago. A different view was held by Wijbrand Blom. He prepared a thick report in which he claimed that his colleagues in the High Government had never had a clear picture of the junk trade with China.[183] He was convinced that with the decline of the junk trade, 'soon a considerable decline' of the urban economy would occur. He pointed out that in addition to tea and porcelain, the Chinese also imported silk and all sorts of 'household trinkets' that the city could not do without. And didn't the junk merchants buy large quantities of pepper, tin, lead, spices, sappanwood, and European manufactures every spring? In his opinion, the balance of trade was always strongly in Batavia's favor, and not a penny had to be spent on this shipping corridor with China. That came at the expense of the Chinese themselves! In Blom's observation, junk shipping formed the umbilical cord by which the Chinese settlements in Java were connected to the motherland, in the same way that Batavia was connected to Patria by the Company's ships. Just like VOC ships every year transported thousands of Europeans from the Netherlands to Batavia, the junks brought thousands of Chinese migrants. Yet, although nobody said so, the direct trade of the VOC ships with Canton must have had great consequences for the bargaining power of Batavia's Chinese mercantile elite vis-à-vis the members of the colonial administration. Until then, all trade with the Middle Kingdom had been mediated by Batavia's Chinese merchants and the nakhodas' of the junks. That exclusive position now came to an end; for the China trade, the High Government was no longer completely dependent on the Chinese elite in town. There is no doubt that this had its implications for the co-colonial relations when one-sided measures were taken against the Chinese in the 1730s.

In hindsight, Blom's reflections on the carriage of Chinese passengers made sense, but in a different way than he could have imagined. When part of the tea trade to Batavia fell away, the Chinese nakhodas realized that they had to derive their income more than ever from passenger transportation. The consequences of this can be guessed, and Diderik Durven immediately capitalized on it. He introduced a new tax of one rixdollar on every Chinese newcomer. There can be no doubt that illegal immigration of Chinese grew into a pressing social problem in the Ommelanden, where unemployed Chinese began to wander at large.

According to the author of the *Chinese Annals of Batavia*, the general situation in the city and the surrounding area was deteriorating daily: 'That year (1731) robbers emerged from all quarters. At night they forced doors and robbed houses. Prodding sticks, they dug holes and crawled inside and rampaged around. The people had no means to make a living.' He then proceeded to describe the rounding up of a Chinese gang of robbers:

> Some people came forward and reported to Captain Guo Maoguan (Que Bauqua): Jin Chaomei has collected a sworn band of brothers around him, several hundred in all. Wherever they go robbing, they behave without any scruples. The captain then immediately went to see the governor general [Durven] and together they hatched a plan. The great king ordered the captain to lead the Dutch sheriff, taking fifty men with him at night to patrol everywhere and secretly investigate the situation around Jin Chaomei's house. If they were joining ranks to rob (people), he should arrest them forthwith. That night the captain went to his house. Jin Chaomei was just preparing a banquet for his followers. The captain immediately ordered the sheriff and his helpers to encircle the house and arrest Jin Chaomei and his robbers, nine people in all. The others crawled over the wall and the roof

> and got away without a trace. The captain thereupon bound the Chinese up and declared them guilty. The following day, Captain Que went to see the governor general saying: 'Jin Chaomei and his robbers have hurt many people. We should make use of the 'candle'(that is, the Judas chair) and let them die slowly, to discourage people from engaging in evil pursuits in the future. The governor general and his councilors deliberated and reached the decision to put Jin Chaomei and his men all together on the candle. Among them there was one man who only two days earlier had joined the band to learn the martial arts, and now he was arrested and punished.[184]

The Chinese Council or Kongkoan

The VOC *plakaatboeken* (registers of official notices) contain various ordinances directed against the smuggling by the Chinese junk network. Judging by the numbers of passengers, the port of Amoy (Xiamen) in Fujian province, was the main supplier of emigrants. On April 22, 1738, the High Government made the decision to curb the influx of Chinese by increasing the cost of the residence permit in Batavia to two rixdollars per person. For unemployed Chinese newcomers, that was a hefty sum that they simply could not pay, and many of them went into hiding as a result. No matter how many government regulations were devised, it was clear that little could be achieved without close cooperation with the leaders of the Chinese community. The Chinese captain and his staff of lieutenants and boedelmeesters gladly collaborated, for without government support, they could not exercise their authority. As early as April 1717, the High Government ordered the registration of all Chinese marriages and divorces. With the introduction of this registration, the Chinese Council or Kong Koan was acknowledged as a semi-governmental institution. It also managed the Chinese cemeteries.[185] As chairman of the Kong Koan, the Chinese captain was assisted by a growing number of lieutenants with whom he met every week to discuss pending matters and take necessary measures. Under Durven's reign, two extra lieutenants were even added to the already existing ones. Each lieutenant was assigned his own town district or suburb.

Ni Hoekong, rising star

The VOC archives occasionally reveal in remarkable detail what went on between the Chinese elite and the High Government. One example is the settlement of the estate of Lieutenant Lian Fuguang (Ni Locko), the wealthy

Chinese referred to earlier in the chapter. When he died on January 23, 1733, his eldest son, Ni Hoekong, informed Governor-General Van Cloon and Director General Westpalm that his father had left the two of them four houses in the Nieuwpoortstraat. Inquiries with the notary revealed that this generous donation had not been included in the will. When this was pointed out to him, Ni Hoekong stated flatly that the gift had been 'verbally testified.' The consequence of this generous donation was that Van Cloon and Westpalm promptly appointed Ni Hoekong to the rank of Chinese lieutenant. This decision elicited from Wouter Hendrix the ironic comment that Ni Locko's son, 'a madman and young loafer,' would never have received the appointment without that miraculous bequest of the four houses. Anyway, Ni Hoekong was not really that inexperienced, because between 1730 and 1731, he had already made himself useful as *boedelmeester*.

According to the author of the *Chinese Annals of Batavia*, Ni Hoekong struck again when he heard that Captain Guo Chunguan (Que Tjoenqua) had died. He left a wagon full of silver pieces at the gate of Governor-General Patras and then submitted an application to be appointed the captain. Needless to say, nothing about this gift can be found in the Company archives. And frankly, it also seems unlikely that such a delivery would have passed inconspicuously through the gate of the Castle. Still, this kind of gossip was not out of the blue either. The private gifting of presents by Chinese to colonial dignitaries was a well-known fact in Indies society and remained so until the end of the colonial era.

Although only about thirty years old, the new captain, Ni Hoekong, was a 'great merchant' who made his fortune trading tea, opium, and Indian textiles. He must have inherited lavishly from his father, for he owned several estates on which thirteen to fourteen sugar mills were in operation. Among those lands was also included a plot in Bekasi that the High Government leased to him. The Babakan estate in Tangerang and a garden west of the Ammanusgracht, however, he had inherited from his father. Within the city walls, Ni Hoekong possessed the immense family home on Rua Malakka that encompassed an entire block near the Portuguese church. It was a sprawling compound, a village almost, in which the different generations of the numerous Ni clan, grandmother, uncles, and brothers with their families were housed. Four of Ni Hoekong's brothers had already served as boedelmeesters and one had yet to become one. A sister had married the son of the Chinese Captain of the city Semarang, Que Anko. During the 1730s, the Ni clan surpassed the Que clan, which had so long ruled in Batavia. Like the Ques, the Nis hailed from the vicinity of the city of Zhangzhou in southern Fujian.[186]

Ni Hoekong could count on little sympathy from his compatriots. When his official appointment as Captain of the Chinese came through, he laid it on thick: 'On the first day of this month (February) he raised a red flagpole and hung on it a flag with a golden dragon on it. Below, he flew a flag with a golden tiger—this means that when dragons and tigers fight, the Chinese will be hurt. The captain and his wife came out of the gate of their house to salute the flags. After that they hosted a banquet and invited guests and entertained them with theater, flute music and drums, proudly showing off for three days on end.'[187] This ostentatious behavior did not befit a Chinese captain, argues a commentator of the *Chinese Annals of Batavia*: he did not show himself a shepherd over his people: 'Here one heard singing, there you heard the moaning of the people. This is not how a superior should behave!'

Following Ni Hoekong's quarrel with one of his lieutenants, Yang Chengguang, it dawned upon the Chinese people that their wealthy headman had little authority among his peers in the Kongkoan. Unable to persuade this older, troublesome lieutenant to fall in line, Captain Ni went to Batavia Castle to lodge a complaint against him and tendered his resignation to Governor-General Valckenier. But Adriaan Valckenier did not accept this. Instead, he summoned the obstinate Lieutenant Yang to the Castle, gave him a scolding for his disrespectful behavior, and dismissed him on the spot. 'Lieutenant Yang heard that with an ashen face,' the *Chinese Annals of Batavia* records. 'Thereupon he went home, but shouted to anyone who wanted to hear: "I may have been fired, but at least I can keep my *payung*. Today's wine I drink today, let the sorrows come tomorrow!"' By this he meant to say that despite his dismissal, he was allowed to keep his parasol, a coveted sign of dignity, and thus had not totally lost face.[188]

On balance, in the 1730s, the Chinese community of Batavia suffered the double blow of the pandemic and the Company's shifting priorities. Yet, the contribution of the Chinese to the urban economy remained as important as ever, although much of their former standing in the eyes of the government was lost as a result of unmanageable immigration, the decline of the sugar industry, and the relative depreciation of the junk trade. A grim mood began to prevail in the city.

We see all this confirmed in a letter to family and friends in Holland in which the Councilor of Justice Reverhorst discussed the position of the Chinese in Batavia. He stated that since the foundation of Batavia, the Chinese were enticed 'with many advantages and privileges' in order to settle down for the sake of the promotion of trade. They had been granted citizenship and been given the freedom to be governed according to their own laws. Two of their officers even had been allotted seats on the board of aldermen. The Chinese population had increased gradually but considerably. There were said to be as many as eighty thousand Chinese outside the city and 'allegedly' as many as twenty thousand lived within the city walls. But, noted Reverhorst, unfortunately, the Chinese had lately been 'shorn, skinned, and stripped to the skin by this government 'since everything is corrupt and for sale.' Yes, Chinese who previously possessed great wealth were now falling into great poverty, while 'a great multitude of the poorer ones fled away to the Bovenlanden [highlands].' That was a dismal, but, as we shall see, all too correct observation.

CHAPTER 12

Small Causes, Great Consequences

On April 21, 1740, Van Imhoff and his wife appeared at the Batavian roadstead, where a hospitable reception awaited him. His entourage of thirty-six European soldiers, a lieutenant, and some other officers provided the necessary decorum. They were decked in red-and-yellow uniforms, something that was reserved for the governor-general's own bodyguard.

Before disembarking from the ship *Goudschalkoord*, the prodigal son received the councilors of the High Government of the Indies and other friends and acquaintances who had been rowed over to meet him. Anyone who stepped on deck had to pass by two grenadiers standing at attention 'with bayonets on their flintlocks.' Months later, looking back on his cousin's jaunty return, a furious Adriaan Valckenier—he was obviously not present himself—wrote that the only thing that Van Imhoff lacked at that meeting was the title of governor-general to put him 'on a par with myself if not above me.' The Chinese were also impressed by Van Imhoff's arrival. They 'warmly welcomed him in town with red banners and music.'

With Van Imhoff's dramatic appearance on Batavia's stage, the tone was set for what was to follow. Hardly had he been installed in the Council of the Indies, when he made his voice heard. He submitted a detailed 'Memorandum of Handover' that he had prepared for his successor in Ceylon and then vociferously interfered in everything that came up for discussion. Valckenier commented afterwards, 'There is sufficiently no meeting of the High Government but he [Van Imhoff] delivers one or another novelty with the noblest propositions and *raisonnements* [rationales].'[189] Entire sessions were spent discussing Ceylon and Malabar, where Van Imhoff emphatically asserted his knowledge and experience. When the reporter on Coromandel affairs, Van Schinne, fell ill—councilors were frequently absent because of the pandemic—the all-knowing Van Imhoff gladly replaced him. Valckenier did not really know what to do with this prima donna but decided to be as pliable as possible.

In July, however, when several cases involving Chinese offenders were heard in the Council of the Indies in quick succession, matters went awry. The first case, on July 8. involved the Chinese, Oeij Toanko, who was suspected of murdering Que Piauko with the assistance of two slave girls. In the absence of evidence, Oeij, as was customary in such cases, was supposed to be banished on the next junk returning to China. When one of the councilors suggested that the accused might possibly get off after the junk's departure and then slip in again via Bantam under a false name, just like 'the great number of that nation here,' it was decided to turn the banishment to China into banishment to Ceylon and to put Oeij to work over there. The two slave girls, however, were sent to the Cape of Good Hope.

Three days later, another Chinese was sentenced, this time to the gallows for manslaughter. A few days later, the alderman's court (*schepenbank*) sentenced a Chinese man to life imprisonment at the Cape of Good Hope for forgery. Ceylon and the Cape were considered to be ideal places of exile owing to their remoteness.[190]

Whether it was because of these three cases in quick succession or not, at the July 25 council meeting, the discussion of Chinese offenders took an abrupt turn. Governor-General Valckenier wondered whether the High Government was not facing a much broader Chinese problem, given the countless Chinese drifters without a livelihood in the city and its surroundings who 'could not be categorized otherwise than as vagabonds and vagrants.' Did they not present a growing threat to the better-off citizenry in their gardens and homes, and were they not sowing panic among the population with murder, robbery, theft, and burglaries? Something had to be done 'to purge this colony as much as possible of that nefarious scum.'[191]

Van Imhoff knew exactly how to deal with the problem. He proposed to have all suspected Chinese elements, whether they possessed a permission slip (identity certificate) or not, arrested by the 'constables, *kaffirs*, the sheriff, and the commissioner for indigenous affairs, and to have them delivered to the city prison for interrogation by the secretary of the aldermen's court.' Illegal elements could then be expelled and transported to Ceylon and set to work there. All this was to be carried out 'the sooner the better, promptly and punctually in order to prevent all evil consequences that might be caused by those unemployed drifters.'

This did not seem like a good idea to Valckenier. He believed that the prosecution of gangs could better be entrusted to European soldiers, reinforced with native troops, since neither the bailiffs, sheriffs, nor commissaries had sufficient personnel to prosecute the hoodlums. In his view, moreover, it was 'altogether impossible that these officials and their underlings [...] could see at a single glance whether Chinese had an honest means of livelihood or not.' He feared that such a crass decision among the Chinese would not only 'create great emotions, but would also cause great harm, as no Chinese merchant would dare to show his face in the streets anymore.' Despite the governor-general's objections, the other councilors nevertheless agreed to Van Imhoff's rigorous approach.

The situation played out exactly as Valckenier had foreseen. The arbitrariness with which the constables and their native underlings proceeded to arrest people led to general confusion among the Chinese. The rumor spread that Van Imhoff had ordered the arrest of all Chinese who were dressed in black 'because they behave properly during the day but turn into thugs at night.' Nor was that the whole story: the message that the illegal immigrants would be exiled to Ceylon was called into question. Another version took its place: the rumor circulated that all those exiles, once at sea, would have their feet washed: that they would simply be thrown overboard.

Here the discrepancy between the imagination of the 'hardliners' in the High Government and colonial reality showed. The Councilors of the Indies took a quasi-rational decision that in reality could not be enforced. For the detention of 'villains' in the Ommelanden, the commissioner, the bailiff, and the sheriff had only native personnel at their disposal, who were now given a free hand to detain anyone they wished. Every councilor must have been familiar with the time-honored Dutch saying '*Schouten and baljuwen grijpen als wuwen*' (sheriffs and bailiffs claw like birds of prey). The manhunt of suspicious elements was arbitrarily carried out and took a turn for the worse. Chinese were even arrested if they had valid papers and were not released until a ransom was stealthily paid.

On August 16, the collector of Jakatra's revenues, Hugo Verijssel, submitted appeals from the Chinese tax farmers of the Chinese poll tax, along with those in charge of the taxation of the vegetable stalls and shops in the city. They asked to be exempted from the payment of taxes for the month of August because many Chinese, fearing arrest, simply stopped showing up. Chinese gardeners no longer brought their fruits and vegetables to the market in the city, and stalls and stores were closed everywhere. Because overzealous officers of the law had also detained the crew of a Chinese vessel from Indramayu, 100 miles down the coast, with a cargo of rice on board, other vessels carrying provisions to Batavia changed course and headed elsewhere to sell their cargoes. Chinese hawkers no longer ventured out into the streets because of the misconduct by the henchmen of the bailiff and sheriff.

Valckenier, who could no longer be physically present at the Council meetings owing to his chronic ailments, suggested via Director General Schaghen that the arrests be discontinued for the time being. They were causing too much unrest among the population in the Ommelanden and were disrupting the city's logistical facilities. This proposal offended Van Imhoff, who believed that the investigation and arrest of undesirable elements should continue as usual, although the highhandedness of the law officers should also be dealt with. Moreover, he was furious that the commissioner of indigenous affairs and the governor-general had not initiated their arrests until a week after the decision of July 25.

On August 25, the commissioner of indigenous affairs, Ferdinand de Roy, reported on the progress of the arrests. What he said was thought-provoking. The Chinese in the Ommelanden no longer let themselves be picked up like meek sheep. In Blitong Jati, his staff had failed to apprehend thirty to forty Chinese, who had fled leaving behind weaponry. When his underlings apprehended ten Chinese without passes at Kali Abang, the Chinese *mandor* (chief) of one of Captain Ni Hoekong's sugar mills intervened. At the head of a troop of ninety menacing-looking Chinese, this Oey Kikoe demanded the immediate release of the apprehended men. He said that he was only willing to accept the authority of his own 'viceroy,' Ni Hoekong. In short, as Valckenier had predicted, the sheriffs, bailiff, and deputies lacked the manpower to carry out the Council's orders in the Ommelanden. In the immediate vicinity of Batavia, the law officers were more successful in making arrests and managed to cram a few hundred men into the crowded city jails to be interrogated by representatives of the aldermen's court. Most of them were released again, but some remained imprisoned awaiting deportation to Ceylon. These measures caused uproar and consternation among the Chinese, but little attention was paid to them.

An outrageous fine

Meanwhile, an entirely different issue arose that brought the governor-general and the director general into conflict with most other members of the Council of the Indies. On July 18, the Council discussed a letter from the Gentlemen XVII in which the directors imposed a fine of nearly 400,000 guilders on the High Government to compensate for so-called lost income at the VOC's auctions in the Netherlands. In the previous year, according to the directorate, Director General Joan Paul Schaghen had shipped an excess cargo of 1,463,173 pounds of sugar and had run 1,394,430 pounds of coffee short in his delivery to the Netherlands. Schaghen explained clearly in the Council why he had done so. Only twenty-four ships had been available for the return fleet. It also needed to be considered that on the way back, many items still had to be picked up from the eight ships that had been shipwrecked at the Cape of Good Hope in the previous season. He had requested and received permission from the Council on July 8, 1738, to use sugar instead of saltpeter as the ships' ballast. Surely the lords were aware that Javanese sugar and Bengal saltpeter were better ballast materials than coffee which should not be exposed to dampness. Van Imhoff, who, owing to his three years' stay in Ceylon, had not been involved in anything, now stated, together with his friends, the councilors Van Schinne and De Haze, that this was a matter for which the governor-general and the director general were primarily responsible. True, the director general was in charge of the trade, he noted delicately, but since the governor-general had also signed the return cargo documents, he held him jointly responsible. Valckenier and Schaghen therefore had to pay 168,493 guilders and 216,656 guilders, respectively, out of their own purse. An indignant Valckenier disagreed and remarked that if any payment had to be made, he was counting on the other councilors to contribute: after all, the entire High Government had signed.

Valckenier proposed to let the matter rest for the time being pending further explanation from the director general to the Gentlemen XVII, but Van Imhoff and his faction wanted to hear nothing more on the matter and managed to push through a resolution that the two chief executives should be held jointly liable for the repayment of these enormous sums of money. For the governor-general, who had already earned so much in the service of the Company, the high fine was peanuts, according to Van Imhoff. 'Dominated by greed for money, however, he [Valckenier] was unwilling to give in,' he wrote to his uncle, the VOC administrator, Balthazar Boreel. He was well aware that he had incurred Valckenier's wrath with his intervention, but he could not care less. The knives were out.

The issue dragged on for another three years until Schaghen returned to Holland in 1742 as admiral of the return fleet and complained in person to the Gentlemen XVII that he was totally ruined by the imposed fine. He argued that at his departure from the Indies, he had deposited the considerable sum of 216,656 guilders for safekeeping. This sum was made up from his earned wages and the capital left by his deceased wives. Reviewing everything again, the management judged in retrospect that the losses suffered actually had amounted to a few tens of thousands of guilders. The matter was therefore settled with a fine of 33,294 guilders—no small sum, but considering all the harm caused by this, one can only conclude that it had been much ado about nothing.[192] Be that as it may, with his tough stance in the Council, Van Imhoff had effectively declared war on Valckenier and Schaghen in August 1740.

The governor-general was no longer angry; he was furious. The harassment campaign had achieved its goal: the atmosphere in the Council room had been completely spoiled, and Valckenier and Schaghen had lost their authority. What perhaps stung Valckenier the most were the simultaneous rumors being spread that in the Netherlands, the decision had already been made to replace him by Van Imhoff. Yes, people even toasted to his election! Thus, Van Imhoff and his followers sawed the legs out from under the governor-general's chair, or as Valckenier wrote in a secret letter of October 31 to the Gentlemen XVII:

'it is evidently his [Van Imhoff's] intention to make me vacate the chair and make room for His Grace, who aspires to it with an ambition that seems to know neither measure nor limit.'

Harmony and conflict

While the factional struggle between Valckenier and Van Imhoff in the Council of the Indies crystallized, let us recapitulate what position the governor-general held in the High Government. In 1724, Reverend Jacobus Canter Visscher, in a letter to his father, very clearly explained how, under the guardianship of Hendrick Swaardecroon, the tasks of the High Government were shared out: at that time, the governor-general still reigned supreme in the Council of the Indies.

> It is well known to you that the head of the High Government is the governor general, who is called His Highness here. He always presides over the meeting, comes up with proposals he deems useful, and, if the votes are tied, has a double vote. Besides, his authority is so great that if he wishes to advance certain matters, no one will oppose him at all, unless it is very important, for the whole militia is entirely dependent on his orders; yea, all the servants of the Company are obliged to take an oath of allegiance to him if he demands it. But the burden of his reign is no less great than his power. One sees him almost always confined in his study, and taking so little recreation, that it is a lot if he appears outside the walls of the Castle at least once a month. But when he appears in public, it is with regal splendor, in order to instill reverent thoughts for the Company among the indigenous nations, who are very fond of outward appearances.

Ten years on, Governor-General Valckenier's position looked considerably less authoritative. As president of the Council, the governor-general was no longer getting his way in the council. Polarization reigned as the opinions of Valckenier and Van Imhoff increasingly clashed during the meetings. It was essentially a matter of two conflicting cultures. The patrician, Valckenier, with his pursuit of a 'soft and indulgent' government, was a typical representative of the 'harmony model,' something that only works when the domination of the strongest party, the governor-general in this case, can provide apparent social peace. As long as his tormentor was at a safe distance in Ceylon, there was no problem with this approach. But when Van Imhoff returned to Batavia and clearly opted for conflict, problems piled up.

How concerned Valckenier was about Van Imhoff's opposition is further confirmed by Joan de Roode in his correspondence with Jan Minne in

Enkhuizen. After Van Imhoff's return to Batavia, 'great things had occurred, which one wished had never happened.' He even suspected that 'if more such histories occur, it may well happen that his Nobleness [Valckenier] repatriates sooner than imagined.'

These and similar observations indicate that Van Imhoff was ruthlessly pulling the cushion from under Valckenier's seat. That he destroyed much in the process did not bother him. He could not wait anymore. This impatience was a character trait that became increasingly apparent. It meant that on the eve of 'the Troubles of 1740,' the High Government of Batavia was effectively paralyzed by the discord in the Council, which itself was exacerbated by the personal feud between the ramshackle governor and his ruthless challenger.

Moreover, there was a pandemic that could not be combated, and the city economy was in crisis. In addition to that, a couple of shortsighted measures by the colonial administration had disrupted Chinese society, and the resulting social unrest had led to uncontrollable migration to the Ommelanden. The sugar industry was in dire straits, and at the head of the Chinese stood a pompous captain who had little concern for the dire condition of his own people. In short, a whole laundry list of dismal developments held Batavia in its grip.

CHAPTER 13

Beyond the City Walls: the Outbreak of the Chinese Rebellion

One of the eyewitness accounts that reached Holland after the Chinese massacre in Batavia opens with the lines:

> The following story will probably cause astonishment throughout the world, but it will also seem incredible to those who have earned their living in this colony and are thus familiar with the local situation and the way of life between the European and the native. How to explain that precisely the Chinese population has lapsed into such ungrateful, malicious, and treacherous schemes against their own benefactors as will be seen in the following narrative? Since the Company established its government and its seat here in these regions the Chinese have been beckoned to Batavia, both because of their commerce and dedication to agriculture and other activities that contribute to the prosperity of this colony, as citizens and subjects, under and beside us, and have thereby grown to a great multitude, nay, they have even has been elevated in wealth, honor, and prosperity to a nearly equal position![193]

The tenor of this and other pamphlets is that the Company had been betrayed by the Chinese who had been *nurtured, aided, and favored* since the founding of Batavia. When I italicize these three words, I do so because the anonymous author of *The Dream of the Rebellion at Batavia* does so himself when he voices the rhetorical question of the river god of Batavia: 'let us face it, have the Chinese recently also been cherished, helped and favored?'[194]

In the previous chapters, we have examined how ill-advised decisions by the High Government under the direction of De Haan and Durven worked out unfavorably for the Chinese community. Seen this way, the Chinese, especially those who lived outside the city or had only recently come to Batavia, had more than one reason to bear grudges. Yet it remains curious how little is known about the motivations and nature of the Chinese rebellion that sprang up in the Ommelanden during the summer of 1740: where did it begin, who were its ringleaders, and what was its course from beginning to end?[195]

Not surprisingly, all authors who have written about the terrible bloodbath in Batavia have relegated everything else that happened before or after to secondary status. The rebellion of the Chinese in the Ommelanden and their mass attack on the city before and during the massacre are described as the direct cause of the massacre. Yet, strangely it has never been identified as a Chinese revolt as such.

There may be a psychological explanation for this: when a terrible incident occurs, it will receive attention first; everything else is considered of minor relevance. Such is the case here: the stormy events inside and around the walls have received much, if not all, of historians' attention, but about the rebels' motives we remain largely in the dark. What may have contributed to this state of affairs is that there are not many useful data available to analyze the Chinese rebellion in the Ommelanden as an autonomous popular movement, let alone to approach it from a Chinese perspective.

This is unfortunate, because in the millennia-old history of China, peasant uprisings are a well-known and frequent phenomenon, and it is obvious that the rebellion of 1740 should also be seen from this perspective. Outside the city arose a Chinese popular protest movement that not only preceded the massacre in the city but continued to play out for quite some time afterwards, even moving onwards to Central Java and unleashing there yet another crisis at the Mataram court. That second phase, the *Perang Cina* (Chinese War) is more a part of Javanese historiography and will not be dealt with here in detail.[196]

As for contemporary local sources, we have to make do with a muddled Sino-Malay poem *Sya'ir Kompeni Welanda berperang dengan Cina* (The Dutch Company battles the Chinese), the Javanese *Babad Tanah Jawi* (The Chronicle of Java), and, of course, the *Chinese Annals of Batavia.*[197] We will combine these data with the VOC material and a handful of pamphlets published in 1741 that also pay attention to the course of the rebellion.

It is striking that the author of the Malay *Sya'ir*—he claims to be a pure Chinese from Sungai Baru and not of mixed Chinese-Malay descent—sees Van Imhoff as the great hero of his story. In this, he is diametrically opposed to the author of the *Chinese Annals* and, for that matter, the *Babad Tanah Jawi*. The first part of his poem is devoted to Van Imhoff's successful exploits in Ceylon. Then follows the siege of the city. Despite the title, very little attention is paid to the subsequent events in Java. For that we must turn to the other two sources. The author of the *Chinese Annals* broadly follows the course of the rebellion but portrays the three protagonists, Ni Hoekong, Valckenier, and Van Imhoff in a rather cliché ridden way: The Chinese captain as a coward, Valckenier as a gutless slob, and Van Imhoff as a bully.

Protest movements

Peasant rebellions were commonplace, if not a primary driver of Chinese history. Over the centuries, dynasties rose and fell as a result of protest movements in the agrarian society on which imperial rule was founded. Spontaneous movements that began as peasant uprisings were, if successful, valorized with the term *ge ming*, literally 'the change of Heavenly Mandate,' that is, a change of power at the top, a new dynasty. Thus, through the centuries, many a peasant son has risen to the Dragon Throne as the 'Son of Heaven' (*tian zi*) thanks to a popular uprising. The cyclical renewal of the Dragon Throne has enabled traditional Chinese society to regroup and consolidate over and over again. Significantly, this term *ge ming* is applied in modern times as a substitute of the Western term 'revolution.'

Apart from Chinese historians, who mostly study popular uprisings from the Marxist point of view of class struggle, Wolfram Eberhard was probably the first to have attempted to provide some structure to the make-up of Chinese peasant uprisings.[198] He explained that in the unruly southern provinces of China—from where the Chinese of Batavia and Ommelanden originated—there were often quarrels between village communities over land ownership. This internecine strife (*xie dou*) was usually fought out with gangs of unmarried and thus unattached youths. The same Chinese 'hooligans' also played a role in religious ceremonies, marched in processions, and provided flagellants who submitted to all manner of ritualistic forms of self-punishment. During periods of unrest, these groups were at the heart of gang formation.

In China's southern coastal provinces, the district official (*difang guan*), the lowest rank of mandarin in the imperial administration, governed the rural land. He did so in cooperation with the local gentry, that is, literate representatives of the village councils. In the case of unjust government such as unfair taxation, protests were usually coordinated by members of the gentry. Out of these protests could arise outright resistance in which the previously rival gangs of the family villages rose in unison against the district capital, so the countryside turned against the walled city where imperial authority resided. When the gangs rose above village level and cried out against injustices in the imperial administration, there was always a need for gang leaders or spokespersons who could articulate the complaints in writing.[199]

In peasant uprisings, religious symbols always played an important role. Oaths of allegiance and brotherhood were sworn before a local deity. Patrons, such as the god of war and trade, *Guanyu*, provided protection, and combatants wore amulets that made them invulnerable.[200] Also, on the sugarcane plantations in Batavia's Ommelanden, day-to-day religious life took place around simple chapels for deities such as the *tudigong* or *dabogong*, the local patron god, and, at a higher level, *Guanyu*.[201]

Much of this is reflected in the revolt of the Chinese in the Ommelanden, perhaps with the added ingredient of internecine struggles between groups originating from different areas of southern China. For although the bulk of the immigrants came from the Fujian coastal region, fortune seekers, like the Hakka's or 'guest people,' who specialized in mining, also came from Fujian as well as neighboring Guangdong. Except in small hamlets of Chinese gardeners and rice farmers in the vicinity of Batavia, there was nothing resembling the original one-family name village in Fujian. However, in the Ommelanden and the hilly Bovenlanden, Chinese communities lived clustered around sugar mills near the sugar cane fields along rivers and streams, like small island populations surrounded by swamps, forests, and native kampongs of Javanese, Buginese, Ambonese, or Balinese. These were by no means static communities, for the mills were moved repeatedly over time, when the surrounding forests had been cleared of firewood needed for the processing of the sugar and the soil of the sugarcane fields had been exhausted.

There can be no doubt that the rebellion was organized from and around the sugar mills. The owner of the mill was usually an absentee owner, a Dutchman or a wealthy Chinese in town, such as Captain Ni Hoekong, who owned several sugar cane plantations with mills. Not surprisingly, quite a few members of the colonial administration in Batavia suspected the Chinese captain and his lieutenants of colluding with the rebels outside the city, especially when one of Ni Hoekong's brothers, the boedelmeester, Ni Tjetkong, chose to champion the cause of the rebels.

The source of the rebellion

Was the rebellion a carefully planned undertaking or was it a spontaneous action in response to colonial oppression? A pamphlet with the revealing title *Omstandig en Allernaeuwkeurigst verhaal Van den Oorsprong, Voortgang en gelukkige ontdekkinge van het vervloekt en Schelms verraad* (Elaborate and highly detailed story of the origin, beginning, progress, and lucky discovery of the damned and villainous treachery) portrays the late boedelmeester, Ni Locko, the father of Captain Ni Hoekong, as the spiritual father of the 'cursed betrayal.' Although Locko's sudden death in 1734 threw a spanner in the works, according to this source, his five sons, all of whom held prominent positions in the Chinese Council, were said to have been bent on rebellion when the time was right. According to other shadowy lore, the rebels would have entrusted the actual leadership of the rebellion to a bastard son of the Chinese emperor who had recruited 'a considerable crowd' of followers around him in the uplands.

According to a more credible version, the direct cause of the revolt was the packet of harsh measures suggested by Van Imhoff. For example, the author of the *Chinese Annals of Batavia* believed that the 'great rebellion at Batavia' (*Baguo Daluan*) was a reaction to the rumors surrounding the deportations to Ceylon: 'What is the use of sitting by? To avoid death we had better revolt.' This same source speaks of two ringleaders, Lian Huaiguan and Lin Chuguan, who distributed black, red, and white rags as badges among their supporters. But after a date for the uprising was set, Lin Chuguan was overcome by fear and revealed the plot to the colonial authorities, who promptly thereafter issued curfews and exit bans for Chinese in the city. The real leader of the rebellion emerged as a certain Huang Banguan—Oey Panko in Company sources—the author of a defiant letter in which he incited the Chinese captain to side with the insurgents.

If there were originally several conspirators, the leadership eventually fell to this Huang Banguan, who was also known as Que Panjang because of his tall stature. The *Babad Tanah Jawi* supports the explanation of the uprising as an act of resistance and also attributes Encik Sapanjang (Que Panjang) the role of leader of the people's movement. In broad outline, this account boils down to the following: this good-natured, valiant man lived among his relatives at a sugar mill in Tanah Gandariyasewu in the Ommelanden (presumably the present-day kampung Gandaria east of Bekasi). After it became clear that the arrested Chinese were thrown into the sea on orders of the evil Van Imhoff (*Baron Pan Émuf*), Encik Sepanjang—furiously tearing his shirt into shreds—summoned his fellow Chinese in the Ommelanden and Bovenlanden to revolt. The Chinese, Encik Limko, 'who lived in the city and was aware that he owed his clothes and food to the beneficial influence of the Company,' informed the governor-general of what was in store. Van Imhoff thereupon sent the Chinese captain (Ni Hoekong) to the rebel leader (Que Panjang) 'with a bowl of gold and a bowl of dung, and admonished to him to choose reconciliation, for if he did not, this meant war and the common people would be the victims.' When the rebel leader reacted indignantly to this, captain Ni Hoekong tried to reason with him: 'Come on, Encik Sepanjang, don't be stubborn. The Company is seeking peace and will be more conscious of its actions from now on. Don't make everyone miserable.'

That statement provoked the furious reply: 'Won't you behave like a real fellow? The Chinese in town do not dare to fight and die. You are not like the Chinese of the sugar mills. They are fine fellows. We dare to fight and die.' Thus, the attempt at peacemaking failed. The Chinese in town were now faced with the choice of staying or leaving town before sunset. 'The Chinese all said they wanted to follow the Company. Then they were ordered to shave off their beards and mustaches.'[202] So much for this Javanese source.

Rumors circulate

What do the Company archives and the leaflets distributed in Holland have to say about the course of events?[203] In early September, little pointed to a brewing popular uprising, but that soon changed. On September 5, the fifteenth day of the seventh Chinese lunar calendar, Captain Ni Hoekong and the members of the Kongkoan prepared to celebrate All Souls' Day with the entire Chinese community. On that day, at each family altar, offerings are made to the 'wandering souls' to guide them to the gates of heaven that temporarily open. An elaborate priest-led ritual takes place in the temples. Bills posted here and there invite wandering souls to gather. Every wandering soul is assigned a place in paper dollhouses set up along with paper money issued by 'the underworld bank' in and around the temple. Once the souls are settled there, they are sent up to heaven, dollhouse and all, in an incineration ceremony. Such was also the case on September 5 and in the evening, paper boats with flickering lights were gently floated down to the sea via the Great River. Heaven and Earth were united on that day. A more peaceful spectacle was hardly possible. But it turned out to be the silence before the storm.

Three weeks later, Governor-General Adriaan Valckenier learned that his gloomiest predictions had come true: in the Ommelanden everything was in disarray: This was not entirely unexpected, for, as he would later admit, 'various displeasures and several disobedient actions' by the Chinese had already been heard about. Again, there are different versions about the initial reporting. According to some, the 'native Christian citizen, Pasquael Andriesz' came to Batavia Castle on Monday afternoon, September 26, to warn Governor-General Valckenier. Another source tells a somewhat more romantic story consistent with the version of the *Chinese Annals of Batavia.* At 5 p.m., an old Chinese Lim Tsouko (Lin Chuguan) asked to be admitted to the governor-general's office. He explained that he had been urged by his countrymen to take up arms against the Company. The plan was to kill all Europeans in the city on a designated night during the wayang performances in the streets. The date set was the new moon, i.e. October 3, when as many as fourteen wayang performances would take place simultaneously throughout the city. Shortly after Lim's visit, the lieutenants, Oey Theko, Khouw Tsinko, and Oey Somko, barged into the governor's office with the same story. Valckenier could hardly believe his ears, but, as he confessed, 'since I am not well acquainted with the Malay language,' he called in the Chinese interpreter Simong. The three lieutenants suspected that Lim Tsouko knew of even more details than he had given.

At 6:30 p.m. the governor-general convened a special meeting of the Council of the Indies. Just at that moment, former alderman Augustine Thornton also presented himself. He had heard from *Landdrost* (bailiff) Vinck that in the Ommelanden, thousands of Chinese were congregating under banners and standards. This was also confirmed by the messenger of the Chinese Council, Uw Jianko, the same man who in the previous weeks had been sent out with a drum to proclaim that anyone without a permission slip would be inexorably arrested.

Trouble in the Ommelanden

The next day, September 27, it was learned that Chinese were setting fires and committing murders in Batavia's hinterland. Bands were already gathering around the military guard posts of Meester Cornelis, Tangerang, the Qual, and Bekasi that in a semicircle protected the city. The governor-general was shocked by this news, but his fellow members of the High Government reacted halfheartedly. No one could believe that 'that nation, which by anyone was considered to be the most cowardly in the world,' would dare to dare to attack Batavia and its outposts.

Nevertheless, when on Wednesday, September 28, it was overheard that 'malicious Chinese' were planning to invade the city that same evening during a wayang performance at the fowl market, immediate measures were taken. The guards at the gates were reinforced and spies went out to scout the situation outside the city walls. When asked what was brewing among his people, Captain Ni Hoekong appeared to be unaware of anything.

On October 1, bailiff, Justinus Vinck, reported that as many as a thousand Chinese had been sighted in Tajoidan, a two hours' walk from the city. Reports also seeped in that at Grogol, a certain Isjong Tsanko was recruiting warriors and distributing blue linen rags among his followers as badges. Another rebel chief named Thioesia or Thiosa was also said to be recruiting men in a garden near the coastal observation post, the Fluijt. It was claimed that he was 'a nobleman by birth who for his evil behavior had to take flight from China to these regions.' An iron smith living near the Utrecht Gate (from whom the insurgents had ordered a batch of hewers) was able to report that *Quintangs* (Chinese from Guangdong Province) and "Mountain Chinese" (presumably Hakka people) were gathering outside the city in groups of fifty to a hundred men. Elsewhere, Chinese appeared to have bought 250 bamboo canes to make spears (pointed *bambu runcing*). Freeburgher Augustine Thornton reported that not only at his estate far from the city, but also at Tjakong, Djatinegara, and Bekasi, gatherings of armed men were scouted. Rumors, rumors, but one thing was clear: groups of rebellious Chinese were gathering everywhere.

On October 2, the spies returned to report that six hundred "Chinese vagabonds" were holed up around the redoubt of Meester Cornelis. It promised no good that the Chinese outside the town were now keeping their road stalls closed. When bailiff Vinck's men exhorted them to reopen their *warongs* (roadside stalls), they were ridiculed. Tension rose by the day.

Two days later, it was reported that the previous evening, two hundred armed Chinese had moved to Paningarang near Grogol and killed the postholder there. Meanwhile, the postmaster at Master Cornelis urgently requested assistance since six hundred armed Chinese with banners and drums were encircling his *benteng* (redoubt).[204] This meant that the insurgents were now becoming a real threat to the ring of forts surrounding the city. In great haste, reinforcements were sent to the entrenchments at Bekasi, Tanah Abang, Angké, Noordwijk, and Meester Cornelis.

On Wednesday, October 5, at 11 a.m., Albertus Steensma came to declare that he had been at the Prigie sugar mill, three hours away from the city. He had found there in the morning a large number of Chinese, all armed with shotguns, huddling at the sugar mill of the secretary of the Chinese Council, Ma Hoekoe. To great cheers, they had gathered there under seven banners. Menacingly, they had informed the native peoples living there in their kampongs that they should stay out of everything. At Li Koenko's sugar mill on Paningarang, too, a troop of Chinese people huddled together. A native sergeant who had gone there on reconnaissance paid for it with his life.

That same evening, council members, Van Imhoff and Van Aarden, along with Captain Jan van Oosten, left at the head of an army unit to Van Imhoff's country estate on Tanah Abang, an hour and a half's walk from town. The Company consisted of twenty-six horsemen, two hundred and thirty European soldiers, and several companies of Balinese, Makassar, and Javanese auxiliaries, with four cannons in tow. They had been asked to appease a large group of insurgents stationed there. Should that fail, they should try to disperse them. Later, another fifty-seven grenadiers, a couple of carpenters with axes, and three hundred Balinese were sent as a reinforcement. Captain Ni Hoekong and four lieutenants also accompanied them, to show their loyalty to the Company and thus remove all suspicion. Because they had quickly returned to the city before it came to an armed encounter, evil tongues claimed afterwards

Governor-General Adriaan Valckenier (1695-1751), holding a command staff in his right hand, with his left arm resting on a book bearing the VOC monogram.

The Valckenier family.

Bird's-eye view of Batavia, circa 1754.

The Chinese Hospital, built especially for the destitute Chinese and supported by revenue from tax farming.

Chinese procession during a pandemic to implore the favour of benevolent spirits.

All Souls' Day temple ceremony, where priests perform an elaborate ritual to gather the 'wandering souls'.

Popular print showing the massacre at the Chinese hospital (right) and the Chinese attack on the Dutch outside the city (left).

Contemporary print showing the burning house of Captain Ni Hoekong by the Roea Malacca canal. In front of the house is a flagpole with a snake.

Governor-General Gustaaf Willem Baron van Imhoff (1705-1750), like Valckenier, is shown half-length with a staff in his right hand.

The coin struck by Governor-General Van Imhoff before his departure for Asia.

that they only had joined the Dutch troops to spy on everything and inform the enemy.

At Tanah Abang, Van Imhoff and fellow councilor, Maurits van Aerden, encountered a carefully formed crescent formation of four to five thousand Chinese under the command of Commander-in-Chief Oey (Que Panjang). The rebels had entrenched themselves in a strategic position behind 'woodworks, consisting of buffalo carts set at length, under which long poles stuck obliquely into the ground, the latter covered with buffalo skins, which were also lined with kapok and thick Chinese paper and filled in between with earth, through which loopholes were made to provide for the [field] pieces.'

Two venerable, elderly Chinese were sent as negotiators to the rebel leader to 'admonish him to refrain from all hostile acts.' The reception at General Oey's headquarters was extremely hostile. He demanded first of all the immediate release of all the Chinese arrested in the Ommelanden and demanded that the Chinese who had been shipped to Ceylon also should return. If the Dutch were unwilling to do so, the insurgents would fight 'as long as there was a drop of blood in their bodies.' Completely empty-handed, the two negotiators did not return, for they were given a letter by the Chinese rebel leader, not for Van Imhoff, but addressed to Captain Ni Hoekong. In his letter, General Oey emphasized that he had sixty thousand men at his disposal in the Bovenlanden.

He wrote: 'The Chinese are maltreated and oppressed here in an insufferable manner. Therefore out of empathy I have appointed myself chieftain and congregated them to wage war against Batavia. I thank God that on the 15th [Chinese calendar] I went out for the first time and gained the victory by which it seems to me that God wants to help me. I have received two envoys who have admonished me to the best of their ability, therefore I am writing this letter so that the prisoners may be discharged and may join me together with the Chinese captain and the lieutenants and then I will consider further action. Therefore my request is that Your Excellency (Ni Hoekong) will please come to meet me and thus assist from within (the city) as well as from without. I have nothing more to say.'[205]

In other words, Captain Ni Hoekong was summoned by Que Panjang to join the insurgents.

The battle at Tanah Abang

After the members of the High Government had taken note of this 'arrogant and offensive letter,' translated first from Chinese into Malay and then from Malay into Dutch, the two councilors, Van Imhoff and Van Baerle, returned to Batavia to report to their colleagues in the Council of the Indies.[206] It was unanimously decided to intervene with the use of arms now that the rioting Chinese 'could not be brought to reason by any amicability.'

The encounter took place before dawn the next morning (October 8), with Van Imhoff on the right wing, and Van Aerden, commissioner Ferdinandus de Roy, and most of the Balinese on the left wing. Almost all accounts describe the battle that followed as an easy victory, but, as 'The Short Day Journal' recounts, the opposite was true: it was a thorny adventure that ended well thanks to brave action by the Balinese captain Babandam.

The Chinese had positioned themselves strategically and approached the Company troops in the formation of a crescent. Captain Van Oosten, who meant to counterattack with his grenadiers via a hastily constructed small bridge, could not get his bearings properly because of the darkness, and was tackled so hard by the Chinese that he had to retreat.

In the meantime, Van Imhoff was also having a hard time on the right flank, where the Chinese tried to surround him with 'his little heap of Europeans of 80 men and as many Balinese.' With utmost exertion, Van Oosten succeeded in dislodging him. 'Seeing that large riotous crowd,' corpulent Van Aarden was hoisted by his six guardians on horseback and, together with commissioner De Roy, he sought refuge in flight and galloped away in the direction of Tanah Abang. Promptly, the coolies who were pulling the field pieces also took to their heels, 'leaving the cannon and ammunition of war behind at the enemy's grasp.'

The Balinese, however, emboldened by their brave captain Babandam, stood their ground: 'He allowed his war party to run amok among the Chinese.' He even succeeded in recovering the abandoned cannons, so that junior merchant, De Windt, could bring them into position. Meanwhile, dawn broke, and only then did it become clear how things stood. The Chinese launched a new attack with 'great clamor and fury' to drag away their dead and wounded, but were stopped by De Windt's cannon fire. They were no match for the firepower of the field artillery.

Out of sheer curiosity, Valckenier's brother-in-law, the councilor of justice, Willem Vincent Helvetius, had ridden from his estate near Jakatra at 5 a.m. to Tanah Abang to check on the situation. There, to his surprise, he happened to meet a trembling Van Aerden, 'sitting on horseback, holding pistols in both hands, with a slave on either side to guide the horse [...] exclaiming with great dismay: "My Lord don't ride any further! I have never been so close to death and have barely escaped! Mr. Van Imhoff has been defeated! I mean to send an express messenger to Batavia to give notice of this disaster".' That was fortunately beside the truth, for Van Imhoff returned unharmed with an escort of horsemen to Tanah Abang a short time later and rode on to Batavia to announce victory over the rebels. The first battle with the Chinese had been won by the deployment of field pieces after several scary hours.

It was agreed that Van Aerden would stay with the cannon and with the Balinese to give them some rest, but he did not remain there for long. At 3 o'clock in the afternoon, he already showed up before the city gate in command of the grenadiers and fusiliers 'with the captured three banners in triumph, as if by his flight he had performed a heroic deed.' To his dismay, junior merchant, De Windt, suddenly found himself charged with the task of watching over the precious field pieces with only a handful of Balinese.

Attacks on the defensive belt around the City

Elsewhere, the Company's affairs developed considerably less favorably. Fifty European soldiers and eighty Balinese had marched to Bekasi on October 5 under the command of Lieutenant Jan Arends and Ensign Christoffel Hempel to take up position there. An expeditionary force sent to Bekasi a little later with extra provisions found only 'heads, arms and feet of our men' along the way. It turned out that Arends and his men had arrived in the pouring rain at a sugar mill surrounded by a wall, where, safely sheltered, they hoped to spend the night. That was a gross miscalculation, for in the middle of the night they were encircled and slaughtered by a large unit of Chinese rebels.

On October 7, some six hundred Chinese also overpowered Post de Qual and killed the postmaster and three soldiers there. Four soldiers escaped and managed to reach Batavia a day later. Ensign Etsart Lammorael Rengers, who had left for Tangerang that same day with a sergeant and twenty-four soldiers, was intercepted by the rebels four hours from the city, near Kadauwang, the former country estate of Governor-General Swaardecroon, and killed along with ten of his men. The others managed to escape by fleeing into the woods.

East of Batavia at the guard posts at the mouth of the Maronda River and at Tandjong Priok, approximately three hours from the city, and further south at Meester Cornelis and Tugu, the former estate of Chasteleijn, the rebels kept house 'with looting, murdering and setting fire to anything they could get their hands on.' An attack by over a thousand Chinese on the post at Angke, on the other hand, was repulsed by the 'terribly amok running' Balinese garrison of two hundred men with enormous losses to the Chinese attackers.

The rebels at the gates

It began with rumblings in the Ommanden; then, the rebels advanced to the fortress belt around the city. The rebellion was getting anxiously close to the walls. Then, on Saturday afternoon, October 8, the anniversary of the Chinese war god Guanyu, the insurgents appeared in the vicinity of the city and overpowered some outposts there. At 6 p.m., they approached the bridge and fence between the Diestpoort and the Nieuwpoort, and set fire to houses. That was meant as the sign for the Chinese inside the city to revolt as well, but there was no response, as the curfew had been imposed on the Chinese by order of Governor-General Valckenier.

In the darkness, the besiegers furiously attacked the bridge 'with continuous shouting and to the sounds of cymbals, drums and other Chinese instruments.' The civilian militia and the Pampanger sentry stationed there tried to hold them back, but were forced to retreat. A Company of grenadiers from the castle under Lieutenant Hemmingson and the civilian cavalry under rittmaster Christoffel Mol came to their aid, but that was of no use either as they had to hastily save their own skins too.

Beyond the walls, the Chinese assailants were in total control until finally, at 3 in the morning, they came under crossfire from the large guns of the Hollandia bulwark, where Van Imhoff was in command, and were forced to break off their attack, leaving behind two field pieces (cannons) and three banners. Withdrawing, they still managed to set fire to the houses outside the Utrecht Gate.

The next morning, the attacks resumed. The rebels now sought cover behind the houses of the suburb and the arrack distilleries outside the city and from there attacked the gate and the bridge near the Diestpoort. When they were on the brink of penetrating the southern suburb, junior merchant, De Windt, suddenly emerged from Tanah Abang like a *deus ex machina* with his field pieces in tow. He managed to bring them into position, aimed at the rebels, and forced them to give up the newly captured bridge again. Later that morning, the grenadiers and fusiliers made a raid outside the city walls. After piloting De Windt and his field pieces safely into the city, they set fire to the entire northern suburb with its arrack distilleries where only Chinese lived. They did so to drive out the rebels hiding there and clear the field of fire in that direction as well. 'It was a terribly sight,' said one pamphlet, 'the flames within that devored everything, the fires outside that consumed everything, as if it was meant to be so, as if the Final Judgment for this city and the colony had arrived.'[207]

Toward the evening of that same October 9, other Chinese troops set upon the gunpowder mills half an hour's walk from the Utrecht Gate, but those attackers were driven off after a tough battle, and so 'this unpleasant and distressing night, which had put everyone in the greatest anxiety possible [...] ended happily thanks to the Lord's never-failing goodness.' To be on the safe side, the garrison of the powder mill plunged the entire stock of 32,789 pounds of gunpowder into the river. That same day, the insurgents also attacked Tugu, setting fire to the church and the houses and drove the native Christians to Batavia.

Thenceforth, it became so quiet outside the city that on October 14, it was decided to send a cavalry Company with several companies of native troops on a reconnaissance mission. Near the Sonthar River, they ran across another band of armed Chinese, which they were able to crush. Five captured banners, a coat of mail intertwined with copper chains, and a breast armor made of buffalo leather were delivered to the Castle upon their return in order to be triumphantly displayed in the front hall of the Council of the Indies.

The brave Chinese attacks had failed because, lightly armed, the rebels proved no match for the field artillery and cannons on the walls of the city. As a matter of fact, it had been a very unequal battle in terms of armaments. In addition, the rebels had to face the Company's belligerent and well-equipped Buginese and Balinese auxiliaries. The rebels also had little sympathy to expect from the indigenous people in the Ommelanden. On the contrary, they found themselves in a hostile environment.

The fate of Chinese women and children

As to the fate of the Chinese women and children of the insurgents, the Dutch sources barely hint at it. Apparently, they were either kept safely hidden in the forests of the Ommelanden for the time being, or had fled. The *Chinese Annals of Batavia*, however, paint a dramatic picture of what happened to them:

> The survivors ran for their lives and scattered in all directions toward the mountains. Some rushed to the rocks, others hid in empty houses but were killed by the native soldiers. Jade and stone [people of high and low descent] were burned indiscriminately. It was heartbreaking and lamentable to see! Truly it is like the saying: There is no way to heaven and no door to earth! They were left to their own devices! The *nyai* of Guo Shou managed to lead a group of men and

> women safely to the plains of Salemba [in Bantam]. Another group led by the estate master Ni Tsietkong also arrived here safely. But the rearguard of them encountered a native chief Raden [Javanese title] who had been ordered by the government to cut them off and kill them. In an instant they were all killed by him. He was a Chinese by birth, but had gone native. How could you renounce the ancestors and become a Bantam chief? The corpses and bones laid scattered across the mountains and the rivers.' [...] 'Some of the fugitives got away safely but still feared they would not be able to find shelter anywhere, until they arrived at a sugar mill. Miller Que thought to himself: "These are all refugees. They certainly have valuables with them." He hatched a plan to kill them and told the refugees, "Good friends, if you have gold and silver with you, you had better give it to me for safekeeping, because soon the native soldiers will come to the mill to rob you. You have already suffered so much. Hide in the sugarcane field tonight." When they heard him saying this, they thought, He is right!, and confidently entrusted him with all their gold and silver. Little did they know that by now Que had secretly informed Raden so that he could encircle the sugarcane fields with his soldiers that same night. The river was filled with corpses. And the booty obtained was divided between the two of them.' [...] 'If someone behaves so heartlessly and unreasonably, heaven and earth do not allow it. Within three days, the miller was caught by the ghosts of the victims. He lost his senses and went stark raving mad and totally lost his way. Heaven's principles are clear and transparent! What is the point of committing crimes?[208]

Testimonies from the countryside

Now that the attack on the city had been successfully beaten off, the next task was to begin with the arduous task of driving out the Chinese troops still scattered here and there in the Ommelanden, for they were far from surrendering, and had merely retreated to the sugar mills in the area. On Friday, October 14, commander Jan van Oosten departed at the head of a troop of soldiers to drive out the Chinese at Tanjong Priok. As it turned out, the insurgents had set pitfalls in the road in which the Dutch cavalry was 'badly trapped.' Upon arrival, Van Oosten found an abandoned army camp with only a group of Chinese women and children, who had been left behind. To his surprise, he also ran into the widow and child of the murdered freeburgher, Salomon Hermenson, who had operated an inn there on the land of the councilor of the Indies, Nicolaas Crul. Hermenson's head stood impaled on a bamboo stake behind his house. Barbara van Amerongen (Hermenson's widow) and her slave Regina of Banda recounted how during the first days of the rebellion, their home had been raided by Chinese rebels. While her husband and his slaves tried to defend themselves and were inevitably trampled underfoot, Barbara had gone into hiding in the attic. This was to no avail, for soon the looters in search of booty came upon her. Begging for mercy, she and her baby were handed over to the attackers' wives with orders to serve them. In the days that followed, she overheard that Batavia had been conquered by the Chinese and that all the Christian men in the city had been beaten to death. Their wives had been made slaves and whores of the Chinese, but Governor-General Valckenier had been enslaved to serve Captain Ni Hoekong as his *payong* bearer. With some relief, Barbara noted afterwards that none of this rumor turned out to be true.[209]

Other testimonies also provide a penetrating look behind the scenes of the rebellion.[210] On November 2, Miss Agatha Rooth, the 27-year-old widow of the freeburgher, Arnoldus de Groot, appeared before the councilors of justice, Helvetius and Woijt, with a blood-curdling story. She had been living with her husband and child in a country house near the Maronde River since 1736 and had never encountered the slightest problems with the local people. In early October, some Chinese had shown up and asked her husband to intercede with the bailiff (*landdrost*) so that they would not be arrested. But her husband had said that this was none of his business and that he did not want to bother that officer about it. Then, on October 8, a certain Malay appeared, known to them as *Bappa* [bapak, father] Sia, who told her that the Chinese were arming themselves to conquer Batavia. Her husband had subsequently called sixty Buginese and Malays under arms to defend his property. Moments later, two Chinese from Nio Tseenkong's sugar mill and a Chinese named Piau came from their own estate to tell them that anybody teaming up with the Dutch would be massacred along with them. But those who kept quiet and aloof in their homes had nothing to fear. From Niai Laij, a Chinese woman employed by her, Agatha learned that the English and the people from Bantam would support the Chinese.

Moments later, the Chinese appeared on the scene but Agatha succeeded to escape with some native women in a canoe. When one of them, Manita, was shot from the riverbank, Agatha and the slave woman carrying her child jumped overboard. Since that woman could not swim, Agatha took the child from her and together they managed to clamber up the bank and hide in the woods. Moments later, some native women and Malays came running up and advised her to surrender, because 'the Chinese had already taken all of Batavia, except for the Castle. The city was in ashes and the ships on the roadstead were ablaze.'

To this Agatha had replied that she would rather be devoured by a tiger than surrender. Thus, she was left in the jungle, all alone with her baby. Another

Malay Bappa Romeni, a close acquaintance, showed up and warned her that a bounty of 50 rixdollars had been put on her head. Fearing that he would turn her in, she fled deeper into the woods and promptly ran into some of her slaves and a Malay called Nero. They told how her husband had been killed by the Chinese and what had happened to their possessions. According to them, the 'lieutenant of the Chinese, Nio Tseenkong' (boedelmeester Ni Tjietkong) had appointed two Chinese, Ti Aijseng and Khe Laij, as agents of her husband's possessions. They had divided the goods and slaves among themselves and given to the natives fifty bunches of the rice stored in the attic. At night, Agatha and her baby, along with two slaves and two slave women, let themselves stealthily drift down the river to the sea where they happened upon a shack standing on stilts, in which some fishermen were staying. After much prayer and supplication, she found them willing to take her to the island of Edam in the Bay of Batavia, where they landed at three in the morning. Agatha had heard from a Chinese woman, that originally captain Ni Hoekong had preferred to wait with the rebellion until the arrival of the junks from China (after the New Year) because they would bring in new weaponry. However, the birthday of their deity (Guanyu) in October had been the deciding factor in the rebellion.

On November 3, an eighteen-year-old Chinese who had worked as a gardener on the land of the free burgher, Pasqual Andries, near Tanjong Priok reported to the Judicial Council. Three weeks ago, four Chinese had forced him to 'join the conspiracy.' If he refused, they would kill him. They said that they intended to wage war on the Company to avoid arrest and deportation to Ceylon. A sharp-pointed bamboo was pressed into his hands and then they went with three hundred men via the estate of Councilor Nicolaas Crul to the Maronde, where there were another hundred or so Chinese waiting for them. There, they smashed a house to pieces, took liquor from the cellar, made an offering with it, and then drank it all.

He had also witnessed the plunder of freeburgher De Groot's home. In Kali Abang, he encountered Ni Tjetkong, the brother of Captain Ni Hoekong, who was in charge there: 'a person of medium height, fairly corpulent, and still youthful.' Occasionally, he saw him passing on horseback with a standard-bearer in front of him and a trumpeter at his heels. There, he saw another tall and gaunt-looking rebel leader named Tsie Thiam. He had heard several times that Ni Hoekong was the instigator of the rebellion, but that he had advised his countrymen to launch an attack on Batavia at night during a downpour when the Europeans would not be able to shoot because they could not keep the gunpowder dry.

A certain Donatus Fransz. of Batavia, 'Christian native of about 20 years,' turned up in Batavia at the end of October and had also a special story to tell.[211] He narrated in detail how the unit of Jan Arends and Christoffel Hempel had been ambushed on their way to Bekasi and had been slaughtered to the last man. Donatus had heard that Captain Ni Hoekong had sent letters to the sugar mills instructing them to resist if Europeans were allowed to pass by. Not much later, fifty European soldiers marched by with a lieutenant, an ensign, two drummers, and a group of slaves carrying baskets of provisions and a keg of gunpowder. They were on their way to Bekasi. Their Javanese guide told that they planned to bivouac on the way at Piesangang on the land of a Javanese lieutenant.

After the departure of the Dutch soldiers, the Chinese miller, Khe Pak, of the sugar mill, Troesan, showed up with a yellow banner and copper cymbals at the head of an estimated two hundred Chinese. At night, they grouped together with others in the forest. The following day they showed up again, this time with two Chinese trumpeters, two drums, and two brass cymbals. They first poured an offering and then left together by midnight to attack the European soldiers at Piesangan. Donatus overheard that the rebels were armed with choppers and as many as forty muskets. The next morning, six to seven hundred men surrounded the mill where the soldiers were bivouacking and set fire to everything. The entire garrison was pummeled, except for six soldiers who managed to take to a boat. But they did not escape either, for after a wild chase they were caught too.

The rebels claimed that they were as many as ten thousand strong. 'They would seek to become masters of Batavia if they had to fight another ten years of war [...] and kill all the Dutch and put the heads of their leaders on stakes here and there on the roads.' Moments later, Donatus learned that all of Batavia was already ablaze and that the governor-general had been sighted atop the Castle tower with a spyglass in hand. As soon as the governor-general observed that the Chinese had taken the city after a fierce battle, he had descended from the tower and fled with most of the councilors and officers to the ships lying at the roadstead, leaving behind all the women and other Europeans in the Castle. The churches within the city and the rice warehouse and many other buildings had been reduced to ashes. Since the Dutch now lacked food and houses of worship, they were forced to abandon Batavia. However, when it later became clear that the city had not been captured at all, the Chinese told him that they planned to attack again in the rainy season, because the Dutch 'would not be able to use their artillery and guns.'

Chased but not yet defeated

After the rebels had been forced to retreat outside the fortress ring around Batavia, they entrenched themselves on the western and eastern borders of the Ommelanden, that is, in a number of sugar mills around the Tangerang River near Bantam and in Que Panjang's headquarters near Bekasi, where about twenty thousand Chinese had built a strong fortress behind a large swamp. Since the turnaround of the rainy season was expected soon, during which it would be well-nigh impossible to conduct army operations with a burning fuse in that swampy area, the High Government decided on October 17 to immediately equip a punitive expedition westward, under the command of Captain Crummel, to the relatively nearby town of Tangerang. The Sultan of Cheribon on the eastern border was requested to keep an eye on the Chinese near him, with the promise that as soon as the wet monsoon was over in May, an army campaign to Bekasi would be undertaken. That Tangerang expedition deserves some attention because it shows how the surviving groups of rebellious Chinese had retreated to their sugar mills.

Captain Crummel's expedition

On the afternoon of October 18, Captain Crummel left Batavia at the head of a Company of eighty-three grenadiers, thirty civilian cavalrymen, twelve carpenters, twelve musketeers, coolies towing four field guns, and several companies of Makassar and Balinese auxiliaries, altogether fifteen hundred men.[212] Although the mopping up operation he had to carry out would be interesting enough to follow on account of all the logistical problems involved, Crummel's comments about the Chinese hideaways, their weaponry, and tactics are even more captivating. Their warfare seems to have come straight from the well-known traditional picaresque novel *Shuihuzhuan* (Tales of the Water Margin) and the *Sanguozhi yanyi* (Novel of the Three Kingdoms), another immensely popular Chinese historical work full of imaginative folk heroes.

On the first day, Crummel's soldiers marched no further than to rittmaster Moll's Piesing country estate and spent the night there. On October 19, they marched to the Kamal sugar mill near the Gedempte Rivier. There, they encountered an entrenched enemy who made furious sorties up to three times, but finally fled. The mill was set on fire. Then the soldiers moved on to the next mill, called Capok, which was another half an hour away. Here too it came to fierce fighting. After three attacks, this mill too was taken, with four banners and a standard held by a Chinese horseman as trophies. In view of his 'considerable outfit and equipment,' he seemed to have been one of the ringleaders of the rebellion. His severed head was sent to Batavia with the banners, the standard, and a red cloth with Chinese characters on it.

Via Kadouwang the army now proceeded westward to the *benteng* (fort) of Tangerang, which was reached on the 20th. There, the tents were pitched to take a rest from this tiring trek through swampy swamps, sugarcane fields, and dense forests. Tangerang's commander reported that along the river down to the observation post Qual by the sea there remained six more sugar mills, 'crammed with Chinese.'

On October 21, the expeditionary force marched on along a narrow and difficult path through the sugar cane plantations to Parankoeda, where they found the Chinese entrenched on a hillside, opposite a sugar mill surrounded with dwellings, 'They began to fire strongly from their hideouts and drove more than 50 to 60 *kerbau* [water buffaloes] in our direction to confuse us, and followed immediately in their wake.' This attempt to embarrass the Company forces with furious buffaloes was inspired by a well-known trick from the Warring States period (third century BCE).[213] However, the galloping beasts swerved into a different direction, so that the Chinese could be shot at with the field cannon and the muskets anyway. After the rebels had pulled out, the mill with its surrounding dwellings was set on fire. 'Here a large musket was captured, more than 10 feet long, shooting bullets of about half a pound, and in addition to that a banner and other field signs, including several choppers and *parring* [machetes].'

A few days later, the Company set out again, after spies had carefully scouted the road. Via a stop at Kadauwang, the men now headed for the Qual, which was still in Chinese hands. On the way, they met with the Chinese interpreter, Simong, who carried the 'Act of Amnesty for the Chinese,' which had been proclaimed on October 23, so that there would be no misunderstanding if 'innocently exiled and wandering subjects of the Chinese nation' came forward within a month. The rebel leaders, however, could not count on amnesty. A bounty of 200 rixdollars had been put on their heads and 500 rixdollars if brought up alive. In one afternoon seven more banners were captured from an army of about five hundred Chinese. Again, a commander was shot from his horse and beheaded. His severed head was also sent to Batavia 'because his appearance seemed familiar.'

On October 26, the 'well known sugar mill Salapadjang' was reached along narrow paths through the forest. Another considerable Chinese army force stood ready for the confrontation. 'Seeing us approaching, the enemy immediately marched up in a irregular way in our direction waving many banners without giving way to the cannon fire.' Heavy hand-to-hand combat broke out between the Chinese and the Company's Makassarese, Balinese, Malay, and Javanese soldiers who ran straight at them shouting amok. After an hour and a half, the battle was decided. The fleeing Chinese disappeared in the direction of kampong Melayu. In the meantime, a Company of Balinese had destroyed the nearby sugar mill, Budjong Renje, and struck down all Chinese except for one old man who was prepared to go to the next sugar mill laden with the letters of pardon to induce its occupants to surrender. After an arduous trek through forest and sugar cane, the troop reached the sugar mill of kampong Melayu on October 27 in the pouring rain, where it was found that the Chinese garrison had already left and escaped across the river into the territory of Bantam.

The weaponry left behind at the mills was a display of Chinese ingenuity as a list of captured weapons shows. In terms of firearms, the Chinese had rifles, muskets, and home-made cannons made from hollowed-out trees studded with iron bands, as well as basses and stone pieces (small cannons). Stabbing weapons were of all kinds: 'very viciously pointed bamboo sticks,' *keris* (Javanese daggers), swords on long stems, swords with short hilts, and large curved pruning knives on long sticks, the so-called man-catchers. The rebels also had man size shields made of buffalo hide and thick interwoven rattan, with a spy hole in the middle. Caltrops had been planted around the mills 'to prevent our people from approaching, at least with the cavalry.'

On November 2, Crummel's little army returned to Batavia, sick and exhausted from marching through water, mud, and swampy sugarcane fields. A month later, on December 14, the insurgents made one last futile attack on Tangerang, but the rainy season put an end to everything, and thus peace was restored on the Bantam frontier.

The Chinese rebellion had cascaded down from the Upperlands like a *banjir* in early October but stopped dead at the walls of Batavia. In the weeks that followed, mopping up operations exterminated the remaining pockets of resistance in the Ommelanden. Only in Que Panjang's home base at Bekasi, did insurgents still bent on revenge refuse to give in and firmly entrenched themselves in a fortress surrounded by marshes. They had to be reckoned with after the wet monsoon was over in spring.

CHAPTER 14

Within the City Walls: Fear and Amok

'O wrath, ghastly to behold!
Corpses were swarming the streets,
the rivers flowed with blood'.[214]
—Reverhorst

What tortured the mind of the Amsterdam patrician, Adriaan Valckenier, as he observed from the castle's parapets the Chinese rebels trooping up, ready to assault the city walls? We cannot fathom his thoughts, but is it an exaggeration to suggest that the ominous October days of 1740 evoked memories of Joost van den Vondel's epic drama *Ghijsbrecht van Aemstel*, which portrayed the horrors of a medieval siege of Amsterdam? What fate would befall Batavia if it were attacked by the Chinese hordes? One thing is certain, Valckenier clearly remembered how his predecessor, Swaardecroon, had nipped in the bud Pieter Erberveld's conspiracy ın 1721, just before his evil plan was due to be carried out on Sunday, when everyone was at church. Being trapped in a city attacked on all sides by furious Chinese rebels must have been an harrowing experience for the Dutch colonizers, even more so because they were living amidst a predominantly Chinese population within the city walls.

Thanks to the studies of Van Hoëvell and Vermeulen, the hard facts are known: in the second week of October 1740, all Chinese men present within the walls of Batavia were slaughtered and a quarter of the city went up in flames. Unlike these two authors, my primary concern in this chapter is not to immerse myself in a detailed account of the bloodbath. My purpose is to demonstrate the inner connections of the occurrences and how these played out in one week's time. It is precisely at this point where Van Höevell seems to have become lost in a forest of details. He insisted on proving that the colonial regime was not to blame for the massacre that took place between October 9 and 11, but that everything was brought about by the faltering Adriaan Valckenier.

Building on the factual knowledge acquired by my predecessors, I will reassess ten surviving 'short,' 'circumstantial,' and 'most accurate' day-to-day reports/pamphlets, check the hair-raising tales by bystanders (and even one participant) of the bloodbath, draw on the account in the '*Chinese Annals of Batavia*,' and compare these with the hard data unearthed from the VOC archives.[215] If I intentionally include all sorts of concoctions from the rumor circuit in the days that preceded the bloody weekend, I do so because they mark the atmosphere of suspicion, fear, revenge, and looting that prevailed *intramuros*. It will in fact amount to a collage of the actions and behavior by three protagonists on the scene—the increasingly desperate Valckenier, the cleverly maneuvering Captain Ni Hoekong, and the incisive and calculating Van Imhoff.

Rising tensions

The High Government received all sorts of signs in September 1740 that something was brewing outside the city, but, as noted above, initially its members did not care much, with the exception perhaps of what was considered the panicking behavior of Governor-General Valckenier. On Saturday, October 1, despite an urgent request by Valckenier, the councilors of the Indies initially even refused to reassemble and discuss the tense situation. Thedens declared that for the time being, he saw no bears on the road; Van Imhoff concurred with him and spoke disparagingly of 'loose rumors,' and Van Suchtelen and Van Schinne also wanted to await further developments. De Chavonnes and Van Aerden were willing to reconvene the next day but only so after first observing the Sabbath. Panicky measures, in their opinion, could only cause more unrest among the population.

They were not entirely wrong in this, for the civilian population was already in a state of terror. When on Sunday morning, October 2, during Reverend Mohr's sermon in the Portuguese church, the *kaffirs* of sheriff Justinus Vinck came marching past the church with fifty-seven arrested Chinese, and there was such an uproar and jostling among the churchgoers that despite the Reverend's soothing words, 'his wig fell off his head, the jabot was pulled off and torn to pieces, and his gown was trampled under the feet of the panicked believers.' Why did the parade of shackled Chinese create such an excitement? They passed by in an almost crucified position, that is, with their arms spread out and tied to bamboo poles.

When the High Government met in an extraordinary session on Sunday after the sermon at the Castle—the weekly outing of the councilors to their country estates was disrupted that day—Valckenier announced that, as a precaution and on his own initiative, he had already doubled the sentry posts at the town hall and at the gates the previous night just to be on the safe side. Sheriff Vinck had informed him that Chinese Lieutenant Khouw Tsinko had hastily returned to Batavia from the countryside of Tajoidan where as many as a thousand Chinese were gathering. Khouw was one of the lieutenants who had already given a warning on September 26. Later that day, spies returned to the city and confirmed that they had observed gatherings of Chinese. One of them reported that a sergeant of the Balinese auxiliaries had been murdered by the Chinese. A certain Koe Sinko also dropped in to reveal the rumor that Captain Ni Hoekong from within the city was secretly maintaining contacts with the rebels in the countryside. Whether that was true or not he left to the members of the Alderman's Court to investigate. 'This time even Messrs. Van Imhoff and van Schinne, who usually contradict me, agreed with me,' Valckenier noted, 'if only because they were eager to cover up their inexcusable lapse of judgement committed by the resolution of the 25 July 1740.'[216]

On Monday, October 3, the Chinese in the city suddenly kept their *warongs* and *tokos* (shops) closed, which meant that no daily food could be obtained any more. In addition, a disturbing sale of bamboo canes was reported from which *bambu runcing*, spiked bamboo spears could be manufactured.

On Tuesday, October 4, a representative of the Aldermen's Court reported about the interrogations that had been conducted among the detained Chinese. One of the arrested men alleged that Captain Ni Hoekong was involved in a conspiracy, but in the absence of further evidence, no credence was given to this allegation. Consequently, an attempt by Valckenier to label the Chinese captain as a dangerous person misfired. To restore calm among the population, the night watches at the city gates and on City Hall square were reduced again to their usual numbers. Postings round the clock had greatly exhausted the civic defense and native troops.

On Wednesday, October 5, 1740, the Council met again in the morning. A message had been received from the garrison at Meester Cornelis urgently requesting reinforcements because an estimated six hundred insurgents had dug in near that defense post. The redoubt at Tangerang also cried for military assistance. By now, none of the councilors were in doubt anymore: they were facing a serious situation. Valckenier therefore asked the meeting whether, in view of all this unrest among the Chinese, the members wanted to 'proceed defensively or offensively.' Would it not be prudent to issue an amnesty to dampen tempers? It was decided to apply 'a gentle hand' first. Van Imhoff and Van Aerden volunteered to go and check out Tanah Abang the next day, where a large number of armed Chinese were said to have gathered. That encounter ended, as we have seen in the previous chapter, in a showdown in which the Chinese were defeated more by good luck than by good management.

On Friday, October 7, the triumphant mood surrounding Van Imhoff's victorious return was soon dampened by disturbing reports that the outposts on the Qual and Tandjong Priok had been overrun the day before. Even Ensign

Rengers' detachment that had left for Tangerang two days earlier appeared to have been intercepted by the Chinese en route. The worst news concerned the slaughter of the entire force of 130 men that had marched to Bekasi on October 5. Angry tongues claimed that Ni Hoekong was also behind that ambush. He allegedly had sent two slaves with a message to his sugar mills near Bekasi to forewarn them about the coming of an expedition force.

Ni Hoekong in a fix

It was not the only gossip circulating about the Chinese captain, and understandably so, for he was in an impossible position: either he had lost control of his constituency, or he was diabolically hobnobbing with them. That same afternoon, Ni Hoekong went to visit Councilor of the Indies Elias de Haze at the town hall, where the latter, as president of the aldermen's court and colonel of the civilian militia, had pitched his headquarters. There, he coordinated all patrols within the walls and oversaw the guards at the gates and outposts beyond. The Chinese captain visited him, curious as he was about the outcome of the armed encounter between Van Imhoff and Van Aerden with the Chinese insurgents that same morning. When he heard that the Chinese had been defeated, he showed himself 'very moved,' according to bystanders. Since this did not escape Mrs. De Haze, she asked him why he looked so dismayed. He replied 'with his Judas face restored' that nothing was wrong with him. This did not satisfy this lady well versed in Malay. She tried to press him hard, 'but that unyielding rock managed to mock her in a scandalous manner and brush aside everything.' Nonetheless, the Chinese captain ventured some clues as to where weapons might be hidden in the city, and acting on this, some buffalo skin made into armor and a collection of choppers were discovered. The suspicion against the captain was understandable. After all, he stood at the head of the Chinese in the city and 'an attack from them was to be feared rather than the attack from outside.'[217]

Suspicious moves

The feeling that something was also brewing within the walls was reinforced by the droves of Chinese women and children leaving the city, while, on the other hand, quite a few men folk were entering the city! That was considered a 'very dangerous sign.' All this running to and fro alarmed the gate keepers, and especially irritated the sailors of the return fleet who had been herded into the city to reinforce the defense. Normally, those sailors were allowed a day of shore leave, but now entire crews were dropped into town without any proper supervision. The men found to their disappointment that Chinese *warongs*, *tokos*, drinking, and other establishments were shuttered. With nowhere to go, the bored sailors lingered aimlessly around the landing spot to await further orders. This situation avenged itself almost immediately: they not only began to 'show rancorous behavior' but started to harass the mysterious influx and outflow of the Chinese, even going so far as demanding money from them. At Van Imhoff's instigation, a decree was immediately issued that anyone who dared to harass, insult, or impede Chinese residents in their doings would be locked up or punished with some other 'arbitrary correction.'

On Saturday, October 8, the 'great festival of the Chinese called "Roode Joosje" [the red faced God of War Guanyu]' was to be celebrated, but strangely enough, the exodus of Chinese continued; apart from women and children, they were now even transporting household furniture in their *perahu*.[218] A sense of danger was in the air, and that impression was confirmed when that same afternoon, gangs of armed Chinese showed up beneath the city walls and began to roam around the southern suburb. To prevent the situation from escalating, Valckenier now ordered a curfew for all Chinese residents in the city and the suburbs. No Chinese were allowed to go out after 6:30 in the evening. Nor were they allowed to show a light outside the house, for it had come to Van Imhoff's attention that the rebels outside the city and the conspirators inside the walls were planning to exchange light signals.

Curfew

The guards were reinforced again, incoming and outgoing traffic was restricted, and at each gate of the city, two members of the Council of the Indies, provided with special orders granting them temporary military authority, assumed supervision of the civilian militia and soldiers stationed there.[219] The garrison of Batavia Castle, consisting of only seven hundred military, was coordinated from the Town Hall and distributed among the various gates, where the civilian militia kept watch. Policing duties within the walls were entrusted to the president of the Council of Justice, Elias de Haze, who could have at his disposal the clerks (pennisten) from Batavia Castle and the sailors transferred from the ships on the road stead. The Diestpoort and Utrechtpoort were closed, although small doors remained open for individual passersby. Posted near the entrance and exit stood the sailors and artisans, armed with muskets, blunderbusses, and choppers, to control the stream of passing

Chinese. The Rotterdam Gate was closed too. Only the Nieuwpoort allowed limited carriage traffic for returning citizens who no longer felt safe in their country houses. De Haze summoned all Castle clerks to the town hall square and provided them with weapons, gunpowder, and bullets. Three companies of forty-eight grenadiers were dispatched to reinforce the outposts of Meester Cornelis, Tangerang, and Tanah Abang. The garrison of the redoubt at Anké also received reinforcements in the form of one hundred Balinese.

The siege begins

Everything was now in a state of war 'to thwart the intentions of the malevolent Chinese,' and that was just as well, because at sunset, amidst loud shouts and cymbal blasts, 'a great heap' of Chinese attacked the city. How that attack was repulsed around midnight at the cost of great losses to the besiegers has already been told in the previous chapter.

On Sunday morning, October 9, at 6 a.m., when the rebels had temporarily retreated, the members of the High Government gathered in the Castle no doubt with eyes red-rimmed from fatigue. It had been a rough night. Valckenier opened the meeting and theatrically raised the question of whether the city should not be purged of the Chinese inhabitants, who could still be found in large numbers within its walls. Had the Chinese not declared themselves the public enemy with their attacks of the previous night?

That was pushing things too far according to the gentlemen. What exactly did the governor-general mean by 'purge'? Chase away or eliminate? Van Imhoff came up with a counterproposal: first let some aldermen and bailiffs escorted by the civic cavalry go on reconnaissance in the vicinity of the city to ascertain the situation there. And as for the city itself, he said, 'Urge the heated tempers to calm down, and have all the Chinese houses searched by the artisans and sailors for possession of arms.' To this only Valckenier disagreed, for who could guarantee that this would be done in an orderly manner? Disagreement ran so high that the councilors broke off without making any further decisions, 'leaving the governor general to his own device, being full of chagrin because the disagreement would bring great harm to the city, now that those who sympathized with the governor general were being shouted down.'

Hardly had the councilors returned to their gates when fire broke out in Utrechtsestraat and shots echoed from the Chinese houses on Groenegracht. Commotion was everywhere! Now the pent-up anger of the sailors erupted. They were embittered about the soldiers killed in action at the redoubts of De Qual, Bekasi, Tanjong Priok, and the Maronde, to say nothing of the massive

Chinese assault on the city during 'this sad and fatal past night.' One spark proved enough. A flaring argument between sailors and a group of Chinese about a Chinese who had been shot got out of hand and exploded into a huge brawl at eight in the morning. Informed of this, Valckenier, 'being alone and assisted by not one member of the High Government,' immediately sent horsemen of his guard to the tumult to try to contain it. But shortly after the grenadiers and horsemen returned to the Castle, the fat was in the fire.

The search operations proposed by Van Imhoff soon degenerated into killing and looting parties in which almost everyone participated. The councilor of justice Reverhorst later wrote in a letter to his friends in Holland:

> Exhausted by staying up several nights in a row, as well as angered by the shedding of the blood of so many Europeans, but also out of desperation about our small force against such an irate multitude of that rebellious nation, [the sailors] proceeded to a total massacre and robbery of these very suspect and certainly for the most part guilty [Chinese] people without being willing to listen to any orders. Nay, on the contrary, these sailors were immediately joined by the entire citizenry and its slaves.[220]

That the sailors took the lead was confirmed by Daniel Nolthenius. They had become bored and weary by loitering around the wharf and, joined by the artisans, they threw themselves on the houses of the Chinese 'with blazing eyes at robbery, broken loose like mad dogs [...] Whereupon those in the other quarters of the city, believing that this was done by order of the government (as some assured them) also put their hands to work and simply committed a ghastly massacre.' Because the sailors and artisans initially set out to loot their homes, many Chinese temporarily managed to survive by going into hiding on the upper floor. But when their homes caught fire, they had no choice but to jump down or perish in the flames, which caused Nolthenius to remark 'that so many Chinese allowed themselves to be killed off like sheep.'

Captain Ni Hoekong, who, after an equally sleepless night, had gone on Sunday morning to the Castle as early as 5:30 a.m. together with one of his uncles to await the outcome of the council meeting, still had the nerve to have breakfast afterwards with Director General Schaghen. However, when the two distinguished Chinese left the Castle Square by carriage, a nasty surprise awaited them at the gate: they were taken at gunpoint by angry members of the Civic Guard. 'Miraculously,' they still managed to make it home. It was estimated that some four to six hundred able-bodied Chinese men had taken refuge in the family compound of captain Ni on Rua Malacca. But if they thought they were safe there they were in for a surprise. Captain Jan van

Oosten had the entire estate surrounded by Company troops and proceeded to bring two cannons into position to set fire to the compound, 'so that the Chinese present there had no choice but to be burned alive or emerge.' When about forty Chinese ventured out through the back yard, they were shot by soldiers waiting for them on the Hoendermarkt. Some of them jumped into the canal to escape their attackers by swimming, but the sailors in their rowboats showed no mercy for them either. 'No harm was done to the women and children, who were allowed to walk away unhindered,' one of the pamphlets asserts, as if to expiate all the horror.

Helped by his neighbor, Alderman Abraham van Dijk, Ni Hoe Kong managed to save his skin one day later. Van Dijk had run into Ni Hoekong's *payung* carrier in the street the night before. When asked where the captain was, the boy replied that his master was hiding 'in very great fear' in his home. In response, Van Dijk had indicated that he would protect the Chinese captain if he came to him via the canal behind his house. At 7 a.m., Ni Hoekong, with his beard shaved off and disguised as a woman, surrounded by some women and children, came wading through the canal where he was met by Van Dijk shouting, 'Don't shoot, don't shoot!' Moments later, Councilor of the Indies Nicolaas Crul came to pick up the Chinese captain and his ladies and escorted them to the Castle, where the Ni Hoekong was detained in the bastion De Parel (Pearl).[221] At 3 o'clock that afternoon, a Balinese guard also fished one of Ni Hoekong's brothers out of a canoe in which he was hiding under a mat. He too was taken away handcuffed to the Castle.

A shocking narrative

What was going through the minds of that marauding and murderous gang? Probably they were utterly *mata gelap* (out of their mind). Significant in this respect is the surviving testimony of a Company servant who, after returning home, wrote down his memories of the massacre. Georg Bernhardt Schwarz was one of hundreds of thousands of Germans who enlisted in the VOC during its two-hundred-year history. On October 11, 1734, he sailed out as a private aboard the ship *Nieuw Walcheren*, but much of his seven-year stay in the tropics was spent in Batavia as a cooper in the *Ambachtskwartier* (the Artisans' Quarter). In 1740, the last year of his employment, he also ran a boarding house together with two slave women.

Schwarz had planned to repatriate with the return fleet on October 15, 1740, but because of the Chinese revolt, the ships' departure was postponed, and the sailors were brought ashore to reinforce the garrison. Along with the workmen of the Artisans' Quarter and the clerks from Batavia Castle, he was seconded to the city militia and thus witnessed the siege of Batavia and subsequent tragic events from beginning to end. Schwarz meticulously recorded his recollections of the Chinese rebellion in his *Reise in Ost-Indien* (Travel in the East Indies). Indeed, he came out roundly that he himself had participated in the plunder. His account confirms that the carnage began with an incident near the square where the sailors were hanging out.

> When a sailor suddenly shot a Chinese man, other Chinese interfered. This led to a serious skirmish between the two sides. But as soon as the governor general and Van Imhoff heard of this *mêlée*, the order was issued to beat to death or shoot to death all the Chinese *sans façon* [just like that] and freely [...]. The sailors started the affair. They banged and hacked open the doors, beat to death all the Chinese wherever they encountered them and looted everything. Women and children, on the other hand, were spared. At 9 o'clock the governor general visited the Artisans' Quarter. He ordered us to march out and destroy all the Chinese in town.[222] This was grist for our mill! In order to obtain good booty, everyone wanted to be the first to have a go at it. The carpenters smashed doors and windows with the axes they carried, and where weapons were found, they massacred the Chinese inhabitants. I myself also had to participate. Since I did know that my [Chinese] neighbor owned a fat pig, I wanted to take it to my house. When the master carpenter saw that, he gave me a thrashing and said, 'You must first kill the Chinese, and only then rob'. Thereupon, lacking a weapon, I took a rice masher, a long wooden stick as thick as an arm, and beat my neighbor to death, with whom I had often eaten and drunk. Although it seemed pitiful to me, I had to do this against my will, since my boss was at the door. After killing him, I went into his room and found a pistol which I took with me, and since there were many bullets lying around that fitted well, I went off with it and shot everything I came across. After I had killed two or three Chinese, I was so used to it that I no longer cared whether I killed a Chinese or a dog.[223]

Looting and arson

By Sunday evening, all the Chinese houses along the Rua Malacca and the Grand River, including the captain's family compound, were on fire. Everything was ablaze. Now the Chinese themselves were the arsonists. Seeing no way out, they preferred to burn in their own homes rather than fall into the clutches of murderers, rapists, and looters. They hung themselves from roof beams or jumped from the upper floor into the fire to be burned alive. The Portuguese city church was also threatened by the conflagration, but the sudden reversal of the sea wind into a land wind sent the flames in the other direction toward the Chinese houses, 'so that the house of God was preserved as a miracle and by God's hand and suffered not the least damage [...] also elsewhere God Almighty once again came to offer His helpful hand to us poor Christians.'

As the whole of Batavia threatened to go up in flames, the city government finally took action on Monday, October 10. Fires were vigorously combated at as many as twelve different places. Meanwhile, the attempts by the Chinese insurgents to break into the South Suburbs were prevented. When they could not succeed, 'the Chinese did their best to obtain by arson what they could not obtain by force, because before the day was over,' the anonymous author of one of the pamphlets wrote, 'the suburb from the Diest gate to the Malay kampong beyond the Utrecht Gate and also the whole of the Western suburb were up in flames causing a horrible spectacle both inside and outside the city. This could truly be said to be the SECOND TROY!'[224]

Although the fire crews were busy all Monday, even during the night of October 10–11, the blaze was still not contained. When all the fires were finally extinguished on Wednesday, October 12, the extent of the damage became all too clear. More than seven hundred Chinese homes had gone up in flames. Curiously, the fire had not spread to a single European home. In a matter of days, the entire southern suburb and a quarter of the city within the walls had been reduced to ashes.

'Even while the fire crews were dousing fires all over the city,' Nolthenius wrote,

> The plunderers continued, fighting among themselves for the booty, until some, maimed in arm or leg, or with a bloodied head, had to leave his loot [to] a stronger one. It is regrettable that many who pass for decent people, prompted by their habitual greed, also defiled themselves with this behavior. Outside the city they went about the same way, wherever a Chinaman was discovered, he was promptly killed, so that many of them took their own lives, mostly by hanging, or burning to death in their houses.[225]

'The sailors gave full rein to their desires,' wrote another eyewitness, 'as they discovered money chests in some houses, dug up jars full of silverware, and also found trade goods and tea.' There was no end to it: 'Ducatoons circulated so easily, I was told, that a sailor gave a ducat for a pipe of tobacco [...] it was below their station to even use small coins. They took pleasure in washing a house clean with wine.'[226] With great difficulty, the authorities managed to restore some discipline in the following days. Two-thirds of the clerks were withdrawn to resume their work at the Castle; one-third remained on guard duty in the city. After the sailors had been sent back to their ships, they left at the end of the month with the return fleet, and those workers of the Artisans' Quarter who were still on guard were replaced by the native citizenry and forthwith piloted back to their quarter, where a huge pile of accumulated loot was stored.

It was not until Friday, October 14, that the civil cavalry and several companies of native troops succeed in driving out the last besiegers. During the afternoon, they returned triumphantly to the city, waving captured banners, as well as guns and pointed weapons. For the next five days, Nolthenius was put in charge of supervising the clearance of rubble and the removal of corpses strewn everywhere amid a terrible stench.

Some 'hard' figures

The pamphlets may have paid much attention to the material destruction wrought, but they could not disguise the tragedy that in those same three or four days, all the Chinese inhabitants (largely apart from women and children) were 'beaten to death like dogs.' Thus Reverhorst wrote in dismay: 'OH WRATH, ghastly to behold! Corpses were swarming the streets, the rivers flowed with blood.'[227] Standing at his doorstep, he had helplessly watched what had unfolded before his eyes, while a 'hail of bullets flew over his head.'[228] Indeed, there was, in Valckenier's words, 'neither a drop of Chinese blood left in the city nor in the suburbs.'[229] Another source presumes that only fifty of all the 'male Chinese inhabitants' made it out alive.

According to the census taken three months later, in December 1740, all 4,389 officially registered Chinese residents within the walls (including the southern suburbs) were gone.[230] Many women and children (about 1,500) had possibly escaped because they were left alive or had already been evacuated in the preceding days.[231] Of the 10,767 Chinese living in the suburbs of the city, only 1,826 remained, according to the same census in December 1740.[232] This means that 8,941 registered Chinese disappeared during the massacre, with the understanding that some of them may have fled during the hostilities. These figures are taken from the official censuses of 1739 and 1740 in the VOC archives. A caveat is in order: these data should be regarded as an approximation rather than an accurate representation of the population, and no account has been taken of the Chinese who had entered the city just before the attack. Also not included are the numbers of rebels who died on the battlefield or later while on the run.

If we compare these figures with the size of Batavia's total population, which strangely enough no one has done, we can see everything a little better in context. According to the (not very reliable) census, a total of 18,476 souls were living in the east side, west side, and southern suburbs of Batavia on the eve of the Chinese massacre. Of these, 11,068 were slaves, far more, therefore, than the 7,408 freemen consisting of Europeans, mestizos, Mardijkers (native Christian), Chinese, Amboynese, Moors and Gentives (Hindus), Malays, Javanese, Balinese, and Makassarese. The Europeans (not counting the military and the Company personnel residing in the Castle, plus the crews on the roadstead) altogether represented only 1,286. Indeed, the 4,389 Chinese numerically constituted the largest ethnic group among the free inhabitants of Batavia, and they were obviously very visible, living in the best parts of the city. But in reality, they were less than a quarter of the entire population, and in hindsight, one might wonder to what extent the Chinese citizens then could have been seen as a real threat.

Drama galore

The members of the High Government initially did not even try or dare to intervene, preferring to look the other way while hysteria ran rampant in the city. Yet, on Monday, October 10, another tragedy occurred in which the authorities were clearly involved. Had the administration still been able to hide somewhat behind the argument that the sailors, artisans, and the townspeople ran berserk and could not be tamed, there is no excuse for what took place in the hospital, the municipal jail (*stadsboeien*), and the Company's jail (*'s Compagnie's boeien*).[233] Henry Abbis, the English chief merchant of the VOC trade in Canton, witnessed how, under the supervision of Judicial Council members Helvetius, Hackenberg, and Munnix, a couple of Mardijkers and 'black boys' (slaves) slaughtered all the Chinese who had taken refuge in the hospital. Only twenty seriously ill patients were spared and evacuated to the island of Edam. Abbis and the hospital's supervisor, Lieshout, could not bear watching the horrid spectacle and walked out. According to his slave, November, the outraged Lieshout had snarled at the judicial councilors, 'Let everybody see how justice is done here! Take them outside because I cannot bear to see the blood here in this house of mine.' The Chinese were chased outside and were promptly slaughtered by the marauding mob. Lieshout was so upset by the carnage that he died a few days later.

No less heinous were the massacres carried out in the municipal and Company jails with the approval, or rather at the instigation, of the authorities. The jailer of the Company's prison, Livinus de Heere, would later confirm during his interrogation that on the orders of the bailiff, Pieter Boockesteijn, all 250 Chinese in the prison had been slaughtered. Shortly before the massacre, Boockesteijn had sent De Heere to the councilor, Elias de Haze, who as president of the Council of Aldermen was in charge of maintaining order in the city, to ask him 'whether he should also kill those Chinese who were being held as hostages.' To this he received the answer 'that anything Chinese should be killed.' When he reported this to the bailiff, the bailiff sent him to De Haze again with the question 'whether the *peranakan* or shaven Chinese also had to be killed,' which elicited De Haze's reply: 'Did I not tell you that anything Chinese should be killed? Yes, the *peranakans* too.' As far as he was aware, the jailer denied that all this had been carried out on the express orders of the governor-general.

A similar drama played out in the municipal prison. According to the jailer who worked there, Andries Retting, the Public Prosecutor Phillips had come over on October 10, after Retting had warned him that the prison was so overcrowded with Chinese that he could no longer accommodate them. One of the jail's marshals, Jan Jurgens, testified that Phillips had growled: 'Is this why I came to this country? To have to carry out such executions? Hurry up, you must come with me.' When the two of them went straight to De Haze for an explanation, they did not find him at home, whereupon the provosts and their underlings decapitated the 232 Chinese prisoners. The provosts estimated that in total, about five hundred Chinese had been killed in both prisons.

During these interrogations, the testimony of the grand cashier, Abraham Abeleven, added another poignant footnote to the whole affair. He confessed that from Sunday morning to Tuesday night, his Chinese friend, Nio Tjienko, had been hiding with him. Because fiscal Phillips' *kaffirs* had seen the Chinese sneaking into his house, Abeleven had no choice but to ask Phillips to put his Chinese friend 'under the protection of the Company.' Phillips, however, had taken exception to this, 'since all Chinese were outlaws.' Abeleven was told that his friend had to leave the house. If not, Phillips would send his *kaffirs* after him. Abeleven then replied that in that case, he would rather let the Chinese out of the barn door. Shortly afterwards, Phillips informed him that one of his slaves had 'administered a stab to the Chinaman.' When Abeleven found Nio Tjienko heavily wounded in the stable, he 'finished him off with his pistol and had the corpse thrown into the canal.'[234]

How to cope with an outrage

There exists an extensive literature on mass murders, ranging from the carefully planned genocide of Jews by the Germans during World War II to the horrific pogroms in Poland, Belarus, Lithuania, and Ukraine carried out largely by local participants. The massacre of around a million so-called supporters of the Indonesian Communist Party in 1965 are also still fresh in our memory.[235] In all these bloodbaths, one may find elements that we encounter in the case of the Chinese massacre at Batavia: the growing frustration and pent-up tension among the local population, the spark that triggers the release, the all-consuming wave of unbridled violence, the impotence of the government that has lost control, and finally the fire with its symbolic 'cleansing effect' by which everything that has been destroyed, looted, and plundered within a short time is forever hidden from view. It is notable, however, that in the case of the Batavian massacre, a group of outsiders, that is, the sailors of the fleet, lit the fuse in the powder keg. Was it in their case perhaps an ugly outbreak of racism?

The processing of such outrages and the public atonement for them is usually a long, drawn-out affair. Oddly enough, little attention has been given to how people and institutions react in the aftermath of such explosions of violence. That alone should make us examine how the Batavian catastrophe was dealt with. The first phase, which spanned about a week, involved the cleanup: removing the corpses from the streets and canals, clearing away the debris, collecting the loot, and punishing excessive instances of looting and theft. Nolthenius, who was charged with clearing the corpses, lay in bed for three days afterwards, sick as a dog, totally exhausted, full of vicarious shame and dismay. The looted items were collected in the Artisans' Quarter, the ringleaders among the looters (including Schwarz) were briefly put under lock and key. Because the ships had to leave, the arrested sailors were released within a few days. No one was really punished.

The second phase, the proclamation of amnesty, concerned those Chinese who had survived the massacre and managed to flee the city in time. The surviving Chinese women and children were provisionally housed in the prisons and in the hospitals—that is, in the same places where their husbands, fathers, sons, and brothers had been slaughtered. On October 22, the High Government, 'moved by fitting commiseration for those of our former subjects of the Chinese nation who are wandering around after have been innocently exiled,' issued a one-month amnesty 'to all the Chinese who have been residing among the rebels either from fear or coercion.'[236] A proclamation was also issued that anyone holding slaves of runaway or murdered Chinese should report them to the Judicial Council.

The role of the High Government

'After 523 captured Chinese had been massacred in the Company and municipal gaols and thrown into the sea in the evening on Monday, October 10, by order of the High Government,' recounts the anonymous author of the "Short Daily Account of the occurrences during the General Revolt and Treason by the Chinese", 'it was decided and promised in this same meeting to give two ducatoons to all natives who delivered a head of a Chinese caught outside the city. For the head of one of their leaders 200 rixdollars were offered, and for that of the mandarin or so-called Chinese prince [Que Panjang] 1,000 rixdollars would be given as a bounty.' Full of sarcasm, the author adds that all this killing was apparently approved of, if not ordered, by the members of the High Government, because it was said to have been carried out under 'the wise direction of God Almighty' for the preservation of the Christian believers, who had almost 'been exterminated by that heathen brood—who have not the slightest knowledge of the true god.' If that would have happened 'the new Dutch church would have been turned from a house of God into a devilish temple.'[237] Did the members of the High Government, the anonymous author seems to be saying, realize what they were doing? Was this behavior worthy of Christians? Looking back at these events, he could only conclude that within the High Government 'everything had been in the utmost confusion, disorder, cowardice and lame behavior. Nay, the disagreements among the council members had been of an indescribable nature.' The resolutions of the council of the autumn of 1740 indeed show in detail how the discord within the High Government continued unabated.

On Sunday morning, October 9, the councilors had parted ways without even agreeing on how to proceed. The next day—by which time the continuous looting and pillaging had been going on for 24 hours—they met again and meekly decided to suppress the ongoing frenzy in town not with a strict order but 'by granting an indemnity,' a reward, to all Company personnel who voluntarily returned to their own houses or positions. With the promise of six ducatoons for each Company servant, and double that for officers, the authorities tried to offer a carrot to the debauched mob. It was all in vain, for seven days later, on October 17, this feeble proclamation had to be repeated. Only then did tempers calm down somewhat because all that could be looted had meanwhile been pocketed. On the same day, Governor-General Valckenier put the question to the assembly 'should not one stop shedding the blood of the Chinese and was it not time to establish order?'[238] Meanwhile the indigenous people in the kampongs around the city had thrown themselves on the Chinese houses, gardens, temples, and sugar mills in their vicinity and had looted everything too. They had even distributed the Chinese women among themselves.[239]

Under those conditions, Van Imhoff, who had already seen the storm coming, submitted a prepared written statement distancing himself from 'the ghastly massacre.' He claimed to have been outside the city when the massacre began (a blatant lie) and shifted the responsibility for it to those 'who had given the orders to that purpose.' He washed his hands in innocence but was willing to 'help restore order and improve what was corrupted and spoiled.' He therefore submitted the proposal to grant a short-term general amnesty to all Chinese who were willing to lay down their arms within a month. Seething with frustration, Valckenier denied Von Imhoff's insinuations 'as if he himself had given orders to beat the Chinese to death.'[240] As for granting amnesty, he felt that it was a far too hasty measure, given the bellicose mood that still prevailed in and around the city. He believed that 'things were not yet in such a calm state that a general amnesty could take place.' Nevertheless, the majority of the assembly agreed with Van Imhoff's proposal, and on October 22, the amnesty was solemnly proclaimed.

The vilification of what had happened could begin. Valckenier during the following weeks drafted a self-defense, or rather launched an accusation against Van Imhoff and his faction in the council. That *oratio pro domo* was written with the assistance of his brother-in-law, the councilor of justice, Helvetius. He needed that assistance because he had lapsed physically and mentally into a very bad shape. As Valckenier had anticipated, the amnesty made little impression on the Chinese outside the city, especially since on November 4, the High Government decided to summarily execute all armed Chinese caught in the Ommelanden. On November 11, it was even decided that the Chinese captured in the hinterland no longer had to be sent to Batavia 'but could also be slaughtered there.' This kind of summary justice later elicited the justifiable comment from the Gentlemen XVII that 'this decision smacked more of murder than the execution of justice.'[241] The amnesty thus turned out to be little more than a formality.

Penance, Thanksgiving, and Day of Prayer

A month later, as the term of the amnesty drew to a close, the third phase began: the government decreed a general day of penance, thanksgiving, and prayer, i.e., a kind of ritual cleansing. The 'increasing plagues of the country and the aggravation of the judgments of the Lord's slapping hand' showed 'the righteous wrath of the Almighty and hitherto all merciful God.' It was all very clear:

in previous years, shipping had already been punished by so many disasters at sea that it threatened to ruin the Company, 'that considerable body, that mighty pillar of the free status of the Netherlands.' And now, Batavia had also been hit by the Chinese revolt! Yes, it seemed as if it pleased God to finally call the Batavian Christians to account, because 'the measure of our sins had become full,' but at the very last moment God had extended His redeeming hand. It was decreed that 'everyone must bow down before His most holy face, confess his guilt, put away deprivations, and give Him glory, so that the Almighty may henceforth assist us to humble what is left of the enemy under our feet [...] to the complete satisfaction of this colony and its restoration.' In other words, the penance and thanksgiving ritual were ritual confessions of guilt in the hope that with God's help, the remaining insurgents could also be dealt with.

The High Government compelled everyone to attend public worship on Wednesday, November 23, and beg the Lord's forgiveness. All this was in the hope that the Almighty would once again have mercy on Batavia and its inhabitants, 'by warding off all further well-deserved plagues and judgments, together with the improvement of the languishing trade, and the prosperity of her colonies everywhere.' That was a mouthful of pious wishes. The colonial government literally bowed its head in sackcloth and ashes for one day before the universe of the avenging (and hopefully forgiving) God of the Old Testament!

Evil tongues

The decision to hold this day of penance, thanksgiving, and prayer almost called down another misfortune upon Batavia. Was it, as people claimed, the widows of the murdered Chinese who spread the rumor that the Europeans, under the guise of this devout occasion, also wanted to do away with their slaves? Or was it because the last paragraph of the proclamation of the Day of Penance, Thanksgiving, and Prayer gave the slaves some food for thought? In that last paragraph, God Almighty was implored 'to give his dearly acquired church a safe refuge among that crooked and twisted race, among whom He has made it reside.'[242]

'Crooked and twisted race'.... The slave population of the city suspected, not unreasonably, that the 'tolling of the bells' and the 'firing of the artillery' announced by the government after the church service might also announce their final hour. According to Reverhorst, 'because of this rumor, a ghastly and triple danger dangled above our heads,' namely that the slaves would either all run away and seek employment by the Chinese, or that, because they were 'much larger in number than their masters, they would do what the latter intended to do to them, or that they would poison all of us Europeans.' When this rumor became known, the government immediately pledged a reward of 300 rixdollars to whoever turned in the scandalmonger. But, Reverhorst added, that, of course, was not enough. Every slave owner felt obliged to have a good conversation with his house personnel. Reverhorst even had to promise his own 'boys' that, in case of danger, he would post himself at the door 'so that attackers first would have to deal with me before laying their hands on them.' This reassured his domestic staff. 'Whereupon they promised me their help, by which and [thanks to] other precautions this very great and dangerous evil has not happened to us, and has been of no use or benefit to the inventors.'[243] Peace was restored in Reverhorst's mansion.

Rivalry

On November 7, the internal schism in the High Government flared anew. A fierce quarrel arose because Valckenier, in his position as captain general, made a decision without consulting the councilors. To show his gratitude to the civilian militia for the services rendered during and after the Chinese revolt, he had decreed that the militia at the guard posts of the gates should be saluted in the same way as the Company's professional soldiers. According to Van Imhoff, this decision should not have been made without consultation. After all, at each city gate, two Councilors of the Indies, in their capacity as specially appointed commissioners, exercised temporary military authority, and they should have been consulted first. Valckenier responded rather clumsily by saying that as governor-general he was free to take this 'domestic measure. [...] He did not, therefore, expect the gentlemen to contravene his given order.' This incensed Van Imhoff, who countered, 'What is this! This looks like a threat! We are thus not secure, my lords! What does the governor general mean to imply!' At the following meeting, on November 11, the Councilors reversed Valckenier's 'domestic measure' behind his back. This was not difficult, because the governor-general was once again absent for health reasons. Informed of the council's decision, Valckenier believed it better to back down 'for the love and preservation of the country and people, as well as the Company's interests, which would have serious consequences if the councilors and the governor general continued to be at loggerheads.' Nevertheless, he instructed Sergeant Major Duirveld to find out who of the officers had refused to obey his orders. He also wanted to find out how Van Imhoff and De Haze, without informing him, had left the city on November 25 with a unit of soldiers, native auxiliaries, and civilian militia, supposedly to attack insurgents near Pulau Gadong.

On November 29, the Council decided, again behind Valckenier's back, that the city gates could be reopened as before. On that occasion, the commissioners of the Diest-and Utrecht Gates, Messrs. Thedens, Van Imhoff, Van Schinne, and Lakeman, let it be known that they had learned of Duirveld's investigation. They were very indignant about this and summoned the sergeant major to explain himself. After much wrangling, Duirveld admitted that he had acted on Valckenier's written order in his capacity as captain general, that is, as his immediate superior, but that he could not produce the written proof: he had lost it. Now it was up to Director General Schaghen, who was replacing the ailing Valckenier, to offer an explanation.

A conspiracy?

Thanks to yet another confidential letter from Joan de Roode to Jan Minne in Enkhuizen, we know the former's inner thoughts on what was going on among Van Imhoff and his 'conspirators.' Whether it is true or not does not matter here; what matters is the perception that prevailed with Valckenier. De Roode began his letter of January 10, 1741, rather ominously: 'Such great vicissitudes have again occurred here that it is almost impossible to describe. [...] One may say, however, that the proverb is true: The world is a stage; everyone plays his part and gets his share. The vicissitudes in these regions are as great as can hardly be imagined. We have almost experienced a second massacre in the city.'[244] De Roode explained that Van Imhoff had continued to stir things up by spreading the news that he had already been appointed governor general by the Gentlemen XVII. Most members of the High Government imagined this to be true and 'clung to Van Imhoff as if he were the rising sun.' Anything that Valckenier proposed was contradicted and rejected if it did not please Van Imhoff, 'so that it seemed that one faced a lord governor general in appearance but not in reality.'

Yes, there were even whispers that on December 16, the return ship *Adrichem* had been fitted out to carry the deposed governor-general back to his native Amsterdam. 'But the pears were not yet stewed,' continued De Roode, because Van Imhoff and De Haze had embarked on an unauthorized short expedition on November 26 with 1,700 men 'to win over the minds of the soldiers.' Preparations had also already been made to replace Duirveld as sergeant major of the troops and the captain of Batavia Castle, Coenraad Muller, with De Haze's brother-in-law, Captain Frank. 'His Honor Valckenier meanwhile kept very quiet, as if the matter did not concern him and as if nothing had happened, so many matters had already passed that a whole book would be needed to describe everything.'

Valckenier indeed kept quiet for some time, but in a letter to his brother-in-law, Cornelis Hop, on December 1, he made no bones about it.[245] He reviewed all his disputes with Van Imhoff in the previous months: quarrels about appointments, about the saluting of civilian officers, the unauthorized expedition, the agitation among the members of the Council of the Indies and, of course, the discord over the payment of the fine that had been imposed by the Gentlemen XVII in connection with the surplus of sugar and the deficit of coffee sent to the Netherlands, by which 'that turbulent gentleman,' Van Imhoff, had even caused a rift between Valckenier and his friend, Director General Schaghen. 'All this,' wrote Valckenier 'has caused me such irritation that I can hardly describe it, and I have wished a thousand times to be dismissed from my position.' How should Valckenier deal with Van Imhoff, who was so eager to pass himself off as God-fearing, 'neglecting no church attendance and never leaving the church except with tearful eyes?' [...] 'How much this moral display corresponds to his way of life,' wrote Valckeniert, 'I will gladly leave to the judgment of the right-minded world, since this gentleman [has] indulged so much in playing dice, drinking and night reveling [...] I even considered whether I should not send him to Holland as a *perturbator* [...] but thanks God I have not done so.' If on December 1, he wisely chose to ignore everything in order to keep the peace, in the following days, he changed his mind dramatically.

Tabula Rasa

At the next council meeting on December 6, the die was cast. At first, everything seemed normal. At 8.30 p.m., Adriaan Valckenier appeared in the meeting room of the Council of the Indies, with Director General Schaghen and Councilor Thedens in tow. As usual, the meeting opened with a prayer, and thereupon, everyone's attention went to the incoming and outgoing mail. Then, when Van Imhoff wanted to raise the Duirveld issue, something amazing happened.[246] At nine o'clock, the door suddenly swung open and 'with stiff strides', Captain Muller, commander of the garrison of Batavia Castle marched into the council chamber at the head of forty grenadiers, 'fully outfitted with grenade and cartridge cases, each equipped with at least six sharp shots, and with the bayonet on snap cock.'

The soldiers lined up in a circle around the conference table so that the councilors could not move. At this, the governor-general took a deep breath and said, 'Do not dismay yourselves my Lords, ye shall hear what it is about. Your Lordships should not feel intimidated.' Thereupon, he fished a bill out of his pocket and handed it to the Secretary of the Council Otto, asking him to read out its contents. Apparently, Valckenier was so emotional that he preferred to leave it to someone else to do the talking. Otto stood up, glanced through the first lines, and spoke: 'The governor general communicates to the gentlemen members, how he has for some time been absent from these meetings owing to a multitude of boils, and skin infections that have made it impossible for him to get clothed, but being almost relieved of them, he finds himself once more able to occupy the governor general's chair and to attend to the public acts in person.' Then he went on to list the responsibilities of the governor-general: 'all the Company's instructions, orders and customs entail that the Governor General must be and remain, the supreme commander here in the country, not only of all the Company's servants in general, but also in particular of all the military and their officers.' Why did Valckenier stress his connection with the military? Because in his position as Captain General, he was directly their superior and fully in command.

Secretary Otto then informed the members of the Council of the Indies that the time had come for the governor-general, in his capacity as captain general to withdraw the special duties that he had delegated to them during the Chinese uprising as commissioners over the military guards at the city gates and the City Hall. He requested that they return the keys to the gates. He took this measure, he said, not only because the Chinese were no longer a threat, but also because of 'the despotic behavior, tumultuous and unqualified appearance of some of the commissioners at the gates,' who, abusing their extraordinary rights, had issued orders that were 'squarely contrary' to his own. For example, his special order to pay ordinary military honors to the civil militia officers had been 'contramandated.' Moreover, it had come to his attention that Councilors Van Imhoff and De Haze had gone chasing after Chinese rebels outside the city without his prior knowledge. In addition, Sergeant Major Duirveld, whom he had instructed to investigate the origins of the order for this expedition, had been taken to task by Messrs. Van Imhoff and De Haze and questioned about who had asked him to collect witnesses on this matter. Because of this and other 'exorbitant incidents,' he now felt compelled to intervene and restore proper relations. Enough! He wanted full disclosure of any decisions taken behind his back, in order to expose the evil intentions of the opposition party 'who, impatient for the Glory of the Supreme Administration, wanted to wrest the commander's staff from him.'

After Secretary Otto had spoken, Valckenier himself took the floor and demanded in a high tone that Otto now read the minutes of the meeting of

December 2, which he had not attended, in order to expose the 'nefarious designs' of the opposing party. Yet, when it became clear from those minutes that nothing to his detriment had been said in his absence, Valckenier lost his temper and branded Otto a 'liar and false minutes secretary.' The councilors remained perplexed and tensely glanced at Director General Schaghen, hoping that he would at least have something to say about 'this cruel and *criant* treatment,' but he too remained silent. A painful, utter silence prevailed. It was clear to everyone present that the governor-general could no longer be reasoned with as he 'blew up in a frenzy, letting no one speak, no longer even speaking himself but just ranting and shouting, a ghastly performance to attend.'

The meeting had spun totally out of control. A tragicomic note to all this was the fumbling around the execution of the order to hand in the keys to the city gates on the spot. A halberdier came in to report that the keys to those gates could not be collected because by order of the captain general himself, the gates of the Castle had been closed. When a solution to this was found, Valckenier again snarled at Van Imhoff and his intimates, Councilors Van Schinne and De Haze, 'making them out in public for ringleaders, agitators, conspirators and the like, and charging and arresting them *ipso momento*.'

The three gentlemen replied wisely that they did not owe their place in the Council to Valckenier, but that they had been appointed by the directors in the Netherlands. They were willing to submit to a decision of the entire Council but not to the 'despotic orders of His Nobleness.' When this was followed by 'an almost unanimous protest from all the members about violence, wrongdoing, and the violation of the freedom of assembly,' the governor-general replied 'that he took full responsibility for all this, yea, that he could be held to account for everything, as captain general of the East India Company.'

Arrested in front of their colleagues, each of the three councilors now had to surrender his rapier and cane to Valckenier's bodyguard—the ultimate insult to gentlemen of standing. When a moment later the keys were handed in, Valckenier walked out of the room and did not show himself again. A few more attempts were made—first by Schaghen, and when that proved to be of no avail, by Valckenier's intimate friends, Crul and Thedens—to bring him to his senses, but all in vain. The only thing the latter two managed to achieve was that Van Imhoff, De Haze, and Van Schinne were not detained in the Castle but were placed under house arrest. Finally, at 4 o'clock in the afternoon, everyone went their own ways. The three illustrious detainees were given the choice of going home that afternoon or waiting for nightfall. Quite unsurprisingly, they chose to leave the same afternoon 'in front of the whole world.'

'Thus this infamous day,' wrote Reverhorst to family and friends, 'the like of which has never yet been experienced in this eastern part of the world, under the *Free State of the Netherlands* and its *Company of the East*, came to an end with general consternation and much muttering and sorrow about such an unprecedented incident within the congregation. *Quod inter arma silent leges*: under the violence of the gun the laws are silent.'

According to De Roode, who had dined with the governor-general just the day before, 'no Christian soul knew of his intention.' He himself learned from his barber what had taken place within the Castle walls—nothing remained hidden from hairdressers, even in eighteenth-century Batavia! Incidentally, he was of the opinion that if Valckenier had not intervened, he would probably have been removed from office by the Council of the Indies and put on a ship to Holland together with his allies (including De Roode himself). So, he was firmly convinced that there had indeed been a conspiracy.

Councilor of Justice Reverhorst left no doubt that all this was unprecedented: 'It was a day the likes of which the Company has not had and probably will not ever experience [again]. A day on which everyone felt so dejected, a day that showed what revenge heaped upon violence can accomplish!' Even the Duke of Alba or any other tyrant, he believed, would never have violated the laws of the sacred conference room, 'since the one who attends a meeting must on account of its sacred freedom be able to come and speak calmly and securely. [...] Who does not shake and tremble when he hears such? I am very curious how these doings and this behavior of the General, who is but head and not sovereign, will be taken up in the Netherlands.'[247] With this indignant statement, Reverhorst hit the nail on the head. How would the Gentlemen XVII respond to this?

Paradoxically, on the other side of the globe, almost simultaneously, the Gentlemen XVII made an important decision. Meeting on December 2, 1740, they decided that 'after twenty-five years of service in various qualities to the Company and finally as governor general of Dutch India, to relieve his Lordship Adriaan Valckenier from that commission' and ... to appoint as his successor, Gustaaf Willem Baron van Imhoff![248]

CHAPTER 15

History at the Crossroads

On December 6, 1741, Daniel Nolthenius wrote despondently to Dirck Trip, one of his patrons in Amsterdam: 'If one observes attentively all the disasters befalling the Company within the space of two years, one should almost have to believe that it is God's holy and irresistible will to finish it off. The loss of so many richly loaded ships, the destruction of this beautiful city by the rebellion of the Chinese and the high disputes that have arisen between Governor General Valckenier and the principal members of the government are all clear evidence of the just wrath of the Almighty!'[249]

The general atmosphere of 1741, the last year of Adriaan Valckenier's administration, was indeed as gloomy and confusing as the man's state of mind. After his tormentors, Van Imhoff, Van Schinne, and De Haze, had suffered the indignity of having to part with their rapiers and canes, they were placed under house arrest, each of them guarded by twenty-four soldiers, four corporals, two sergeants, and an ensign in front of and behind their house. On January 12, the three gentlemen were escorted to three different ships of the return fleet on the roadstead, that lay ready to hoist their sails. In the preceding weeks, the deportees had been forced to sell their real estate at lightning speed. Needless to say, the proceeds from the forced sale of their houses and estates were meager. A clause in the contracts of sale, however, allowed them—should they return within three years—to buy their property back at the same price.

Even at sea, the exiles remained under guard. Twelve servicemen, a sergeant, and two corporals were supposed to see to it that the prisoners did not leave their cabin, a fool's errand that no skipper complied with. In a sealed box addressed to the Gentlemen XVII, the confiscated rapiers and canes were sent along, to be restored to their owners upon arrival in Holland. The ship officers were ordered not to call at the Cape of Good Hope, but if they had to, the three passengers would not be allowed to go ashore. As if all that was not enough, Valckenier even requested Hendrik Swellengrebel[250], who in the meantime had risen to the position of Commander of the Cape, not to receive Van Imhoff, Van Schinne, and De Haze, but 'keep them shut up in the skipper's quarters or cabin.' That order distressed poor Swellengrebel so much that he apologized afterwards for his meek behavior to his patron, Jan Minne, in Enkhuizen. Hoping 'not to have given displeasure to either party,' he had avoided the gentlemen when they did go ashore. Like a Cape ostrich, he had stuck his head in the sand. 'How extremely embarrassed I shall be,' he wrote, 'when the Honorable Mr. Valckenier repatriating next year will call me to account for this.' Little did he know what was in the offing.

Back to normal?

With the deportation of his opponents, Valckenier expected to create 'pleasant peacefulness and unity' again. But that remained a pious hope, for too much had occurred within the Council of the Indies in the previous months. The councilors resented how their rights had been trampled upon during the infamous meeting of December 6. Accordingly, the governing elite in Batavia were saddled with a governor-general who, perceiving threats all around him, continued to ail physically and mentally until his departure in the fall of 1741. More out of pity and loyalty than conviction, his old friends Thedens, Schaghen, and Crul did not let him down completely, but they were honest enough to tell him that he had done wrong by stripping the councilors of their rights. With much give and take, they managed to keep the tensions within the High Government under control.

It gradually dawned on Valckenier what he had gotten himself into. He must have wondered what kind of reception the deportees would receive in the Netherlands. What would they tell the Gentlemen XVII? When rumors began to circulate in town that Valckenier would soon be dismissed, the by now paranoid governor-general posted a notice against slanderers: 'Warning against the spreading of untrue messages regarding Governor-General A. Valckenier,' and offered a substantial bounty for whoever disclosed 'the galling tongues of slander.'[251] The immediate entourage watched all this with shaking heads. It even elicited the Council of Justice Reverhorst's sigh that in Batavia now 'ruffians and godforsaken rascals play their part and, forced by usurpation, the good and well-meaning do not dare to speak out.' A couple of questions continued to haunt the minds of the members of the High Government: what impact might the rebellion have on Batavia's relations with the Javanese court in Kartasura? And what about the trade relations with China? How would the authorities in Canton or even the court in Beijing react?

As an appendix of the 'General Missive' of October 31, 1740, which reported on the rebellion and the massacre, Adriaan Valckenier had already sent a secret personal letter to the Gentlemen XVII in which he held Gustaaf Willem van Imhoff responsible for the outbreak of the Chinese rebellion.[252] According to him, the revolt had been caused by Van Imhoff's reckless proposal of July 25,

1740, 'to have Chinese dressed in black arrested at random.' In a second letter dated December 1, Valckenier further accused his rival of insubordination. On January 8, 1741, Valckenier sent a third letter that listed in 1,120 (!) points, the reasons why Van Imhoff, De Haze, and Van Schinne had been placed under military arrest on December 6.[253] A final indictment followed on March 25.

In drafting all these letters, Valckenier was assisted by his brother-in-law, the Councilor of Justice Willem Vincent Helvetius. At least that is what his colleague Reverhorst claimed: 'Mr. Helvetius is prime minister, counselor, and inquisition master general, and has two other inquisition masters under him such as the infamous Monsieur de Roode and Monsieur Hakkenberg.' One may wonder indeed, how Valckenier, chronically tormented by all manner of ailments, resentments, and fits of rage, could have composed such aptly worded cunning legal charges. Helvetius remained a firm supporter of his brother in law and would go on to provide Valckenier with legal advice until the very end, with unpleasant consequences for himself, as we shall see.

Because Valckenier was aware that he was held responsible for the massacre by his opponents, he was at pains to deny that he had ordered the extermination of the Chinese. As Vermeulen also concludes after careful investigation, there is no written evidence anywhere to suggest that he gave that order. But in order to substantiate his own charge against 'the opposition party'—as Valckenier invariably called the *kongsi* of Van Imhoff, Van Schinne, and De Haze—he requested the Alderman's Court to gather all kinds of (questionable, according to Reverhorst) testimonies, hoping to show that the Chinese had revolted because of the arrests in August and the banishments to Ceylon. Because it would serve him well if it could be proven that the Chinese captain was directly involved in the uprising, he ordered the prosecution of Ni Hoekong.

The 'interrogation' of Ni Hoekong

It was the task of Public Prosecutor Cornelis Phillips to indict the Chinese captain, and it was up to the members of the Council of Justice to interrogate him.[254] The gentlemen did not waste any time. In January 1741, Phillips filed charges against Ni Hoekong on a *crimen perduellionis* (charge of high treason) consisting of 102 counts. This put Ni Hoekong, who had narrowly escaped death during the massacre, on trial for a charge punishable by death. The trial that followed is interesting because the accused proved to be not at all the weak character that he was made out to be, but was on the contrary, a tough nut to crack.[255]

Phillips asked the Judicial Council to have Ni Hoekong tortured when questioned (a demand *ad torturam*) and thus force a confession of his crimes.

On January 21, 1741, the Chinese captain was ushered into the pain chamber and ordered to confess his role in the rebellion. After all, the facts spoke for themselves: how could the captain claim to have known nothing of the rebellion when his own messenger, Uw Tjamko, already knew about it? Had his brother, Ni Tjetkong, not been spotted on horseback as one of the leaders of the rebellion, and had the Chinese who were arrested not shouted, 'It's the captain's fault!'

After the Chinese captain had been tormented for over six minutes, he was lowered and then picked up again with a weight on his right toe. He did not budge, however. Then Phillips changed tack: 'Was it not true that the captain had lived in close friendship with his brother Ni Tjetkong, one of the ringleaders of the rebellion?'

'Yes indeed,' was the reply, 'because he was my brother.'

'And had he not also kept good friendship with Ni Waijko, and had he not been with the others daily?'

'No, with him specifically he had not kept a great friendship.'

'Had he not been in his garden before the rebellion?'

'Yes!'

'Had he not then read a poster or bill written in the Chinese language that was taped [to a post] in his garden?'

He had seen the bill but had not read it because it was raining and because he believed that it was the same annual announcement inviting people to make an offering to the departed. When the bill was shown to him, Ni Hoekong noted that he had seen it before and that it contained no evil or inflammatory content.

The captain was then tortured with two weights on both big toes for another five minutes. After a few questions about the offerings in his garden, the questioning continued: 'Did he not know that Ni Wayko was head of the rebels, and that the latter had distributed patches of blue cotton for people to tie around their heads? And hadn't the Chinese lit lanterns in front of their houses to distinguish them from the houses of the Dutch?'

'On whose orders had the great wayang theater been erected at the night market in the city?'

He knew nothing about all that.

Time again for ten minutes of even more severe torture. Now screws were applied to both shins. Meanwhile, the captain's brother Ni Lienkong was ushered in, shown the same Chinese poster, and asked what its purport was. But according to him, there was nothing at all harmful about it.

As the shin screws were tightened once more, the interrogation continued mercilessly: 'Didn't Ni Hoekong know that in response to the Chinese attack from outside, the Chinese rebels inside the city would burn and kill everything around them?'

'No, he had not given orders to kill Dutchmen.'

'And then, didn't he give orders to massacre the fifty or sixty soldiers at Bekasi?'

Ni Hoekong knew nothing about all this.

After the prisoner had been tormented for another 11 minutes—thus, altogether for 32 minutes—the Judicial Council decided to suspend the torture.

The next day Ni Hoekong, most likely with severe pain in his limbs, was arraigned again to clarify matters, but he continued adamantly to deny everything. No matter what Phillips tried, he could not establish complicity in the rebellion conclusively. The interrogation in the torture chamber was the heavy-handed overture to a drawn-out trial in which three successive prosecutors tried to prove that Captain Ni had been 'the chief instigator and author' of the rebellion and had therefore committed treason. His brother, estate master Ni Lienkong, was also implicated in the charges. On August 29, 1742, Cornelis Phillips called for the exile of Ni Lienkong and the death penalty for Ni Hoekong.

Given the lack of evidence, the indignant lawyer of the Chinese captain and his brother, Mr. Cras, found those sentences a mockery of justice and demanded their acquittal. The charge, he said, was 'like a rumbling bladder full of conceited fart' that rested on nothing but 'old nag tales.' This was also obvious to the members of the Judicial Council who considered the case, although they dared not say it aloud. On July 31, 1743, their verdict followed: Ni Hoekong was exiled to Ceylon for 25 years, but his brother was released immediately. Lawyer Cras appealed, but the final verdict followed on May 18, 1744. The banishment to Ceylon was commuted to Ambon, where Ni Hoekong died on Christmas Day 1746 leaving behind wives and children who had remained in Batavia.

A severe Chinese judgement

How did the Chinese themselves assess the Chinese captain's behavior during those fateful days? Lin Cuipu, one of the Chinese commentators of the *Chinese Annals of Batavia*, had nothing good to say about the unfortunate captain and lashed out in a bitter philippic:

> The Great Captain was the head of the Tang people. He should have had sufficient power to overcome the problems. When the people were in distress, and the officials perverted the laws, he should have remonstrated and clarified to the officials

> that good and bad did not depend on black and white clothing. He should have tactfully intervened and opened a compassionate heart to move the authorities to listen. Then it could have been done. I think that it could have helped. Moreover, the family of Great Captain was the wealthiest in all Batavia.[256]

He continued, addressing the Captain directly:

> Given that the officials were strictly checking the permits, you should have explained how weal and woe alternate, and you should have warned the Chinese. In that case, would not many people then have purchased the (identity) permits? If they really did not have the money to buy the permits, then you, Captain, you could have exercised compassion and paid for them! The amount of money spent would have been limited, but not a few would have received your compassion. And many people would have sung your praises! Why did you not think of this?' [...] You stupid captain! You served as if you could not wield your sword and cut with it. The losses were very big. If you had opened your mouth to save the people, and if the Dutch officials stubbornly did not listen, then you could have lessened your responsibility for what happened. How could you, with a closed mouth, be too scared to speak out? Why did you sit still like a dead body? Lives were lost, because an ignoramus was the leader of the people. How tragic! How lamentable! [...] Every time I think this over, I have to stop writing and lament! I say that the foreigners, although they sit in an elevated position, behaved like wolves and dogs. This is how it was: The Dutch officials committed self-indulgent crimes, but you, Ni Hoekong, also committed a great crime by ingratiating and submitting yourself [to the Dutch].

Que Panjang's lair at Bekasi

Batavia may have been 'emptied' of Chinese, but during the rainy season, a large number of insurgents were still entrenched in a fortress at Bekasi under their formidable leader, Que Panjang. They could only be dealt with after the turn of the monsoon in May. Meanwhile, spies had to explore how the rebels had fortified themselves there. A first attempt to send some vessels via the river failed. But in late February, two Bantam nobles were willing to go on an investigative tour, and through a middleman they actually managed to arrange a meeting with Que Panjang at his headquarters.

Upon their return to Batavia, they gave a precise description of the enemy's army camp and seem to have been much impressed with the fortifications that they had visited.[257] After meeting at an agreed-to rendezvous, they were escorted by two to three hundred armed Chinese to Bekasi, where they entered through a gate with a trap door into the Chinese army camp, which was strategically located between a swamp and sugarcane fields. The roads leading to it were littered with traps. Soon they saw the ramparts of the camp with armed people posted on top and fluttering banners. Surrounded by a ditch, the ramparts were made of clapboard wood and the palisades on them were reinforced inside with firewood and earth, and lined on top with wheels from buffalo carts as parapets. Every so often, muskets and basses fired salutes.

A few courtesy gifts from the Sultan of Bantam were carried in front of the visitors: 'a bottle of *zakkie* [*sake*, rice wine], two bottles of wine, a large drinking glass, a bottle of tea, ten dried fish, ten Tonkinese salted eggs, ten oranges and four pears.' Through a double line of as many as three thousand combatants carrying banners for each Company, they reached the gate of the *pagar* (enclosure) of the sugar mill house, where they were welcomed with drum and cymbal beats and as many as a hundred musket shots.

Que Panjang came out to meet them and led them inside where two hundred warriors had taken up their positions on either side. The reception took place around a square table in front of the statue of a Chinese deity. After tea was poured and the two baskets of gifts were handed over, Panjang inquired about the letters received from China and about the Chinese of Batavia, whereupon one of the emissaries, Raden Badjo, told him that many letters had arrived with the junks from China, but no one knew to whom they now could be delivered. Then 'suddenly a silence, great dejection, and sadness was detected among the bystanders.' So many men had perished and clearly a lack of contact with the home province in China was felt.

The leader of the Chinese rebels boasted that there were as many as a thousand iron smiths in the camp and that another twenty thousand men were stationed at other guard posts and sugar mills nearby. The Chinese manufactured their own gunpowder with snow-white saltpeter, but judging from the sound of the fired salute shots, its quality was inferior to that of the Company. All around, the visitors saw stalls selling Javanese tobacco, salt, and salted fish. Provisions abounded. Rice was cooked in huge sugar pans. At the sound of the cymbal, everyone came with a basket to get his or her portion. All the Chinese looked healthy; yet it was not lost on the visitors that a dejected mood prevailed in the camp. Provided with letters for the High Government in which some of the Chinese from the camp expressed their desire to surrender but did not know how to go about it, the two Bantamese envoys returned to Batavia and reported what they had seen and heard.

On May 19, 1741, after the turn of the monsoon, the decision was taken to attack this fortress of the Chinese rebel leader to quell the last remnants of the rebellion once and for all. An expeditionary army consisting of European and native soldiers, civilians, cavalry, and one hundred sailors, altogether six hundred and fifteen men, left Batavia on June 4 under the command of Abraham Roos. They returned three weeks later without having met with the insurgents, for at Bekasi they had found a completely deserted camp.[258] Que Panjang and his followers had not long before packed their things and had marched eastward to Central Java to join a Chinese uprising that had broken out there too.

A slumbering volcano

It cannot be denied that in the Company archives, the Chinese adventurers, the Javanese, and the other Indonesian peoples who settled in the Ommelanden, as well as the slaves and the freeburghers, Mardijkers, and mestizos in the city, only figure in the background. If they show up at all as individuals, it is usually because they appeared before a notary, lodged a petition, or because they committed some kind of offense: plotting conspiracy, running away, or perpetrating a crime.

What did the colonial authorities actually know about what was lurking among the Javanese *tani* (farmers)? A one-sided, declared peace and order atop a slumbering volcano—that is how the colonial *condition humaine* can be best characterized. How else can we explain the fact that the commander of Java's northeast coast, Bartholomeus Visscher, stationed in Semarang, could report in 1739 that Javanese society 'was flourishing peacefully and under God's blessing and would remain so for many years to come, as everyone shunned war,' while in the following year tempers flared all over the island![259] That affairs in central Java were anything but peaceful was suddenly discovered by the High Government when, in the spring of 1741, disturbing news arrived from Semarang.

What had transpired? Que Panjang migrated eastward to the Pasisir with his men in May 1741 to join restless Chinese who were now also rebelling in this region. Led by their own captain, Tan Sinko (Singseh), they had revolted just like their brethren in the Ommelanden. The Chinese from the coastal region had every reason to revolt, not only because they feared that they would suffer the same fate as their fellow townsmen in Batavia, but also because they wanted to take advantage of the longstanding tense relationship between the beach regents and the court in Kartasura. Within a few months, the rebels overpowered all the smaller Company settlements along the Pasisir: Japara, Juwana, Rembang, and Kuala Demak and then raised a siege at Semarang.

The Chinese War 1741–1743

Relaxed within the walls of his fort in Semarang, Visscher appeared oblivious to the local situation until June 1741, when he faced a sudden frontal attack by Chinese and Javanese troops who, unlike the poorly armed insurgents before the walls of Batavia, were equipped with modern artillery. Visscher then committed the same mistake as his superiors in Batavia of distrusting and imprisoning the local Chinese officers of Semarang, thus antagonizing all the Chinese. Only with military assistance from Batavia could the siege be broken five months later. Initially, there was only minimal help because Valckenier believed that the situation around Batavia had not yet stabilized enough to relinquish part of his garrison.

The Chinese War that broke out in the spring of 1741 would fester for another two years until the VOC was able to restore order thanks to help from Cakraningrat IV, the regent of Western Madura. While the Chinese War was a side effect of the Chinese revolt in Batavia, it was in fact the catalyst for yet another Javanese civil war centered on the court in Kartasura, where once again there was a power struggle going on between different factions and prominent personalities around the throne. At the end of this war, Que Panjang and Tan Singseh are said to have gone down in the fray together with the men who remained loyal to them, although Que Panjang may have escaped to Bali.[260]

Reconstruction

In the aftermath of the massacre, the public and economic life in Batavia was totally disrupted. There was a severe shortage of all kinds of foodstuffs. A tangle of disconnected supply lines had to be laboriously reconstructed piece by piece. But how could daily life start again without the Chinese on whose shoulders the urban economy had rested?

The High Government made every effort to restore 'this once sumptuous colony to its former glory and thus allow the Company to enjoy such fruits as have been plucked from the womb of this capital in the days of old.' The estate and orphanage trustees worked day and night to catalog the losses and put accounts back in order. With the loss of Chinese middlemen, the food supply had collapsed, and although the administration exempted the trade in rice from import duties, distribution had to be subjected to strict quotas. Only in early 1742 was the situation again under control. Regarding the reconstruction of the heavily damaged city, Councilors Nicolaas Crul and Maurits van Aerden presented a blueprint 'to redress and repair this very dilapidated colony' as early as November 11, 1740. An important part of their plan was the establishment of a Chinese kampong outside the walls of Batavia—'situated under the range of our cannons and by the fear of the same kept in deep obedience'—to serve as a residence for all Chinese.[261] The move to this 'Chinese kampong' was a memorable step, for it drew a line under the ideas of Jan Pietersz. Coen, who had kept Europeans and Chinese together within the walls, unlike the Spanish practice in Manila. From now on, no more houses within the walls were to be sold to 'heathens and Muslims,' although those who already had a house in town could remain there as long as they lived. Further attempts to replace the Chinese in Batavia with native merchants and artisans ended in utter failure.[262]

Since about a quarter of Batavia had been reduced to ashes, and Chinese were no longer welcome, plans were made to change to a different spatial arrangement. A market was now envisioned on the spot where the Ni family's sizeable family residence had previously stood, but this was not a success. The square remained empty for a long time. Because no more Chinese were allowed into the town, there was no commercial activity at the new *pasar* at all.

After some time, Chinese merchants were allowed back into the city gates during the day. With that typically Dutch adherence to the idea of social engineering, the Council of the Indies first spent months arguing over the ideal quota of Chinese who could be allowed back into and around the city. On August 1, 1742, they agreed on a total of 5,934 Chinese. There was, of course, no way to control that. How this figure was arrived at, however, is interesting, if only because the figures give a fine impression of the indispensable role that the Chinese played in the city's economy. For the sugar industry, the Company envisioned sixty sugar mills, with forty Chinese personnel each, which meant 2,400 men. The arrack industry was also considered indispensable. The annual requirement was estimated at two thousand *leggers* (400–500 liters), and at least 224 workers (or 14 per distillery) were considered necessary for this. Furthermore, eight hundred gardeners and farmers, one hundred blacksmiths, thirty shoemakers, fifty (clothing) dyers, thirty tailors, twenty barbers, forty plumbers, forty chair and box makers, twenty *sombreel* (parasol) makers, thirty varnishers and gilders, twenty gold and silver smiths, sixty cattle butchers, fifty leather workers, sixty carpenters and masons, thirty stone cutters, fifty lime burners, two hundred brick and tile makers, forty charcoal burners, one hundred oil pressers, ten *kamine* (chimney) makers, ten lantern makers, one hundred basket makers, ten doctors, six hundred merchants, shopkeepers, tenant farmers, hawkers of all kinds, four hundred woodcutters, three hundred candy cooks, fifty coopers, ten schoolmasters, thirty potters, and finally ten coppersmiths.[263]

The China trade

Trade with China was another pressing point on the agenda of the Batavian administration. After all, what implications would the Chinese massacre have for the Chinese shipping to Batavia and for the Company's shipping link with Canton? It was to be feared that the *nakhodas* of the Chinese junks would turn around as soon as they heard what had happened to their compatriots in October. And who could accommodate them in Batavia now that the Chinese captain and his officers were imprisoned or killed?

Some ships were sent to the Singapore Strait to meet the junks arriving from China and escort them to Batavia. There, again, Henry Abbis brought relief. This indispensable Englishman who had also helped to set up the VOC trade from Batavia to Canton in 1735, was temporarily assigned a residence at the harbor where he could be useful thanks to his linguistic accomplishments, tact, and experience. But judging from the Chinese reports, he only partially succeeded in that mission. The nakhodas of the junks complained about the filthy and unhealthy place outside the *boom* (customs office) where they were received. They felt intimidated (in all likelihood justifiably) by the special arrangements made.

Governor-General Valckenier felt deeply concerned about the backlash that the Company's trade might suffer in Canton. This compelled him to write an unctuous letter to the Chinese emperor in which he tried to gain his compassion for what had happened in Batavia.[264] He justified his letter with the concluding words:

> We have deemed it necessary to give your Imperial Majesty a true and circumstantial account [...] for we firmly trust, that, now that your Imperial Majesty has been fully informed of the truth of this *facheus* [tragic] occurrence, Your Imperial Majesty, in accordance with His High Wisdom, will approve what we have done, and order his Ministers in Canton, that neither our trade over there should be hindered, nor our personnel be caused any inconvenience.

The epistle, written in Portuguese, was sent with the merchants from the *Huis te Foreest* and *Enkhuijsen* because none of the Chinese who remained in Batavia could or dared to translate the contents 'into the official court language.' The idea was to have the message properly translated in Macau or Canton, but after consulting the authorities in Canton, it was finally decided not to forward it to the imperial court.

The situation in Canton

When the two ships anchored on August 4 at the roadstead of Portuguese Macau, at the mouth of the Pearl River, they were welcomed by the supercargo, Jan van Rijckevorsel, who had spent the so-called 'quiet time' (the six months in which trade was at a standstill) in Macau with two assistants and a surgeon. They explained that nothing had happened to them when the first tidings of the revolt on Batavia trickled in.[265] However, while walking in the city, Van Rijckevorsel had repeatedly heard rather disturbing shouts of *Hollanda Batavia*. The Portuguese commander had informed them that he could not protect the Dutch sailors ashore, because he was under Chinese jurisdiction and was rather apprehensive 'of the unreasonableness of the Chinese rabble' ashore. He recommended that the crews stay on the ships for as long as possible until it became clear how the *hoppo*, the emperor's representative in Canton, reacted. However, he did make sure that the two Dutch ships were supplied with provisions so that, if necessary, they could leave immediately.

In September, to everyone's relief, twelve or thirteen Chinese merchants appeared on board of the *Huis te Foreest* and assured the Dutch that they could proceed to the usual anchorage of Whampoa near Canton. When the two VOC ships arrived there on September 26, eleven European ships were already awaiting delivery of the cargoes of tea. The other European merchants had spoken ill of the Dutchmen to the Chinese authorities to get rid of their competitors, but their slander fell on deaf ears. The *hoppo* even had the locals warned that no one should harm the Dutch. 'Even the Chinese rabble who are accustomed to spit on all foreigners when they meet in the street and pull them by the clothes and similar buffoonery,' left the Dutch sailors alone. Some Chinese war junks anchored next to the VOC ships at a pistol shot's distance, but they turned out to have come to protect them rather than to do any harm. Indeed, it had been learned that several vessels carrying Chinese 'malcontents' had arrived from Amoy in Canton to take revenge for the massacre of their fellow brethren, but they did not get the opportunity to do so now.

Before departing on December 20, it was reported that the Emperor of China, upon learning of the revolt in Batavia, had rejoiced that the Company had 'disposed of that scum, pack of vagrants, that he did not regard to be Chinese.' This was a rather simplistic representation of events, for it is known from the Chinese court chronicles that the reports from Batavia had caused quite a stir at the court.[266]

A heated debate around the Dragon Throne

The governor of the coastal province of Fujian—from which most Batavian Chinese hailed—understandably had written an indignant memorial to the throne about the horrific events in Batavia. Although he agreed that the Chinese who had been slaughtered had lived in Batavia for generations in defiance of imperial decrees, he proposed that the perpetrators of the massacre should be severely punished. He argued that the cruel red-haired barbarians had dared to strike only because they lived so away far from the emperor. All trade with Batavia should be banned henceforth, he believed.

In contrast, the governor-general of Guangdong and Guangxi provinces, Duke Qing Fu, submitted a memorandum emphasizing the importance of foreign trade to the southern coastal provinces. He believed that without overseas trade, the inhabitants of his provinces would turn into beggars. This view was supported by the court mandarin, Cai Xin, a member of the imperial academy and also a teacher of the crown prince.[267] This Fujian-born scholar was not only well acquainted with the importance of the Nanyang trade for his home province, but it so happened that, coincidentally, he had run into an old friend in Beijing who was visiting that city not long before. And that was none other than Cheng Xunwo, the good fellow who had gone to seek his fortune in Java to settle his parents' debts! At Cai Xin's request, the latter then wrote the *Galaba jilue* (the Concise Report of Galaba), which has been extensively cited in Chapter 11.

Cai Xin agreed that what had occurred in the Southern Seas was abominable, but added that the overseas Chinese who had been victimized had disobeyed the imperial edict: 'Since they had lived there for a long time, they placed themselves outside the borders. Although they are called Chinese, they are in fact no different from the barbarians living there,' he mused. 'Taking this into consideration, what happened did not damage our [Chinese] civilization.' Thus, the discussion rippled back and forth between supporters and opponents of continuing trade with the Dutch until the debate at court was summed up as follows:

> Some mandarins request that we not prohibit overseas trade. Others, on the contrary, request a temporary suspension of trade with Java. Although opinions are divided, they have in common that they all subscribe to Your Majesty's lofty principle of benevolence toward those who are not part of our civilization. If the king of Java [Valckenier] expresses his regrets and is willing to repent in order to receive Your Majesty's all-embracing mercy, we, Your servants, request that the various kinds of barbarians still be allowed to trade with us.[268]

And so it happened: the emperor stroked his hand over his heart—after all, this was all bickering about the death of degenerate former subjects. And thus the overseas trade of the coastal provinces with faraway Batavia remained as it was. Of course, no one in Batavia was aware of this court discussion. Only when the junks, after a year's absence, reappeared on the roadstead in 1743 and the VOC ships in Canton were not hindered in any way, was it understood that the catastrophe of October 1740 would have no further consequences for the China trade.

The reaction back home

In the Netherlands, meanwhile, the true dimension of the bloodbath in Batavia was slowly sinking in. The first stories and rumors of the massacre reached the country in early August 1741, with the arrival of the fleet that had departed from Batavia on November 3, 1740. Those ships must have brought Governor-General Valckenier's first report of October 31. The taverns in Holland and Zeeland buzzed with tall tales from the sailors who had made such a racket in Batavia. But only in the first days of September, when the Gentlemen XVII met in session, did they realize what a tragedy had occurred one year earlier.[269]

The minutes of the September 7, 1741 board meeting of the Gentlemen XVII mention that a few days earlier, the councilor of the Indies, Elias de Haze, had arrived completely unexpectedly aboard the ship *Nieuwerkerk* on the Texel roadstead and that in the near future, the arrival of the newly elected Governor-General Van Imhoff and the councilor of the Indies, Van Schinne, could also be expected. The sailors arriving from the Indies also brought with them all sorts of writings about the Chinese uprising. On September 8 and 11, 'the secret letters and enclosures of Governor General Valckenier' were read with astonishment. Also on the table now was the 'Brief discourse serving as the main justification, against the assertions made in a certain account by the governor general Adriaan Valckenier' written by Councilors Chavonnes, Guillot, and Berendrecht, dated December 6, 1740, in which they protested against Valckenier's actions.

On September 19, news broke that Van Imhoff had also arrived. On Monday, September 22, he and De Haze met with the Gentlemen XVII, who restored the rapiers and canes that had been taken from them in Batavia. The gentlemen complained about the treatment that they had suffered and, not being aware of the accusations brought against them, requested to see the documents that had been dispatched from Batavia. In the meantime, a pressing letter from the secretariat of the States General had also reached Director Westerveen, demanding clarification of 'the events in Batavia about which so many countless versions have been told and rumors spread.' As is evident from the many pamphlets and even newspaper reports already circulating at the time, the Chinese massacre caused a great shock among the Dutch population. It is no wonder that the highest levels of government were now also involved, especially as the Company's charter was due for renewal.[270]

On September 29, Isaac Van Schinne at last arrived on the ship *Watervliet*. On October 3 and 4, after the Gentlemen XVII had once again carefully reviewed Valckenier's letters of October 30, 1740 and January 10, 1741, they gave the deportees the opportunity to have their say. That happened the next day. They 'summarily' gave their comments with the promise to submit their objections in writing at short notice. That happened as early as October 12, when Van Imhoff, De Haze, and Van Schinne presented their *Remarques* on the documents sent by Valckenier, adding their own version of what had happened during the fateful meeting of December 6, 1740.

On October 20 and 21, 1741, having also read the last *Generale Missive* of March 25, the Company directors agreed that the decision to deport the three gentlemen had not been made according to the rules and was therefore 'of no value whatsoever.' This compelled the assembly to request Van Imhoff, who they had appointed governor-general almost a year before, and the two councilors to prepare for their return to the Indies 'to purge the ingrained abuses and evil practices of some Company servants there.' At the end of the day, the three took their leave with the promise that they would soon pass on their thoughts on the matter.

After reading the documents that they had requested, the special committee of the States General also concluded that much had gone wrong in Batavia. To make this known to a wider circle, a remarkably sharply worded 'Extract from the Register of Resolutions' was published on October 30, 1741.[271] On the basis of the information provided to them, the country's supreme administrators determined that they could not perceive 'where and how the horrible and lamentable massacre had found its origin.' Whether that massacre had occurred spontaneously or by order from on high was not clear to them. And although it was claimed that the governor-general had ordered the massacre, the records that they had seen did not show this. What was clear, they cynically noted, was that people in Batavia had worked with all their might to put out the fire in the city but that apparently no one in the government had attempted 'to appease the tumult and stop the massacre.' In particular, the special committee expressed disgust at the execution of all the Chinese prisoners in the jails of the Company and the Bench of Alderman, 'an action that cannot be considered without horror.' They also concluded that disagreements and disputes had arisen over the power and authority of the governor-general, especially his position as captain general of the armed forces. All this needed to be subjected to close scrutiny. In their opinion, there remained many 'facts and allegations that demand more clarification' and trusted that all this should be handed over to the Council of Justice in Batavia to pass judgment. The decision to put the case in the hands of the Batavian Council of Justice was based on the charter that the VOC had received at its founding in 1602. All legal problems within the Company had to be dealt with by the appointed Council of Justice. As a result, all the documents were returned to the Gentlemen XVII, so that they could act as they saw fit 'for the maintenance of justice, for the preservation of good order and for the most benefit and prosperity of the Company.'

Valckenier's 'close friends and kinsmen' in Amsterdam had already seen the storm brewing and, arguing that he could not be assured of neutral judgment in Batavia, they petitioned the States General to prevent the Batavia Council of Justice from trying the former governor-general. But that request was in vain. The Directors gave more credence to the comments of the three exiles and concurred with the conclusions of the States General. The case was placed in the hands of the Council of Justice of Batavia.

The Considerations of Van Imhoff

Based on the adage that attack was the best defense against Valckenier's allegations, Van Imhoff had already put most of his thoughts on paper during the return trip to Holland. Learning that he had been appointed governor-general, he came up with an integrated campaign plan. On November 24, he handed over to the directors of the Company a blueprint for the reorganization of the East India Company's business in Asia, the *Considerations on the present state of the Dutch East India Company in relation primarily to its management, trade, shipping, and household in the Indies.*[272] It was a voluminous commentary on the shipping, trade, and possessions of the VOC in Asia and the administration thereof. With this monumental document—in printed form and without appendices 114 pages—Van Imhoff intended to make it clear that *only he* could make the 'redress' (reform) of the Company possible. Diagnosis was not enough; a leader was needed who was willing and able to carry out this turnaround with renewed vigor!

Van Imhoff identified the following factors as the main causes of the 'decline' of the Company: the excessive size of the organization, the inadequate quality of the ships and their crews—far too many ships were lost en route—and the major changes in the political and economic climate in Asia due to increasing English and French competition. It was therefore important to remain on good terms with the Asian rulers by dealing cordially with them. Last but not least, heavily damaged Batavia had to be reanimated to function as the beating heart of the entire trade network.

According to Van Imhoff, the 'languishing state' of the East India Company was due to the fact that it had lost its way as a combination of merchant and sovereign because the merchant had to pay ever higher administrative costs than it had to bear as sovereign: 'the Company was no longer a mere merchant but a trading power.' Or as Van Imhoff's successor Jacob Mossel would put it ten years later, 'What the Company consumes as sovereign, it must pay as merchant.'

Was Van Imhoff's diagnosis of the 'present languishing state' of the Company as new and original as it was thought to be at the time? No. In a way, it harkened back to the Van Hoorns, who had warned fifty years earlier about Rijckloff van Goens' expansionist policy and the rigid monopoly of the Gentlemen XVII, which made the Company less competitive against its European competitors. But that had fallen on deaf ears, as the rejections of the Gentlemen XVII showed. Van Imhoff noted that the Company should set trade priorities, that is, focus on a few main products on which it had a monopoly, and leave other trade to private initiative as the English did.

What was original, however, were Van Imhoff's insights into the Company's difficult financial situation in Asia. For example, he proposed an end to the complicated method of calculation in 'light' and 'heavy' money, based on the different value of silver money in Europe and Asia.[273] And regarding the political situation in the Indonesian Archipelago, Van Imhoff stressed the importance of the Company, as a ruling territorial power, dealing properly with native elites and the populations indebted to them. If the Company could have well-educated administrative officials with knowledge of the languages and customs of the Asiatic people, he said, it would not have to spend huge sums of money on defense (or rather offense) as the English and French did in India.

On December 7, Van Imhoff, Van Schinne, and De Haze appeared once again before the Gentlemen XVII in Amsterdam. The president welcomed them and again emphasized how indignant the board was about the treatment that they had suffered in Batavia exactly one year earlier, not to mention the insulting manner in which they had been deported to the homeland. The Company Board declared 'the actions of the former Governor General Valckenier, baseless, null, powerless and of no value, and therefore non-existent.' Following this, the board announced some further points of interest that were important for the legal settlement of the case in Batavia. Finally—the venom was in the tail—the meeting decided to instruct the commander of the Cape of Good Hope to 'detain certain persons arriving at the Cape until Mr. Van Imhoff will have arrived.' By this they of course meant Valckenier and his entourage. As the meeting drew to a close, the three councilors expressed their gratitude for the 'honour and esteem' they had received from the meeting. Incidentally, another ten months would pass before Van Imhoff actually left for the Indies to shoulder the governorship. First, the necessary measures in the field of shipbuilding and navigation had to be taken in response to his 'Considerations.'

The formal farewell finally took place on August 28, 1742. The new governor-general gave a fine 'farewell address.' The Directors honored Van Imhoff with a silver tea set worth 15,000 guilders. De Haze was assigned a gift worth 5,000 guilders. It is doubtful whether he received this gift, because at the last moment, De Haze, like Van Schinne before him, chose to stay home because he was not offered the position of director general. This was a wise decision in retrospect, because during the judicial inquiry in Batavia, he was found to have played an extremely questionable role in the slaughter of the Chinese in the prisons. On October 27, 1742, Van Imhoff departed for the Indies aboard the ship the *Hersteller* (The Repairer).

Meanwhile back in Batavia

According to his letters to his brother-in-law Hop, despite the disapproving reactions of the members of the Council and even of his closest friends, Helvetius and Crul, Valckenier was greatly relieved to have rid himself of his three enemies.[274] That the mood in the Council of the Indies remained depressed even after the departure of the three gentlemen is evident from a letter from Councilor of Justice Reverhorst to family and friends in Leiden. 'It is miserable and sad here,' he wrote at the end of March 1741, 'ruffians and godforsaken rascals are calling the shots in the city. Violence and tyranny reign supreme, good-willed and benevolent souls dare not utter a sound. Valckenier will threaten people who contradict him with transfer to the isle of Banda or brand them fools or idiots.' Some members of the Council of the Indies went so far as to jokingly call Valckenier 'our king.'

The list of abuses recited by Reverhorst was long: Public Prosecutor Phillips was 'drunk every day' and had recently fallen into the canal while urinating—'like a Pharisee that fellow wants to deceive the world.' Helvetius, 'that Kraut and arselicker,' was forwarding everything that was discussed in the Judicial Council to his brother-in-law, Valckenier. Nobody dared to speak aloud anymore because of Helvetius, De Roode, and other spies. If this continued and no measures were taken, Reverhorst believed, the Company would soon be finished, and the consequences would 'shake all of the Netherlands!'[275]

Valckenier himself was of a different opinion. He announced in the General Missive of March 25, 1741, that the High Government was proceeding with all caution to restore order. Five months later, on August 17, the letter arrived in Batavia in which the Gentlemen XVII announced Valckenier's resignation and Van Imhoff's appointment. Four days before, Valckenier, again felled by illness and unable to appear in the council room, had announced his intention to repatriate in the fall. But even though the Gentlemen XVII in the Netherlands had determined on December 2, 1740, that Johannes Thedens would succeed him ad interim, should Van Imhoff be absent for any reason, Valckenier 'extremely aggrieved and expressing himself in very unbecoming utterances,' refused to formally relinquish his title. Thedens indicated that he was willing to assume the administration immediately, which led to all sorts of squabbling, especially since Director General Schaghen announced on September 1 that he too wanted to resign in order to return home with Valckenier. The two gentlemen were suddenly in a hurry, as they did not want to meet Van Imhoff in Batavia under any circumstances. Valckenier wished to leave as early as October 18, but expressed his willingness to wait at the Cape of Good Hope for the other return ships that would leave after him. On November 6, he boarded the ship *Amsterdam* after wishing the High Government 'a prosperous state and splendor.' That sounded rather wry considering that in his last General Missive, he had informed the Gentlemen XVII of 'an unprecedented revolt and rebellion of the Chinese' in all of Java. The councilors waved Valckenier off with the pious wish that 'Jehovah would from now on look upon them with a more favorable eye.' Thedens could not resist the temptation to send a second missive shortly after Valckenier's departure in which he attributed the perilous state of the Company and of 'Java, which is the main supplier of our food,' to the recently departed governor. Never since time immemorial, according to him, had things looked so bad!

Arrest at the Cape

On March 15, 1742, the commander of the Cape of Good Hope, Henrik Swellengrebel, wrote to Valckenier's brother-in-law, Cornelis Hop, that Valckenier had arrived at the Cape on January 25 'in a very bad constitution both of body and brain.' Those ailments had considerably aggravated when Swellengrebel had been forced to take him into military custody. Indeed, on February 11, the English dispatch boat *Swift* had arrived with orders from the Gentlemen XVII to arrest Valckenier and send him back to Batavia. This had 'greatly dismayed' Swellengrebel himself because Valckenier had always been a patron and friend of his family. His 71-year-old father Johannes remembered how a very young Valckenier had been his guest 27 years earlier on the recommendation of Mayor Nicolaas Witsen. According to Swellengrebel, Valckenier was in 'such a deplorable condition' that he might not even be able to leave the Cape. He provided 'His Nobleness, considering the circumstances, as much honor and decency as he owed to a man of birth and decency,' and had taken him in as a lodger.

Now it was up to Valckenier to turn in his rapier and cane. All of his 'precious and voluminous goods' were brought ashore from the hold of the *Amsterdam* to be inventoried. Most were sealed, but items for daily use, such as golden shirt buttons, shoe buckles, and garments, were returned to him. Chief merchant, Gerrit Hackenberg, the former administrator of the medicinal store at Batavia, who, as surgeon and intimate friend, accompanied Valckenier on the trip home, added his diagnosis of Valckenier's poor condition. He was suffering from 'double malaria, seizures and failing strength, in addition to compressed nervous fluids which necessarily had to clog up the cerebral conduits and thus impeded a clarity of mind.' Hackenberg understood that the order to return to Batavia also had consequences for himself: 'How my affairs will work out with me poor devil, I shall have to await with due patience.' Not thinking long about it, he took to his heels and thus evaded prosecution.[276]

Here again, *la mano de dios* seems to have played a role, for the *Amsterdam*, the ship on which Valckenier and Hackenberg were to continue their voyage, sank with all hands (including the bulk of Valckenier's possessions) off the Shetland Islands a few months later. The arrest warrant had actually saved the lives of Valckenier and Hackenberg.

In August, Swellengrebel had better news for Hop. His guest had visibly recovered and, according to his surgeon, had not been this well in ten years. Valckenier would have preferred to stay at the Cape a little longer, but Swellengrebel had advised him against it. He had better leave as soon as possible, or else Van Imhoff would 'so to speak take him along in triumph under his own flag.' Valckenier therefore returned to Batavia on September 5 on the *Sara Jacoba*. Taking leave of the Cape commander's children, he said: 'How fortunate you children are to see your parents, as mine may never experience such happiness again!' And exclaiming 'My God, what can a man come to! Solon, O Solon! Help me!' he stepped into the sloop that took him to the square rigger.[277] He realized that no warm welcome was in the offing. It turned out that way, for on arrival in Batavia, he was whisked away directly to the Ruby Bastion (Punt Robijn) of the Castle, where he was put under strict custody.

CHAPTER 16

Peripetia and Catharsis

So, who were the perpetrators of the massacre? We need not ponder that question for long: in an atmosphere that had been simmering for days and nights, one fatal brawl between Chinese and the sailors of the fleet was enough to provoke the carnage in the city. In an instant, virtually the entire population of Batavia lost its bearings and minds. If we focus the question more closely on those ultimately responsible, we inevitably end up with failing Company authorities who provoked with shortsighted measures a Chinese revolt in the Ommeland.

His honor restored and back in Batavia on May 26, 1743, Van Imhoff set out to execute his 'reform' program and at the same time tried to settle his personal accounts with Valckenier. This meant that two lawsuits were involved, a civil and a criminal one. The civil suit was launched by Van Imhoff, Van Schinne, and De Haze against Valckenier to demand reparations for the social and financial wrongs that they had suffered. They sought to recover the losses that they had suffered as a result of the deportation, and therefore tried to have Valckenier's property in Holland and Batavia seized pending the judges' ruling. The criminal case was brought by the Council of Justice against Valckenier and his supporters on the grounds of their direct involvement in the massacre and, more specifically, the murder of the Chinese in the hospital and the two jails. This lawsuit was initiated by the Batavia public prosecutor. Upon his arrival in Batavia, Van Imhoff therefore cautiously inquired about the status of the criminal trial, although obviously 'by virtue of his authority' he had to keep himself as neutral as possible.

Carrying out the reforms

But before we address the legal proceedings, let us first tackle Van Imhoff's role as the great reformer, the *Hersteller* (redresser) as he styled himself. After his arrival in Amsterdam from Batavia in the winter of 1741, Van Imhoff was introduced by his nephew, Jacob Boreel, to the 'Saturdaegse krans' (Saturday Club), a select Company of Amsterdam regents. Even in the spring and summer of 1742, when he and his wife enjoyed Boreel's hospitality at his country estate, 'Beeckesteyn,' Van Imhoff remained in close touch with this urban elite. Through forging such personal contacts, the self-assured Van Imhoff must have impressed the directors of the Company with his expertise and charisma. Stadholder William IV of Orange-Nassau, who in 1742 entertained Van Imhoff at his Soestdijk hunting lodge, saw his guest leave with sorrow: 'Je n'ai pas pu voir partir le digne homme sans une extrême regret' (I cannot see such a worthy man leave without great regret). Van Imhoff had such a great time in Amsterdam that he afterwards sometimes wondered why on earth he had gone back to the East Indies. Had he not already angled for citizenship in Amsterdam in the hope of becoming a member of the alderman's bench? Yet, the goalposts had been moved. He no longer had a choice. He had already been appointed governor-general on December 2, 1740, and he had stuck his neck out by submitting the 'Considerations.' It was a matter of honor for him to return to the tropics and 'redress' the Company's affairs there.

Just how high the expectations of the Gentlemen XVII were is evident from the congratulatory letter sent by the West Frisian Company director, Jan Minne, to the newly appointed councilor of the Indies, Nicolaas van Berendregt (presumably the author of *The Dream of the Rebellion at Batavia*). Under the leadership of 'the wise and much admired' Governor-General Van Imhoff, Berendregt was now put in a position to help restore 'the dilapidated and moribund Company' and all this 'in service of the shareholders and in support of the dear fatherland that was also suffering bad times.' Minne mentioned a whole laundry list of disasters such as the damaging storms that broke the dikes, the harsh winter, the floods in Holland and Zeeland, the lack of food—one long litany that showed that even in the Low Countries, affairs were in disarray. Those clearly were not the best of times.[278]

On October 27, 1742, Van Imhoff left the Texel roadstead with a squadron of five ships. Compared to the other East Indiamen, the admiral's ship the *Herstelder*, built at the Amsterdam VOC shipyard to the design of English master shipbuilder, Charles Bentham, proved innovative but was by no means perfect. The ship, Van Imhoff noted, 'steered like a boat and sailed excellently, but it could also sway and pitch to perfection.' During the crossing, all sorts of nutritional and hygienic measures were taken to combat the pathogens on board. This attention to food and drink for the crew indeed paid off. On three of the squadron's five ships, there was not a single case of illness or death before Table Bay was reached on January 21, 1743.

Never before had a governor-general in office visited the Cape, so this had to be celebrated, not least because Van Imhoff was very fond of ostentation. Soon the ships were dressed with their signal flags flying. On land, preparations were feverishly made for the solemn reception of the esteemed guest. When the governor and his wife set foot ashore the next day, the entire garrison was standing with fluttering banners. Governor Swellengrebel greeted the couple a bit nervously, because two years earlier he had ignored Van Imhoff, treating him as a 'state prisoner,' and had in the meantime also extended hospitality to the latter's archenemy, Adriaan Valckenier.

With a carefully prepared speech, the governor-general addressed the Cape crowd. He outlined the vicissitudes of his own destiny in Biblical terms. Was he not 'like another Joseph' first cast aside only to 'come to the aid of Egypt and Canaan in the greatest need? [...] So many a time it pleased the Almighty to glorify His power in the weakness of His flawed creatures!' Van Imhoff rounded off these grand words about the role of providence with the moralistic exhortation that the audience should be thankful that they could live 'free and un-afflicted in the shadow of their vine and fig trees.'

Swellengrebel informed his esteemed visitor of all that had happened during Valckenier's stay at the Cape. In his next letter, Van Imhoff informed his cousin, Boreel, sardonically that his predecessor had been 'entirely out of his mind.' Nevertheless, he had spent his time going over all the precious items that he had brought with him, at times muttering something along the lines of, 'If only I had returned to Holland sooner.' Also, when he had recovered his senses, he had given Swellengrebel three 'salutary counsels: Fear God, do not be stingy, and do not rely on evil counselors.' This advice provoked Van Imhoff's ridicule: 'It would have made more of an impression if he had come to that discovery earlier. It proved that he must not have been so entirely mad.'

The tidings that reached Van Imhoff at The Cape from Batavia, however, did not cheer him as much: 'Thus I find myself as if looking down from a dangerous precipice and that is a weakness that I shall still have to learn to master.' With these gloomy forebodings, the governor-general set sail on February 28, but not before first presenting his hosts with several gold and silver medals with his own effigy on one side and the uplifting inscription *spes meliorum temporum* (hope for better times) on the other.

The assumption of government

After a long voyage with many lulls and headwinds, the ships anchored in the Batavian roadstead on May 28, 1743, and that very afternoon, Governor-General Van Imhoff assumed his authority with a passionate speech that caused many to reach for a handkerchief. Although he found a 'besotted and confused estate' over the next few days, he did not let anyone know that it was difficult for him to take up his calling. Indeed, he set a new meeting schedule for the Council of the Indies, namely Tuesdays and Fridays at 4 o'clock in the afternoon, so that each could carry out his daily work in the morning with zest and fresh courage.

Nonetheless, Van Imhoff shuddered at the thought of 'the redress such an inaccessible mountain of work and a narrow pass in which 100 malcontents could block the way of as many as 10,000 well-wishers.[279] Yet if God be with us, who shall impede us?' God-fearing as he was, the governor-general organized an extraordinary day of thanksgiving and prayer on June 12 to stir up public life. On that occasion, he delivered a moral sermon in which he reminded the sinful community that the Lord's Almighty hand had been making itself felt for more than twenty years, first through losses at sea and then through 'the smiting of this city and its surrounding territory with all manner of sicknesses and deaths, which have now been going on for twelve years [...] increasing the plagues by steps and degrees.' And as if that were not enough, he added, 'the righteous Judge, seeing the insensibility and wickedness of His reluctant children, had added on top of that his great and terrible judgment of the of year 1740, which will make both ears ring for many centuries to come [...] but in spite His long suffering, it has pleased God to now grant a great change in government, and that is to be celebrated.'[280]

Did Van Imhoff succeed in implementing his program to 'redress' the Honorable Company's affairs? To begin with shipping, the Gentlemen XVII went a long way toward meeting his recommendations. Full of admiration for British and French shipbuilding and annoyed with the old-fashioned craftsmen of the VOC, Van Imhoff wished to establish a construction program to build faster and more versatile ships. His proposals on navigation, however, were craftily stifled by the conventional shipyard bosses and the hardy jack tars on whom he had set his sights. In the end, only a few ships were built to the new designs. The VOC's shipyards clung to the beamy 'return vessels' with lots of cargo capacity: 'show-offs on the roadstead, drifters at sea' (*Pronkers op de ree, dwarsdrijvers op zee*). Van Imhoff also wanted to address the training and selection of ships' officers. To this end, he established an *Académie de Marine* in Batavia for the training of cadets. Sadly, this training center had to close its doors in 1755 because the mortality rate among the students in Batavia was so high. Summing up, Van Imhoff correctly pointed out various weaknesses, but attempts at reform yielded little in the long run.

Fortunately, the new governor-general was able to rely on excellent helpers for the direction of the colonial administration's day-to-day affairs in the East Indies, although he made no mention of this anywhere in his correspondence. He could turn to the shrewd Jacob Mossel as director general, a man with vast experience in the Indian subcontinent, where during the last decade, the Company had ceded much of its market share to English, French, and Danish competition. Mossel, who would later succeed Van Imhoff, was among other things the founder of the Amphioen (Opium) Society, by which the High Government hoped to limit smuggling in opium imported from India. By sharing his participation in this extremely profitable private venture with others, Van Imhoff was able to shield himself from possible criticism from the administrators in the homeland; he even donated a number of shares to the recently appointed Supreme Commander of the East India Company, Stadholder Willem IV, to strengthen his personal ties with the house of Orange.

To quell the turmoil of the civil strife in Central Java, Van Imhoff could rely on such experienced people as Commissioner Hugo Verijssel, the commanders of Semarang and Surabaya, Elzo Sterrenberg and Reinier de Klerck, respectively, and the commander of the VOC troops Baron von Hohendorf, the officer who single-handedly rescued the susuhunan from the beleaguered *kraton*. Thanks to them, not to mention the military support of Madurese Prince Cakraningrat IV, by the autumn of 1743, peace had already returned to the extent that the Company was able to conclude an extremely advantageous 'peace treaty of reconciliation' with Susuhunan Pakubuwana II. In gratitude for the sovereign's rescue, the VOC received the coastal territory of Java with all its revenues, in return for payment of a fixed annual fee with which the susuhunan could maintain his court and family.

Van Imhoff had the signing of this treaty publicly celebrated with a day of thanksgiving and prayer. For the first time, this celebration included the non-Christian population groups of Batavia, albeit with pressure from above. 'Everyone was exhorted to adorn the front door of their homes with lanterns and garlands. Violators faced a fine of 25 rials.[281] Bewildered and filled with fear, everyone followed the orders.' In subsequent years, as if they were incantation ceremonies, similar days of thanksgiving and prayer were observed on the departure of all return fleets, not unlike the annual custom of the Chinese who celebrated the arrival and the departure of the junks with *wayang* performances dedicated to their sea goddess, Mazu.

Day in and day out, Van Imhoff decreed how things should be improved, but before any of this was fully implemented, he was already immersed in the next task. He established a number of useful institutions, such as a seminary for prospective ministers, a city printing office, a post office, a pawnbroker's shop, and the newspaper *Bataviase nouvelles* (which was promptly banned by the Gentlemen XVII, fearful as they were of foreign prying eyes). Many initiatives seemed promising, but the sticky world of the East made it difficult to make them work well. Nonetheless, some of the ventures were useful such as the construction of a church for the Lutheran congregation, the foundation of a sanatorium at the hot springs of Tjipanas where 'impotent' Company servants could recover, and the settlement of European (mostly East Frisian) farmers in the pleasant, temperate climate of Kampong Baru at the foot of the mountains. Unfortunately, during the uprising in Bantam in the early 1750s, those scattered cattle farms were again razed to the ground by roving *rampokkers* (roving armed gangs of robbers). Although angry tongues claimed that on the basis of all these events, the *Hersteller* could be more aptly called the *Versteller* (bungler), Van Imhoff did succeed in restructuring the lease system of the city taxes and supervised the construction and repair of numerous useful infrastructural works, such as the deepening of canals and other civic sanitation measures. Thus, he only partially succeeded in restoring Batavia to its former glory.

If little came of Van Imhoff's good intentions, it should be conceded that he lacked the necessary resources: the promised capital for trade and the promised sending of new ships and crew never materialized. Add to this, perhaps somewhat anachronistically, through the fact that every modern management program 'transforming insights into practical use' insists that making plans is one thing and executing plans and consolidating another, the weakness of the 'reformer' was exposed.

Some trading ventures that Van Imhoff initiated to revitalize the Company while filling his own purse failed miserably. For example, he attempted—in complete violation of the Treaty of Münster (1648)—to establish direct trade relations between Batavia and silver-rich Mexico. Two failed expeditions ended in a costly debacle, but also led to a diplomatic crisis between the States General and the Spanish king.[282] In 1745, Van Imhoff purchased from English privateers three French vessels *Jason, Dauphin,* and *Hercules* that they had captured on their way back from China. When he sent these ships with their rich cargoes on behalf of the Company (and for himself) to the Netherlands, this created another major diplomatic incident, this time with the French king himself. That crisis could only be defused by payment of a hefty fine of 3.1 million *livres* by the Company. It was not until 1753, well after Van Imhoff's death, that this matter was settled.[283]

In his 'Considerations,' Van Imhoff had advocated a hard line with regard to private trade with the Netherlands, with one exception: he wanted to leave open the possibility for private individuals to load on their own account the Company's return ships with cargoes of tea 'up to a quantity of two or three ship cargoes.' In this way, the government could take the wind out of the sails of the 'spillage' (smuggling) in that highly priced commodity, and at the same time encourage the sailing of the Chinese junks as suppliers of tea to Batavia. This also offered private individuals the opportunity to transfer substantial sums of money in the form of tea after it was no longer permitted to use bills of exchange to transfer large sums of money to the Netherlands. Judging from his correspondence with cousin Boreel, Van Imhoff himself took full advantage of this arrangement. With the sale of tea in the Netherlands by his Amsterdam business agent, Robert Hendrik Armenault, he was able to boost his private capital considerably. Upon his death, he left behind in cash and securities 1,825,615 guilders, a capital that in today's terms can easily be multiplied by eighty.

When it gradually became clear to Van Imhoff that he might never be able to realize his dream of acquiring an estate in the Netherlands, he had a vast area of land reclaimed for himself in the Bovenlanden, which he appropriately named Buitenzorg (*sans souci*, or carefree). This personal country retreat, where he increasingly withdrew with his loved ones, was to be further expanded over time by his successors and went on to serve as the palace of the governors-general of what would later become the Dutch East Indies. Renamed Bogor, it has been home to Indonesia's president since independence.

Political flaws

In his interactions with the native princes with whom he wished to deal cordially, Van Imhoff was not that diplomatic at all. During a triumphal tour through Java from March 24 to June 10, 1746—about which he left a magnificent travelog—he bruised the ego of the susuhunan's proud brother, Prince Mangkubumi, by lecturing him publicly at the court. That same evening, the offended prince took refuge in the surrounding mountains and gathered a large number of followers around him. Together with another prince, Mas Said, he caused the susuhunan and the Company so many headaches in the following years that at the Treaty of Giyanti in 1755, the kingdom of Mataram had to be divided in two.[284] In Bantam, Batavia's other neighbor, political affairs also went awry. Van Imhoff had the mentally disturbed sultan locked up and replaced him with his wife, the sultana Sharifa Fatima, with whom he had maintained close relations since the 1730s. By putting forward a son of her brother as the heir to the throne instead of the legitimate pretender, the sultana antagonized the population to such an extent that a large-scale revolt broke out in Bantam as well. Not until years after Van Imhoff's death could order be restored in the sultanate.[285]

Van Imhoff's most startling intervention was his about-face in favor of the Chinese. He could hardly have done otherwise, either. How else would it be possible to revive Batavia's moribund local economy? Ironically, he was left with no choice but to appeal to Chinese free enterprise. One important measure was increasing the number of passengers allowed to arrive with the junks from China each year, 'because those people cannot be missed in this colony; moreover a good number of them die every year [because of Batavia's unhealthy climate].'[286] He not only gave the Chinese free rein, but also helped restore their mediating role within the colonial economy.

Initially, the captain of the Chinese of Cheribon, Oey Tiensieuw, and Lieutenant Tan Iko refused to accede to Van Imhoff's request to revive the Chinese Council, but after long urging they agreed. The Chinese Council or Kong Koan, with its captain, lieutenant, and boedelmeesters was formally established in 1747, and provided with its own office, including a secretary paid by the government. This new Chinese official was given the task of carefully recording and archiving the meetings and other activities of the Chinese Council so that no future misunderstandings could ever arise.

Initially there was little willingness among the remaining Chinese foremen to take the lead again as captains and lieutenants, because they were terrified of reprisals from the imperial regime once they had returned to China. Those fears were borne out when several years later, lieutenant Tan Iko returned home with his family. He was promptly apprehended and detained upon arrival. On charges of shadowy trading activities and collaboration with a foreign ruler, all of his property was confiscated and he and his wife and children were exiled to the western border regions.[287]

Remarkably, even a critical contemporary Chinese commentator on the *Chinese Annals of Batavia* praised Van Imhoff for his decisiveness:

> The provoker of the Batavian rebellion was Van Imhoff, who behaved at will like a tyrant and violently rounded up Chinese and massacred innocent people, bringing about the great disaster. Given his administration in later days, however, he laid the foundations of the country's government. One might say he was an outstanding minister who brought peace and prosperity. But he had an evil conscience and was ruthless in character [...]. When Van Imhoff arrived in Batavia he forged all kinds of plans that preceded the days of unrest. The people were terrified day and night. If only Valckenier had shown a stronger and more decisive character [...]. But after Van Imhoff usurped the throne, he introduced new tax leases, built a fort on the island of Onrust, repaired bridges, and had locks built. His reign and his building projects benefited the country and its people. All this proved that he was an able administrator in peacetime, but an unscrupulous schemer in hard times.[288]

Van Imhoff himself rather gloomily drew up an account of his reign: 'We have faced the sad effects of a longstanding decline of affairs resulting in that great reverse of the year 1740; but if I bring to mind the succession of events since that time, I become distraught, fearing much more than hoping, and seeing little improvement therein, since it appears to me that everything is equally cramped and difficult to spin a good yarn from it; for breaking threads and knotting them again, provides weak linen to the weaver….'

Denouement

As he had already done in Holland, upon his arrival in Batavia on May 28, 1743, Van Imhoff requested that the Council of Justice immediately seize all of Valckenier's remaining movable and immovable property. That request was granted, but until a verdict followed in the criminal case, these civil proceedings made no progress. When Van Imhoff was warned by his cousin, Boreel, that the tough position that he was taking in the civil actions might work to his disadvantage and damage his reputation—had he not been restored to his honor and had all his possessions in Batavia not been returned?—he responded as if stung by a wasp that on account of the injustice suffered, he had every right to take the stand as the offended party: he felt fully entitled to claim compensation. The sum he claimed constituted the money that he needed for his future life in the Netherlands. Since Van Imhoff also received advice from legal scholars from Holland to settle the civil case quickly, he must have felt that in the circles around him, a certain empathy was gradually building up for Valckenier, imprisoned in Batavia Castle.[289]

Although Van Imhoff could not interfere with the criminal proceedings against Valckenier, he had every interest in a quick conviction, so that he could also polish off the claims of the 'riotous Chinese' who blamed him for causing their rebellion and whom he 'recommended, after Solomon's biblical example concerning Simeï, to keep quiet.'[290] It had clearly not escaped his notice what the Chinese thought of him.

The criminal proceedings[291]

As we have seen, the Gentlemen XVII in the Netherlands ordered the High Government of Batavia, *in casu* the Council of Justice, to take legal action against ex-Governor-General Adriaan Valckenier and his associates. These were, respectively, his brother-in-law, Councilor of Justice Willem Vincent Helvetius, who was suspected of having written the Governor's secret letters; the inspector of the leprosy care, Nicolaas Munnix; Public Prosecutor Cornelis Phillips, and bailiff Pieter Boockesteijn, in connection with the murders in the prisons and the Chinese hospital. Also were included the administrator of the pharmacy, Gerrit Hackenberg, and auction master, Jan de Roode, both confidants of Valckenier; the military men, Hendrik Duirveld and Coenraad Muller, because they carried out the arrest of the three councilors on December 6, 1740; and, finally, the freeburgher, Jacob Kool, and the native officer, Pasqual Andries, who were allegedly involved in trafficking in offices.

Not a word was spoken of the mutineers and looters who had been allowed to run their murderous course for a week in October 1740. That was apparently a hopeless task. About Duirveld, De Roode, Munnix, and Hackenberg we can be brief: the first three died before they could be heard, and Hackenberg, as mentioned above, disappeared in Cape Town. More and more suspects fell by the wayside. Since Phillips himself was among the accused, he had to be replaced at short notice by an interim public prosecutor. On July 19, 1742, Nicolaas Jongsma, secretary of the Board of Aldermen, was selected.

Locked up in the Ruby Bastion, Valckenier was in total misery. In a letter to his beloved children, sisters, and other family members, he wrote, 'Only God knows whether this [letter] will possibly be my last to you or not.' But he did not lack local support. His mother-in-law, Catharina Massis, his old friend the councilor, Nicolaas Crul, and his brother-in-law, the former governor of Ceylon, Willem Maurits Bruijnink, regularly tried to cheer him up with a visit to the Ruby Bastion until this was forbidden. Bruijnink reported that Valckenier was in a serious condition: 'Being better one day than another, without us being able to judge the outcome. He does show peace of mind, and so little affectation about the accidents, that one must say that in these circumstances he shows an extraordinary greatness of mind.'[292]

When Bruijnink told Valckenier a few months later that his daughter, Sanna Caatje, had died, 'this tiding nevertheless showed that His Honour was not deprived of all affection and feeling and unable to restrain himself from shedding tears, but shortly afterwards he was composed again feeling himself at ease in God's will and pleasure.'[293] Until the end of her long life (86 years), Catharina Massis continued to provide her son-in-law with treats and uplifting notes, and acted, together with brothers-in-law, Helvetius and Bruijnink, and bosom friend, Crul, as a mediator with the home front in the Netherlands.

An endless trial

On August 1, 1742, Public Prosecutor Jongsma had taken Valckenier into custody. On October 3, he further demanded that Helvetius and Phillips be held hostage in their own homes, because he considered them guilty of the murder of the Chinese in the hospital and prisons. Helvetius immediately hit back by filing a petition for 'recusation' (challenge) on October 11 because both the president of the board of justice, Lakeman, and the aldermen, Jongsma and De Haze, had been involved in approving the murders in the hospital and prisons. That request was denied. An attempt by Jongsma on January 29, 1743, to convert Helvetius' house arrest into incarceration was not granted, and that was just as well for Valckenier, because in this way, he could continue to count on the effective legal support of his brother-in-law. Meanwhile, large numbers of people were being interrogated by the Council of Justice in order to gain a better understanding of what had taken place between October and December 1740.

During his interrogation, Phillips asserted that on October 11, 1740, he had been verbally summoned by Valckenier to execute the prisoners in the Company and municipal prisons. He had then instructed bailiff Boockesteijn to carry out that order in the civilian prison, while he himself had taken care of the Company prison.[294]

Questioned about his presence at the executions in the hospital, Helvetius denied having taken part in them. He had only watched as the Chinese, who had been rushed out, were slaughtered in the street by the angry population. Given the chaotic situation, it was quite understandable that he had held a rapier in his hand. During his interrogation, he explicitly distanced himself from the hot-tempered conduct of his brother-in-law, Valckenier, during the council meeting of December 6, 1740. He had not been present there, but he could at least understand why the governor-general had reacted impetuously given the precarious situation into which he had been maneuvered by Van Imhoff and his faction.

When Valckenier was summoned to be heard in March 1743, one year and five months after his incarceration, he argued that he had neither ordered the massacre on October 9 nor been involved in the sale of offices. He had not ordered Phillips and Boockesteijn to murder the Chinese prisoners, but on the contrary had referred them to the president of the Board of Justice Lakeman for the Company jail and the president of the Bench of Aldermen, De Haze, for the jail under the town hall. He had only given orders to expel those who feigned illness from the hospital, but two dozen really ill Chinese had been allowed to stay and had later been transported to the island of Edam. As to the arrest of the three councilors of the Indies, for that he took full responsibility, believing that they had rebelled against his authority. 'It was better to prevent than to cure.' And yes, for his secret letters to the Gentlemen XVII of October 31 and December 1, 1740, he had appealed to Helvetius, Duirveld, and others. Also, with Helvetius's legal assistance, the secret letters of January 8 and March 25, 1741, had been drafted.

After this, a lull in the procedures occurred, not in the least because the prosecutor, Jongsma, accused of prejudice by Valckenier's lawyer, chose to step down on account of ill health. Jongsma was replaced by the bailiff, Hendrik Jacob van Suchtelen, but since the latter did not consider himself qualified for this job, he was in turn replaced by Cornelis Rosenboom, who, with fresh courage, injected new life into the proceedings. On March 13, 1744, after 28 months of arrest, Valckenier was brought to the town hall 'with as much decency as can be given to a man of his birth and character in those circumstances,' to be *formally* charged with selling offices, killing Chinese, falsifying a resolution, and finally *lèse-majesté* and an assault on fellow members of the government. The death penalty was demanded. Now it was up to Valckenier and his counsel, Johan Joachim Oly, to defend themselves. That answer, because of Valckenier's declining health, came with much delay on December 18, 1744. What may also have played a role in this is that they had been preparing an extensive defense containing no less than 12,233 articles. Helvetius's turn came on August 4. He faced a fine of 25,000 rixdollars and lifetime banishment from the East Indies.

Delaying tactics

The legal playing field was already beginning to thin out, but the Valckenier case dragged on. Rosenboom filed his rejoinder to Valckenier's lengthy answer on October 12, 1745, maintaining his claim for conviction for 'homicide, falsity and *lèse-majesté* mixed with armed and public violence.' When Mr. Willem Cras replaced Oly as Valckenier's attorney, he was given three months to respond. For this purpose, Cras requested to have a large number of witnesses for the defense of Valckenier interrogated. This was granted to him in March 1746. The hearing of witnesses became increasingly difficult, because many of those involved had in the meantime died or left Batavia. On August 16, Mr. Cras obtained another eight-month reprieve. He took the opportunity to request two hundred 'authentic copies' of the resolutions of the governor-general and council that Valckenier believed that he needed for his defense. Here Van Imhoff committed a procedural error by personally intervening in the matter and asking Valckenier what documents he actually needed, to which the latter replied that this was none of his business, as he was in discussion exclusively with the Council of Justice. Valckenier received 150 of the 220 documents requested, which gave him the opportunity to draft a letter of complaint in which he once again explained at length that he could prove from the requested but still lacking documentation how dangerous the situation had been in October 1740. He again pointed out that in those days, the High Government had unanimously offered bounties to the native populations in the Ommelanden to cut off Chinese heads. In addition, he repeated the old grievance that Van Imhoff had knowingly spoiled the mood of the Council after his arrival from Ceylon and had plotted in November to depose him and send him to the Netherlands.

On June 5, 1747, Valckenier announced that his rejoinder was ready, but in the meantime, he had petitioned the administrators in the Netherlands to obtain the documents refused by the Council of the Indies. When, in April 1748, Rosenboom stepped down as prosecutor and Mr. Albertus Waals was appointed in his place, this gave Cras the opportunity to challenge this appointment because Waals had previously acted as attorney for Van Imhoff. Helvetius characterized Waals as a lightweight: 'a funny Bremen fellow from the heart of Westphalia in 1743, who came drifting over here on a little straw.' There was no alternative for the Council of Justice but to appeal again to Van Suchtelen, who had already been briefly involved in the case in 1743 but then did not consider himself qualified. When Van Suchtelen summoned Valckenier on December 24, 1748, the latter requested suspension and postponement pending a response from the Netherlands to Cras's claims at the Court of Holland.

By this time, even Van Imhoff began to despair of a verdict in the criminal case. 'The law case is stretched to a long term, probably hoping that I meanwhile shall die or repatriate, and that they [Valckenier and his faction] will then get away with it as they like,' he wrote. Van Imhoff had seen this correctly, for by the time of his death on November 1, 1750, things had not moved an inch.

The 'creolization' of Van Imhoff

Meanwhile, Van Imhoff had suffered two severe personal setbacks. After his youngest brother, François, and his wife were shipwrecked aboard the VOC ship *Hollandia* off the Scilly Islands in 1743, he himself remained the only male member of the family. On July 22, 1744, his wife, Catharina Magdalena, also died. All four children, two boys and two girls, that she had given birth to had died young. Since then, she had suffered from ill-health for years. Consequently, the governor-general had lost all hope 'of reproducing a line of descent.'

Taking all this into consideration, he concluded that 'my affairs have taken a different shape [...] and that consequently I may also be obliged to adjust myself, and henceforth work on other principles then before.'[295] This obscure but significant phrase in a letter sent to the widow of Isaac van Schinne on March 31, 1748, can be interpreted in two ways. Did he mean that he was now going to work even harder, or did he wish to beget children by other means according to a method not uncommon in the colonies? Or perhaps he meant both? 'The affairs and people here in the country have by death, departure and change of times become of such a different shape,' he continued his letter to the dowager, Van Schinne, 'that you would hardly know Batavia any more. Of the hundred, hardly anyone of those you and I have known here are left.' So many people had left for Holland with their belongings that even money had become scarce.

Van Imhoff initially wished to return home after the death of his wife. But this was not granted to him, 'since the gentlemen directors have requested me to continue a bit longer.' This caused him to change course, even in his personal life. Not a word can be found about this in his correspondence. About a year before the death of his wife, Van Imhoff had received a pretty slave girl as a gift from the queen of Boni (on the island of Celebes). He had then purchased this attractive present from the Company and enfranchised her. After the young woman was baptized with the name Helena Pieters, she moved in with him and in the years that followed she gave him four children, two boys and two girls, of whom the eldest, Jan Willem (1747), and his sister Isabella, a year younger, survived childhood.

The governor-general was still based in the Castle, but most of the time he spent with his family in his garden estate along the Jakatra road, or the country house on Tanah Abang about five kilometers from the city. Two or three times a year he also took them to 'a country still higher up [...] to enjoy the fresh air of the mountains and the beautiful vistas. Some make shift bamboo dwellings are standing there, with which one must make do for the moment,' he wrote. Apparently, Buitenzorg was not yet a big deal in 1748, but that did not prevent him from greatly expanding his building activities there. He no longer paid attention to the fata morgana over the horizon, i.e., a distinguished country estate in the Dutch Republic, but set his sights on a new rural property at the foot of the *Blauwe Bergen* (blue mountains) in order to enjoy a carefree old age surrounded by his young wife and children. In the last years of his life, Van Imhoff seems to have opted for a more introspective existence, leaving the day-to-day affairs of the Company to Director General Mossel. This did not escape his gossiping environment, as evidenced by a letter from a contemporary in which he claims that Van Imhoff, 'carried away to his own disrepute by the temptations of his black concubine,' was quite under the thumb of Leentje Pieters.[296]

Personal ambitions

During the second half of his seven-year administration, Van Imhoff concentrated more and more on his social position after his resignation. His pre-existing selfish traits now tended toward megalomania. Thanks to cousin Boreel and mayor Van de Poll and other influential people in Amsterdam's city council, he had already obtained citizenship of the city in 1745, but that was not enough. In 1748, when the *Staatsgezinden* (Republicans) in the Amsterdam administration were replaced by the pro-Stadholder faction, Van Imhoff could reap success from the carefully cultivated ties with the House of Orange.

And then something odd happened. Whereas a few years earlier Van Imhoff had made fun of Valckenier's claims to the rank and military authority of captain general of the Dutch East Indies, he now believed that by virtue of his rank as captain general on land and water he could lay claim to the rank of 'general of infantry or cavalry' in the Netherlands. Thus, upon his return to Holland, he hoped not to pass for a *quantité négligeable*, like Governor-General Durven in his home town of Delft, or Joan van Hoorn, who met a nasty end as a 'forgotten citizen' in Amsterdam. That wish, too, was fulfilled: on March 22, 1748, Van Imhoff was appointed general of infantry. It did not stop there, for once he was informed of the change of government in Amsterdam (which also cost his nephew, the alderman, Jacob Boreel, his position), he directly addressed Stadholder Willem IV in his position of 'Supreme Director of the Company' with a basket full of special demands.

End of life

In his last letter to cousin Jacob Boreel, Van Imhoff had complained that he had not yet received a letter relieving him of his position from the Gentlemen XVII. He sorely needed one, for he 'labored severely with dysentery and hemorrhoids' and this weighed heavily on his body. Would he be allowed to see his homeland again? Was his future actually in the Netherlands, or was it better for him to stay in Java? Could he present himself at all with his *nyai* and children in the Netherlands? And who would take care of them after his death? He must have pondered these questions for months, because the content of the letter which he wrote on September 9 to the Stadholder is patently clear: after first exhausting himself in 'remerciements respectueux à Votre Altesse sérénissime,' Van Imhoff came up with an astonishing set of demands, each of which suggests that they sprang from a fevered brain, but which, on closer inspection, are nevertheless understandable: Van Imhoff had become his own prisoner. For surrounded by his loving companion, Helena Pieters, and small children, whom he could not possibly show off in Amsterdam, he understood that there was really no way back to the Netherlands: *Adieu*, seigniory Zeist and his friends of the Amsterdam 'Saturday Club'! From now on, his future lay in Buitenzorg.[297]

Of course, Van Imhoff could not put it that way. He therefore did so in the form of a list of extravagant wishes: he requested that Buitenzorg be ceded to him in ownership. Should he be unable to acclimatize to the cold climate after his possible return to the Netherlands, he wished to return to Batavia as a former governor-general and be granted access to the meeting of the High Government with a 'second concluding vote after that of the reigning governor general, without therefore wishing in the least to be a burden to the Company.' Finally, he requested for his Buitenzorg estate 'a church, a school, a guard, and what belongs to it, a personal physician and surgeon, and a choice of servants including a minister from Batavia.'

This was truly a set of extraordinary demands, which the Prince and the Gentlemen XVII must have read in utter amazement, were it not for the fact that this letter was delivered on May 5, 1751, simultaneously with the news that Gustaaf Willem baron van Imhoff, 50 years old, had died on November 1, 1750, 'after a wasting illness of two months' in his country house on Tanah Abang. 'An irreparable loss to the Company' was Willem IV's comment.[298]

Van Imhoff's last wish was to be buried without pomp and circumstance. Because of 'the splendor of his ministry and the strange thoughts which the Indigenous would form about such simplicity,' the High Government decided to bury him anyway 'with full pomp.' The corpse was followed by a long procession from the castle to the church in the center of town. Shortly before his death, Van Imhoff had put three-year-old Jan Willem ('Jantje') with his wet nurse and *ayah* (servant) Melathi on a return ship to the Netherlands to be raised by his sisters. The heavily pregnant Helena Pieters was left behind all alone.

In his will drawn up in January, sealed and handed to notary, Albertus Domburg, on October 24, Van Imhoff made sure that his loved ones, friends, and surroundings would not lack anything. He requested the Stadholder 'by a favorable open letter of legitimization' to recognize his surviving children as his legitimate descendants with full name, title, and coat of arms. The legitimization was carried out seven years later for the not inconsiderable sum of 30,000 guilders making the little baron, Jan Willem, the founding father of the still flourishing Van Imhoff family in the Netherlands.[299]

Helena Pieters was also well taken care of. She inherited as life insurance a garden at Manggadua, a house in the city, and one of the estates outside the city, at first forty, and later sixty slaves, a lot of gold and silverware and, not unimportantly, a steady income from three *tokos* (shops) to be leased to the Chinese, outside the Diestpoort in the Chinese kampong, which she herself was allowed to manage. Should the thought arise that we are dealing with a life companion who had to be happy with what was left to her, this certainly was not the case. The will shows that Helena was quite capable of looking after herself. She effectively tightened the screws on her husband in his last months. Van Imhoff initially left her 6,000 rixdollars, but just before his death, the sum was raised to 10,000! We also see considerable adjustments in the will regarding the jewels, houses, and numbers of slaves allotted to her.[300] Ruling over the grave, Van Imhoff did try to keep her in line, however, by installing supervisory guardians. He had no objection if Helena remarried 'to a man of good and irreproachable, clean as well as bourgeois descent.' Also, this gentleman had to be protestant, and of no lower rank than junior merchant. Helena found that ideal marriage candidate in Lieutenant Duurkoop from her husband's dragoon guard.

Governor-General Jacob Mossel commemorated his predecessor in the Council as a man who 'not only was gifted with uncommon talents and great qualities, but who right from the beginning of his reign, had always exerted and concentrated all his faculties with the utmost zeal to restore the Company to a prosperous state, if possible.'[301] That could not be denied. Van Imhoff did not lack good ideas; the problem was that with him everything had to be done too quickly. Also, many of his ambitious concepts were difficult to realize because of a lack of money and resources, or because he made an ill-considered step at decisive moments. The other side of the coin was that his pushy behavior, his lust for money, and wounded pride caused much suffering and damage around him.

The tug of war for Adriaan Valckenier's estate

In 1752, Isaac Adriaan Valckenier in Amsterdam received a letter from a certain R. de Laver of Batavia informing him that on June 19, 1751, 'God Almighty had pleased to dissolve his father from his so tortured body and, we hope, will receive him into his eternal kingdom.' After nine and a half years of captivity, Adriaan Valckenier, 61 years old, had survived his archenemy by more than seven months. De Laver could not refrain from commenting on this: 'Your father had the blessing of seeing his mortal enemy, who so yearned for his death, pass away before him [...]. Defamatory tongues said Valckenier had spoiled everything, Imhoff would fix it, but alas! How wrong they were!'[302]

De Laver was biased, but he was right: civil war had erupted in Bantam, and unrest reigned at the court of Mataram. Van Imhoff had created much mischief in Java with his undiplomatic actions.

What began as the trial of the suspected perpetrators and those responsible for the Chinese massacre ended in a war of attrition between Valckenier and Van Imhoff, in which both collapsed like exhausted boxers in their own corners, Van Imhoff surrounded by his loved ones in his home, Valckenier lonely at the Ruby Bastion. Vincent Helvetius, his son-in-law, Jeremias van Riemsdijk, and P. J. Bangeman requested permission from the Council of Justice to transfer Valckenier's corpse from the Ruby Bastion to the residence of his mother-in-law, Massis, who had stipulated in her will that her house should not be sold before Valckenier's death. From there, the gentlemen wanted to arrange the funeral. This was granted on the condition that Valckenier be buried without pomp and circumstance. Not satisfied with this, they turned to the High Government, and by order of Governor-General Jacob Mossel, a proper burial ceremony was allowed at which, De Laver wrote, many people 'and to the annoyance of Valckenier's enemies very many Chinese,' were present.

Mossel felt that the whole matter had dragged along enough and therefore intervened when, on July 27, 1751, the Council of Justice wanted to snatch the handling of Valckenier's estate from the hands of the administrator. He feared that all sorts of objects were being embezzled by the members of the Council of Justice and wanted to be done with the whole matter. The disputes between the governor-general and the Council of Justice led to such an epic quarrel that it was decided to temporarily halt the proceedings surrounding Valckenier's estate pending a ruling on the matter from the Gentlemen XVII themselves. After much legal wrangling, on September 24, 1755, the judgment was passed that 'the criminal proceedings against Valckenier had been extinguished and abolished by his death.'

Thirteen years of house arrest

Should anyone ever venture to get to the bottom of the litigation surrounding the Chinese massacre, she or he will encounter Willem Vincent Helvetius everywhere. On March 17, 1750, the Judicial Council decided to 'keep in state' the case against Helvetius, who by now had been confined in his own home for seven years and would not be released from his house arrest until five years later. Helvetius filed a petition on February 4, 1755, in which he argued that Public Prosecutor Rosenboom's claim had been 'calumnious, outrageous, and enormous, founded only on his erroneous conception, spiteful prejudice, and self-serving assumptions.' The verdict followed on May 28: Helvetius was acquitted of all charges, financially compensated for all trials and, by a decree of June 13, 1755, reinstated as a member of the Council of Justice with payment of the income foregone between October 3, 1742, and June 2, 1755. On October 20 of the same year, Helvetius informed Valckenier's son that he had been completely exonerated and restored to his former position. He said he did not intend to exact his wrath on anyone. One wonders on whom he could have done so, because upon his return to the Council of Justice, Helvetius found none of his former adversaries present. Save a few who had returned to the Netherlands, all the others had already passed away. In his case, the saying that 'slow and steady wins the race' rings true: when he died on January 20, 1771, he had risen to the position of president of the Council of Justice of Batavia.

The Revenge of Heaven

All that remained was to settle Valckenier's estate with the VOC's trustees in the Republic. After all, it was in the Company's treasury that all his seized assets were administered. In November 1742, a meeting of the Gentlemen XVII had revealed that a total of 262,153 rixdollars was outstanding in bills of exchange in Adriaan Valckenier's name. Twenty years later, on March 31, 1760, the trustees, Temminck and Calkoen, and the Company's lawyer, Mr. Van der Hoop, were commissioned by the Company directors to conclude a contract with Isaac Adriaan Valckenier, the universal heir.[303] That agreement provided Adriaan Valckenier's son with 725,000 guilders. In addition to this, the Amsterdam court of justice declared the civil actions (by Van Imhoff, De Haze, and Van Schinne) against Valckenier's heirs also ended, with the public prosecutors being ordered to pay the costs of the trial!

Does money make one happy? Not in the case of Isaac Adriaan. Judging from the correspondence that he maintained with his imprisoned father over the years, he at first seemed to be doing well. He went to study law in Leiden in 1748, and after completing his studies, he joined the Amsterdam Town Hall as an accountant in 1753. Three years later, he married Sara Johanna Vultejus and by the time he was 28, he was appointed alderman of Amsterdam. This job does not seem to have been a success, for one year later he continued to serve in lesser offices. After receiving the huge inheritance, the couple moved to a double dwelling on the respectable Gouden Bocht (Golden Bight) of the Herengracht.[304] Of the five children born to this marriage, three girls and a boy reached adulthood. During the course of the 1760s, Isaac Adriaan gradually lost his bearings, until things went horribly wrong in 1768. The famous *Chronicle* of Jacob Bicker Raije describes in detail how, on March 14, 1768, Isaac Adriaan fired a pistol at his wife, with the bullet luckily missing her and ending up in the wallpaper behind her, 'whereupon he took another pistol from his chest, thinking to shoot himself in the head with it, but that bullet also flew past into the ceiling.'[305]

Declared insane, Isaac Adriaan was placed in a specially purchased safe house aptly named 'Vredelust' (peace of mind), where, like his imprisoned father, he spent the rest of his life—he died in 1785—in solitary confinement. His only surviving son, Adriaan Cornelis (1760–1813), remained a bachelor all his life. Upon his death, the illustrious Valckenier family came to an end in the male line.

If it were up to Chinese folklore, this tragic end would surely have been explained as the revenge of heaven down to the third generation.

AFTERWORD

Prospero and Caliban

> Views, interpretations may change, not excluding
> those of the participants. The history itself
> is graven permanently in stone.[306]
> —John Kenneth Galbraith

After the curtain has fallen, here are my final comments: Unlike Van Hoëvell and especially Vermeulen, who have meticulously reconstructed the horrific events of the October days of 1740 on the basis of the VOC archives, I have focused primarily on the historical context of the Chinese massacre and the question of how it could have come about. Why did the Dutch and Chinese diasporas, which seemed so well suited to each other in Batavia, end up clashing first outside and then inside the walls of the city?

The Gentlemen XVII's advice to Jan Pietersz. Coen had seemed so wise. Had they not told him that there was nothing to fear from the Chinese, 'a zealous, industrious and unarmed people'? They would never revolt to make themselves masters of the country, provided that 'all the administrative functions were performed only by the most distinguished and able of our own nation.' A hundred years later, this advice had fallen on deaf ears; the 'most distinguished and able,' the patricians Valckenier and Van Imhoff, had dramatically failed in their duties.

A unique form of collaboration between two colonial models took place in and around Batavia in the seventeenth century. The Dutch settlement in Batavia became the headquarters of the United East India Company, which sought to acquire and maintain trade monopolies in tropical export products. At the same time, a Chinese overseas trading network spread across the Eastern Seas to the Indonesian archipelago. In Batavia, these two forms of overseas economic expansion became intertwined in a model of cooperation in which the Chinese, although under the domination of the Company's administration, played a crucial role.

A new chapter in this cooperation was opened with the development and exploitation of the Ommelanden. While a vibrant social life in Batavia was unthinkable without the participation of the Chinese in the urban economy, the development of the Ommelanden also seemed impossible without their contribution to the sugar industry. However, the Company's administration managed to antagonize these 'industrious and hardworking' people when colonization began to spread to the border of the hinterland and beyond. This development is reminiscent of Shakespeare's *The Tempest*. Although Prospero had supposedly 'nurtured, supported and favoured' Caliban, he was astonished to find that he still rebelled against him.

By the 1730s, critical tensions were beginning to emerge in Batavia amid a toxic mix of dissension within the High Government, a malaria epidemic, and unchecked large-scale Chinese immigration. On top of all this, the destruction of virgin forest to make way for sugar plantations ruined the ecosystem in and around the city. Sadly, within a few years, the factionalism between Valckenier and Van Imhoff wiped out what the Van Hoorns, father and son, had painstakingly built up over the previous century. Shortsighted and impulsive measures by the colonial administration led to a spontaneous Chinese uprising.

The Chinese rebels' attack on Batavia unleashed an uncontrollable frenzy in the besieged city. The orgy of violence unleashed by the sailors spilled over into the terrified urban population. The government sat by and did not lift a finger when the rampage began. Impersonal influences may have been at work, but human agents, from high to low, were complicit in the carnage and looting of the city.

Nevertheless, after the massacre of October 1740, there was no abrupt end to more than a century of collaboration between the two communities. On the contrary, within a short space of time, mutual relations were re-established—at first with some reluctance, but soon with increasing willingness on both sides; there were too many mutual interests at stake. Van Imhoff, who had been partly responsible for the terrible events of 1740, realized that he could not go on without the Chinese and arranged for a cooperation to be formalized again in the Kong Koan, or Chinese Council.

But it was not a return to 'business as usual.' The amicable intertwining of interests that had characterized the mutual relations in the days of father and son Van Hoorn gave way after 1740 to a cautious colonial policy that aimed to integrate the Chinese into hierarchical structures as 'foreign Orientals,' with restrictive measures such as travel passes and strictly controlled China towns. In the nineteenth century, this situation of 'apartheid' was largely formalized in colonial legislation that enshrined the special position of 'foreign Orientals' apart from indigenous society. Although the colonial government attempted to intervene in the position of Chinese communities in the Dutch East Indies, and although ethnic branding through all kinds of special measures continued in Indonesia under the regimes of Sukarno and Suharto, there is no doubt that Chinese immigrants and their descendants have continued to play a vital role in the economic and social life of the Indonesian archipelago. The old colonial ties may have disappeared, but the Chinese presence, adapted to the current conditions, has remained very much alive.

Notes

1 Willem van Haren, 'Gedicht op den moord gepleegd aan de Chineesen te Batavia den ix Octob: Anno 1740', in J.Th. Vermeulen, *De Chineezen te Batavia en de troebelen van 1740*, pp. 142–143.

2 W.R. van Hoëvell, 'Batavia in 1740', *Tijdschrift voor Nederlandsch-Indië* 3-1 (1840), pp. 447–556. Zie ook 'De moord der Chinezen te Batavia, een woord aan den heer A.J. van der Aa', *Tijdschrift voor Nederlandsch-Indië* 8-3 (1846), p. 114.

3 J.Th. Vermeulen, *De Chineezen te Batavia en de troebelen van 1740.*

4 The archives of the VOC are kept in the National Archives at the Hague.

5 A.R.T. Kemasang, 'The Massacre of Chinese in Java: Curtain Raiser for the Dutch Plantation Economy', in *Bulletin of Concerned Asian Scholars*, vol.14-1, 1982, pp. 61–71; Remco Raben, 'De Chinese Oorlog in Batavia in 1740' in J.Th. Lindblad and Alicia Schrikker, eds, *Het verre gezicht. Politieke en culturele relaties tussen Nederland en Azië, Afrika en Amerika*, pp. 106–123.

6 W.R. van Höevell en Pieter Meijer (red.), 'Chronologische geschiedenis van Batavia, geschreven door een Chinees, uit het Chineesch vertaald door W.H. Medhurst', in: *Tijdschrift voor Nederlandsch-Indie* (1840) 3-2, 1–145. For a recent translation of the original, see: Leonard Blussé en Nie Dening, *The Chinese Annals of Batavia, The Kai Ba Lidai Shiji* (开吧 历代史纪) *and other stories (1610–1795)*, Leiden: Brill Publishers 2018.

7 See Manjusha Kuruppath, *Dutch Drama and the Company's Orient. A Study of Representation and its Information Circuits, c. 1650–1780.*

8 Joost van den Vondel, *Zungchin, of ondergang der Sineesche maatschappye (1667).*

9 Onno Zwier van Haren, *Agon, sulthan van Bantam (1769).*

10 The standard work on the VOC is: Femme S. Gaastra, *The Dutch East India Company, Expansion and Decline.* Zutphen: Walburg Pers 2003.

11 Johanna van Riebeeck wrote in 1709 to her father, Governor-General Abraham Riebeeck, that the ship on which she and her husband, the former Governor-General Joan van Hoorn, sailed was so over loaded with private goods, that the crew had to sleep on the ship deck. Her husband even asserted that the cargo on the captain's account even exceeded the Company's account. E.C. Godée Molsbergen, *Geschiedenis van Nederlandsch Indië* IV, p. 20.

12 J.C.M. Warnsinck, *Reisen van Nicolaus de Graaff. Gedaan naar alle gewesten des Werelds. Beginnende van 1639 tot 1687 incluis; Oost Indische Spiegel*, p. 25.

13 See J. de Hullu, 'De matrozen en soldaten op de schepen der Oost-Indische Compagnie', p. 70.

14 H. van Malsen, 'Briefwisseling van den Gouverneur-generaal Gustaaf Willem baron van Imhoff met den advocaat-fiscaal der Amsterdamsche Admiraliteit enz. Jacob Boreel Janszoon (1738–1750)', p. 378.

15 Els M. Jacobs, *Merchant in Asia, The Trade of the Dutch East India Company during the Eighteenth Century*, pp. 6–8.

16 Letter to N. van Reigersberch 1640, 9 juni. Hugo de Groot, *Briefwisseling van Hugo Grotius*, Vol. XI, nr. 4687.

17 J.C. van Leur, *Indonesian Trade and Society* (1967).

18 André Gunder Frank, *Reorient* (1988).

19 See, for instance, N. Steensgaard, 'The Companies as a specific Institution in the History of European Expansion' in L. Blussé and F.S. Gaastra (eds.), *Companies and Trade. Essays on Overseas Trading Companies during the Ancien Régime*, Leiden: Leiden University Press 1981, pp. 245–264.

20 François Valentijn, *Oud en Nieuw Oostindiën*, Vol. V-a, p. 25.

21 Bantam is nowadays called Banten. See Johan Talens, *Een feodale samenleving in koloniaal vaarwater. Staatsvorming, koloniale expansie en economische onderontwikkeling in Bantam, West-Java (1600–1750).*

22 H.A. Breuning, *Het voormalige Batavia*, p. 18.

23 As W.E. Wertheim put it, 'The Company stepped in the place of oriental port rulers', *Indonesië van vorstenrijk tot neo-kolonie*, p. 20.

24 Leonard Blussé, 'Amongst Feigned Friends and Declared Enemies' in Solvi Sogner ed., *Making Sense of*

Global History. Oslo: Universitetsforlaget 2002. pp. 154–168.

25 Remco Raben, *Batavia and Colombo. The Ethnic and Social Spatial Order of Two Colonial Cities 1600–1800.*

26 Bondan Kanumoyoso, *Beyond the City Wall. Society and Economic Development in the Ommelanden of Batavia 1684–1740.*

27 P. Meijer, *Verzameling van Instructiën, Ordonnanciën en Reglementen voor de Regering van Nederlandsch Indië.* 'Ordonnancie en instructie', August 22, 1617, Artikel 74, p. 44.

28 See Leonard Blussé, *Strange Company, Chinese Settlers, Mestizo Women and the Dutch in voc Batavia*, pp. 75–96.

29 Gerret Vermeulen, *Gedenkwaardige Voyagie naar Oost-Indiën 1668–1674.* Cited in J. Semmelink, *Geschiedenis der cholera in Oost-Indië voor 1817*, p. 334.

30 F. Valentijn, *Oud en Nieuw Oost-Indiën* Vol. IV, p. 230.

31 For security's sake, Javanese were not allowed to live in the city.

32 J.S. Furnival, *Netherlands India, a Study of Plural Economy.*

33 Bodo Wiethoff, *Die Chinesische Seeverbotspolitik und der private Űberseehandel von 1368 bis 1567.*

34 The Fujianese mandarin Zhang Xie was commissioned by the imperial court to write this treaty.

35 Xu Guanmian, *Pepper to Sea Cucumbers. Chinese Gustatory Revolution in Global History*, 900–1840.

36 See the local gazetteer of Amoy. Zhou Kai, *Xiamen zhi*, Vol. 2, *shang chuan* (trading ships) section', pp. 166–179.

37 Leonard Blussé, 'Trojan Horse of Lead: the Picis in Early 17th Century Java', in: *Strange Company*, pp. 35–48.

38 'Around the city of Manila live more than 20.000 families, mostly Chinese but also Japanese and the natives of the country. The Castilians, living within the walls of this city, levy tribute, taxes and other emoluments on these people, to maintain themselves'. H.T. Colenbrander, *Jan Pietersz. Coen, Levensbeschrijving*, p. 641.

39 For the Formosan case, see Tonio Andrade, *How Taiwan Became Chinese, Dutch, Spanish, and Han Colonization in the Seventeenth Century.* New York, Columbia University Press 2009. But also elsewhere in Southeast Asia co-colonization occurred. See, for instance, Leonard Blussé, *Strange Company, Chinese Settlers, Mestizo Women and the Dutch in VOC Batavia.* Verhandelingen KITLV 122, Dordrecht 1986; Matthew J. Bowser, 'Partner in Empire, Co-Colonisation and the Rise of Anti-Indian Nationalism in Burma' in *Journal of Imperia; and Commonwealth History*, Vol. 49, 2021-1, pp. 118–147.

40 Andrade, *How Taiwan Became Chinese* describes this development in detail, pp. 122–125.

41 Letter of January 31, 1623, H.T. Colenbrander, Jan Pietersz. Coen, Bescheiden omtrent zijn bedrijf in Indië Vol. I, p. 293.

42 Blussé en Nie, *The Chinese Annals of Batavia*, 60. For Bencon's biography see B. Hoetink, 'So Bing Kong. Het eerste hoofd der Chinezen te Batavia' and 'Een Nalezing'.

43 Missive by Coen dated October 26, 1620 in De Jonge, *Opkomst* Vol. IV, p. 218, en Resolution October 9, 1620, p. 235. 'On the request of the Chinese community in our territory to lighten and liberate them from the corvée imposed on them for the strengthening of the fortress', October 9, 1620, *Plakaatboek* Vol. I, pp. 76–77.

44 For his biography, see Leonard Blussé: 'Testament to a Towkay', in: Leonard Blussé, *Strange Company*, pp. 49–72.

45 Placard of May 26, 1640 in Van der Chijs, *Plakaatboek* Vol. I, p. 438.

46 August 13, 1640, *Plakaatboek* Vol.I, p. 446.

47 May 15, 1648, *Plakaatboek* Vol. II, p. 123. A few years later the capital tax was imposed again. January 3, 1658, *Plakaatboek* Vol. II, pp. 25, 314.

48 The experiment with Chinese laborers in the Formosan sugar should have warned the Batavian government, because Caron's successors faced in 1652 a Chinese peasant rebellion. See Johannes Huber, 'Chinese settlers against the Dutch East India Company; The Rebellion led by Kuo Huai-i on Taiwan in 1652', in: E.B. Vermeer (red.), *Development and Decline of Fukien Province in the 17th and 18th Centuries*, pp. 265–296.

49 'Een smeekschrift van de Bataviasche burgerij', in: N.P. van den Bergh, *Uit de dagen der Compagnie*, pp. 30–63.

50 See J.K.J. de Jonge, *Opkomst van het Nederlandsch gezag in Oost-Indië* Vol. VI, pp. vii–xxvi.

51 See Hoetink, 'Chinese officieren', p. 22

52 Blussé en Nie, *The Chinese Annals*, p. 73.

53 *Ibidem*,p. 72.

54 As a reward for his loyalty, Zheng Chenggong received from the Mingpretender to the throne the title Guoxingye, 'he who bears the name of the dynasty'. In the Minnan dialect of Fujian province, this honorary title was pronounced Koksengya.

55 Joan (ten), Margarita (eight), Govert (five), Catharina (four), Pieter jr. (18 months).

56 Adam Clulow, *Amboina, 1623*, p. 50.

57 Most of these exported slaves were captured in the frequent wars between the Balinese principalities.

58 Yves Giraud, *Voyages et aventures du Capitaine Ripon aux grandes Indes*, p. 146.

59 See Bataviase Statuten (1642): 'Slaeven ofte lijffeijgenen', in: *Plakaatboek* Vol. I, pp. 572–676.

60 F. de Haan, *Priangan* Vol. I, p. 3.

61 https://www.mdpi.com/2504-3900/83/1/60.

62 Jan Nieuhof (John Ogilby transl.), *An Embassy from the East India Company of the United Provinces to the Grand Tartar Cham Emperor of China*. London: John Macock 1669.

63 Martinus Martini, *Novus Atlas Sinensis.*(1655).

64 A quadrumvirate of regents at the court under the leadership of a Manchu nobleman, Oboi, suddenly turned against the presence of Catholic priests in China. All churches were closed, and the priests were banished to Macao. See Arthur W. Hummel, *Eminent Chinese of the Ch'ing Period (1644–1912)*, p. 891. Wills, *Embassies*, p. 91.

65 John E. Wills has described with some irony the naive Dutch attempts at rapprochement. John E. Wills, *Pepper, Guns, & Parleys. The Dutch East India Company and China, 1662–1681.*

66 'Rapport over Indische zaken aan de Staten Generaal', in: W.M. Ottow, *Rijckloff Volckertsz van Goens. De carrière van een diplomaat 1619–1655*, p. 226.

67 VOC 1269 (1669), 'Consideratiën of rapport wegens de Pekinse ambassade', f. 281.

68 Olfert Dapper, *Gedenkwaerdig Bedryf der Nederlandsche Oost-Indische Maetschappye, op de Kuste en in het Keizerrijk van Taising of Sina: Behelzende het tweede en derde Gesandschap*, p. 232.

69 Dapper, *Gedenkwaerdig Bedryf*, pp. 296, 334.

70 *Daghregister gehouden int Casteel Batavia anno 1668–69*, pp. 9–15.

71 VOC 1269 (1669) f. 273–302. 'Consideratiën off rapport wegens de Pekinse ambassade'.

72 Councilor Anthonio Hurdt succeeded him. This was the first time that Company troops moved into Java's interior. See H.J. de Graaf, *De expeditie van Anthonio Hurdt, Raad van Indië, als admiraal en superintendent naar de binnenlanden van Java, Sept.-Dec. 1678 volgens het journaal van Johan Jurgen Briel, secretaris.*

73 For the treaty's content, see *Bataviaas Daghregister anno 1677*, pp. 365–371.

74 'Preparatoire Consideratiën ende advys wegens de Nederlantse Colonie in dese Indische gewesten, tot examinatie en correctie voorgestelt aen d'Ed. heer Gouverneur Generael Joan Maetsuycker en d'Ed. Heeren Raden van Indië, door d'E. Pieter van Hoorn (1675), see De Jonge, *Opkomst* Vol. VI, pp. 130–147.

75 De Jonge, *Opkomst* Vol. VI, p. xxii.

76 De Jonge, *Opkomst* Vol. VI, p. xxxix.

77 Van Deventer, *Geschiedenis van de Nederlanders op Java*, p. 312.

78 'Eenige voorname eygenschappen van de ware Deugt, Voorsichtigheydt, Wysheydt en Volmaecktheydt, getrocken uyt den Chineschen Confucius.' He probably made use of the Latin translation by father Couplet.

79 Xu Guanmian, 'The "Perfect Map" of Widow Hiamtse: A Micro-Spatial History of Sugar Plantations in Early Modern Southeast Asia, 1685–1710', pp. 97–126.

80 J.W. de Klein, *Het Preangerstelsel (1677–1871) en zijn nawer*king, p. 13

81 14 Mayi 1686, 'Last voor de Bovenlandsche, Javaansche of andere hoofden en voor de Preangers', in: *Plakaatboek* Vol. III, pp. 177–178.

82 Van Dam, *Beschrijvinge, derde boek*, pp. 116–117.

83 23 July 1680, *Plakaatboek* Vol. III, p. 52.

84 Leonard Blussé, *Bitters Bonds*, p. 56.

85 An Kumar, *Surapati, Man and Legend: A Study of three babad traditions.*

86 Nonja Peters, *The Christian Slaves of Depok. A Colonial Tale Unravels.*

87 'Memorie van C. Chastelein van 30 juni 1708', in: J. Faes, *Geschiedenis particulier landbezit op Java*, Batavia, pp. 221–258.

88 De Jonge, *Opkomst* Vol.VIII, p. 132.

89 This practice is called *Bindungan.*

90 M. Peters, *De wijze koopman. Het wereldwijde onderzoek van Nicolaes Witsen (1641–1717), burgemeester en voc-bewindhebber van Amsterdam*, p. 231

91 The *Chinese Annals of Batavia* record the date as November 1718. Blussé and Nie, *The Chinese Annals*, pp. 100, 101.

92 See F.W. Stapel et al. (red.), *Indië schrijft zijn eigen geschiedenis*, pp. 94–95.

93 Leonard Blussé, 'Doctor at Sea: Chou Mei-yeh's Voyage to the West (1710–1711)' in Erica de Poorter (ed.), *As the Twig is Bent... Essays in Honour of Frits Vos*, pp. 7–30.

94 Petronella, the only surviving descendant of the Van Hoorn family, died in 1764, as the mistress of her country retreat, Rosendael Castle, near Arnhem. A charming sketch of her life can be found in Bea Brommer, *To My Dear Pieternelletje. Grandfather and Granddaughter in VOC Time, 1710–1720.*

95 Tsoa Wanjock/ Cai Huanyu. See B. Hoetink, 'Chineesche Officieren te Batavia', p. 29.

96 Quee Congko/ Guo Junge. See B. Hoetink, 'Chineesche Officieren te Batavia', pp. 31–33.

97 Leonard Blussé, *Strange Company*, 'The VOC and the Junk Trade to Batavia: a Problem in Administrative Control', pp. 97–155.

98 Gang Zhao, *The Qing Opening to the Ocean. Chinese Maritime Policies 1684–1757*, pp. 79–98.

99 Leonard Blussé, 'No boats to China. The Dutch East India Company and the changing pattern of the China Sea trade, 1635–1690', *Modern Asian Studies* 30–1(1996), pp. 51–76.

100 *Plakaatboek* III, May 21, 1690, pp. 262–269.

101 *Plakaatboek* IV, p. 16.

102 Blussé en Nie, *The Chinese Annals*, p. 96.

103 Valentijn, *Oud en Nieuw Oost-Indiën*, V-a, p. 250.

104 François Leguat, *De gevaarlijke en zeldzame Reyzen van den Heere F. Leguat met zijn bijhebbend Gezelschap naar twee Onbewoonde Oostindische Eylanden.*

105 Blussé en Nie, *The Chinese Annals*, p. 251.

106 *Ibidem*, pp. 74,75.

107 *Ibidem*, p. 92.

108 Many thanks are given to Dr. Irina Katkova who photographed these letters in the Russian Academy of Science in St Petersburg.

109 Unfortunately, this tombstone was badly damaged during the Cultural Revolution, but was recently restored to the extent possible.

110 For more details see Xu Guanmian, 'The Making of the Sino-Dutch Sugar Frontiers in Early Modern Asia'; N.P. van den Berg, 'De suikerindustrie op Java onder het bestuur van de Oost-Indische Compagnie', in: *Uit de dagen der Compagnie*, pp. 305–349.

111 Ulbe Bosma, *The World of Sugar. How the Sweet Stuff Transformed our Politics, Health and Environment over 2000 Years.* Cambridge: Harvard University Press 2023.

112 J. Mossel, *Aanmerkingen over de zuykermolens rondom Batavia, in 't Bantamse, Ceribonse, en langs Java*, December 31, 1750.

113 De Jonge, *Opkomst* VIII, pp. 324–327

114 'Uittreksel uit een rapport en uit bijlagen over de suikerindustrie in de Ommelanden van Batavia door de Raden van India Christoffel van Swoll en Hendrik Zwaardekroon, 20 juni 1710', in: De Jonge, *Opkomst*, pp. 157–165.

115 Letter to the Gentlemen XVII of February 10, 1708 in De Jonge, *Opkomst* VIII, p. 143.

116 F.S. Gaastra, *Bewind en beleid bij de voc 1672–702.* Zutphen: Walburg Pers 1989.

117 H.S. van Lennep, *Genealogie van het geslacht Valckenier 1512–1934*, Naarden 1983.

118 Bruijn, Gaastra, *Dutch-Asiatic Shipping*, vol. 2, p. 324. *Linschoten*, 804 ton. Departure from Texel October 22, 1714, at The Cape March 19, 1715 until April 19, 1715, arrival in Batavia June 23, 1715.

119 Valentijn, *Oud- en Nieuw Oost Indiën*, IV-a, p. 348.

120 De Jonge, *Opkomst* IX, pp. xvi, 34–37.

121 L.W.G. de Roo, 'De conspiratie van 1721', in *Tijdschrift voor Indische Taal-, Land- en Volkenkunde van het Koninklijk Bataviaasch Genootschap van Kunsten en Wetenschappen*, pp. 362–397.

122 B. van der Pol (ed.), *Mallabaarse Brieven. De brieven van de Friese predikant Jacobus Canter Visscher 1717–1725*, Zutphen: Walburg Pers 2008, p. 268.

123 Anonymous, *Verzameling van verscheide echte stukken/De DROOM*, p. 115

124 NA VOC 327, 'Patriase missieve', July 21, 1725. The directors surmised that the Javanese nobles would purchase fire weapons from the proceeds of the coffee deliveries.

125 Anonymous, *Verzameling van verscheide echte stukken/De DROOM*, p. 117.

126 The following paragraph is based on an article by H.J. de Graaf about Van Imhoff's letter: H.J. de Graaf, 'Gouverneur-generaal van Imhoff's broeder en de Académie de Marine', pp. 369–378.

127 Coolhaas, *Generale Missiven* VIII, p. 239.

128 NA 1.11.01.01, inv. 167, (ascribed to Wouter Hendrix) 'Memorie', p. 36.

129 Coolhaas, *Generale Missiven*, XI, p. 3.

130 Westfries archief, Oud Enkhuizer Archief 1535, 'Wederleggingen van ternedergestelde positiven in nevensstaande missive, 15 oktober 1740'.

131 De Jonge, *Opkomst* IX, p. 163.

132 For a summary of the tragic events in Ceylon, see Godée Molsbergen, *Geschiedenis van Nederlandsch-Indië* IV, pp. 121–136.

133 'After the sentence was pronounced, his clothes were stripped by the executioner and then, being tied backwards on a chair, his throat was cut with a curved knife, without causing the condemned any confusion, from his arrival at the place of execution until his death'. See Godée Molsbergen, *Geschiedenis van Nederlandsch Indië* IV, p. 136

134 Hendrix's devastating criticisms can be found in the anonymous and unfortunately incomplete 'Memorie' that Hendrix wrote after his return to the Netherlands. NA 1.11.01.01, inv. 167.

135 14 February 1732, Van Goor, *Generale Missiven* IX, p. 324.

136 Westfries Archief, OEA 1535.

137 NA VOC 1.04.02, inv. 328, *Patriase Missive*, September 14, 1731.

138 A.K.A. Gijsberti Hodenpijl, 'Het ontslag en het opontbod van den G.G. Mr. Diederik Durven op 9 october 1731', pp. 178–218. See also Westfries Archief, p 1010731–34, 'Specificaties van de pretenties van Durven'.

139 Had they known that he had been promoted to the position of water fiscal by Durven so that he could cash a hefty sum from the seizure of the English smuggler *Success* at the Batavian roadstead, they might have been less indulgent.

140 NA 1.11.01.01, inv. 167. 'Memorie', p. 3: 'Over the past few years they (the Directors in Holland) have maliciously done their utmost to deal the final stab to the Company.'

141 Vermeulen has sorted out this particular bone of contention. See *De Chineezen te Batavia*, pp. 50–51.

142 'The Essay on Diseases Incidental to Europeans in Hot Climates, with the Method of Preventing their Fatal Consequences, 1768' cited by Semmelink, *Geschiedenis der cholera*, p. 334.

143 De Jonge, *Opkomst* IX, p. 206.

144 March 31, 1738, Van Goor, *Generale Missiven* X, pp. 107–108.

145 Blussé en Nie, *The Chinese Annals*, p. 108.

146 Peter H. van der Brug, *Malaria en malaise: de VOC in Batavia in de achttiende eeuw.*

147 Van Gorkom, 'Ongezond Batavia', p. 189.

148 August 18, 1729, VOC 327, Patriase Missive.

149 NA 1.11.01.01, inv. 167. Hendrix, 'Memorie', p. 50.

150 March 31, 1734, Van Goor, *Generale Missiven* IX, pp. 583–584.

151 Anonymous, 'Droom van de Opstand te Batavia', p. 134.

152 Johann Wolfgang Heydt, *Allerneuester geographisch-und topografischer Schau-Platz von Africa und Ost-Indien*; Claudine en Denys Lombard-Salmon, 'Paysage et exotisme à Batavia, la villa du gouverneur-général Valckenier (1737–1741)', pp. 103–117.

153 W.R. van Hoëvell, '"De moord der Chinezen in Batavia", een woord aan den heer A.J. van der Aa', p. 118.

154 Vermeulen, *De Chineezen te Batavia*, p. 47.

155 NA1.10.05.05, inv. 5, p. 267. Letter to Jan van Holst.

156 Four hundred crewmembers went down with their ships on September 17, 1737, VOC 329, *Patriase Missiven* 1737–1741.

157 NA 1.10.05.05, inv. 1, 2 (Registers with letters from family members and others), and 5 (Letterboek with letters to family members and others).

158 NA 1.10.05.05, inv. 1, Letter of October 4, 1738.

159 NA 1.10.05.05, inv.5, pp.593–594. Letter of February 2, 1739.

160 NA 1.10.05.05, inv.5, pp. 531–566. Letter of January 30, 1739.

161 Letter of December 20, 1736, *Het geslacht Nolthenius*, Vol. 2, p. 991.

162 Westfries Archief, OAE 1682–271, letter J.A. de Roode to Jan Minne, Batavia, October 24, 1735 (1010868).

163 Van Goor, *Generale Missiven* X, p. 388.

164 April 2, 1737. Van Goor, *Generale Missiven* IX, p. 829.

165 Lodewijk Wagenaar, Anke Galjaard, Marianne Nierop, Marleen Speelman (red.), *Gouverneur Van Imhoff op dienstreis in 1739. Naar Cochin, Travancore en Tuticorin, en terug over Jaffna en Mannar naar Colombo (zondag 25 januari tot zaterdag 18 april).* Zutphen: Walburg Pers 2007.

166 December 15, 1738. H. van Malsen, 'Briefwisseling van den Gouverneur-generaal Gustaaf Willem baron Van Imhoff met den advocaat-fiscaal der Amsterdamsche Admiraliteit enz., Jacob Boreel Janszoon (1738–1750)', p. 325.

167 October 1, 1740. Van Malsen, 'Briefwisseling', p. 333. Publius Terentius Afer (ca. 195 BC-159 BC) was a Latin play writer.

168 For the full English translation, see Blussé and Nie, *The Chinese Annals of Batavia*, pp. 205–218.

169 See *Zhangzhou fuzhi*, 1878 edition, *juan* 49, pp. 31a, b.

170 Anonymous, *Droom van de opstand te Batavia*, p. 130.

171 Salt fish, called *karwaat* in South African, stems probably from Portugese cravado.

172 Discussed in the Council of the Indies on December 30, 1729 and sent to the Company directors as an attachment to the General Missive of January 31. Van Goor, *Generale Missiven* IX, p. 91.

173 NA 1.11.01.01. 'Memorie', pp. 173–191.

174 NA 1.04.02 VOC 329. 'Patriase Missiven' 1737–1741, September 4, 1739

175 The term 'informal empire' is used as it was introduced by the British historians, Ronal Robinson and John Gallaghe. See Ronald Robinson, 'Non-European Foundations of European Imperialism: Sketch for a Theory of Collaboration', pp. 117–140

176 Van Deventer, *Geschiedenis van de Nederlanders op Java*, Vol. I, p. 102.

177 Peter Carey has analyzed this situation in a slightly later period in Javanese history: 'Changing Javanese Perceptions of the Chinese Communities in Central Java, 1755–1825', pp. 1–47.

178 Luc Nagtegaal, *Riding the Dutch Tiger, The Dutch East India Company and the Northeast Coast of Java, 1680–1743.*

179 Joan van Hoorn, 'Corte Beschryvinge van het Noord-Oostelijckste gedeelte van Java's opkomst ende voortgangh' (1700–1703), Manuscript collection KITLV, Leiden No.H 73, pp. 15, 31–32.

180 May 23, 1740. See Gijsberti Hodenpijl, 'Govert Cnoll', 4. 23 mei 1710.

181 Van Goor, *Generale Missiven* IX, December 31, 1736, p. 789.

182 J. de Hullu, 'Over den Chinaschen handel der Oost-Indische Compagnie in de eerste dertig jaar van de 18de eeuw'.

183 NA VOC 2216, March 17, 1733. 'Consideratiën van de Raad ordinaris Blom belangende den Chinesen handel', f. 6596–6607.

184 Blussé en Nie, *The Chinese Annals of Batavia*, p. 108.

185 P. de Roo de la Faille, 'De Chineesche Raad te Batavia en het door dit college beheerde fonds', pp. 302–324.

186 Ni Hoekong was appointed on September 11, 1736. For his biography, see Hoetink, 'Ni Hoekong. Kapitein der Chinezen te Batavia in 1740', pp. 447–518.

187 Blussé en Nie, *Chinese Annals*, p. 122.

188 Blussé en Nie, *Chinese Annals*, p. 122.

189 Krom, Van Imhoff, p. 57.

190 July 8, 1740, NA VOC 765, 'Resoluties Gouverneur-generaal en Raden', f. 776; 11 July, f. 852; July 25, f. 780, f.781.

191 July 25, 1740, NA VOC 765, 'Resoluties Gouverneur-generaal en Raden', f. 781.

192 NA 1.11.01.01, inv. 165, (e) Verweerschrift aan de gecommitteerde bewindhebbers van Joan Paul Schaghen, oud-Directeur-generaal van Indien mitsgaders admiraal der laatste retourvloot in het verleden jaar gearriveerd.

193 NA 1.11.01.01. 173.d. 'Relaas wegens het voorgevallene gedurende den opstand en ontstane rebellie mitsgaders het gesmeede verraad door de Chineese natie tegens de Nederlandsche Oostindische maatschappij en dies hooftstad Batavia met den resorte van dien, een begin neemende met den 26 september 1740 tot eind december 1740'. (Account of what had happened during the rebellion and the treason by the Chinese nation against the Netherlands East India Company and its capital Batavia and environment beginning on September 26, 1740 until the end of December 1740).

194 *DROOM; waar in veele aanmerkelijke zaaken voorkomen*, p. 113

195 Correctly argues Remco Raben that these are the questions that should be posed and answered first. See his 'De Chinese Oorlog in Batavia in 1740', pp. 106–123.

196 W.G.J. Remmelink, *The Chinese War and the Collapse of the Javanese State, 1725–1743*.

197 J. Rusconi, *Sjaír Kompeni welanda berberang dengan Tjina*; Willem Remmelink, *Babad Tanah Jawi, The Cronicle of Java, The Revised Prose Version of C.F. Winter sr.*

198 Wolfram Eberhard, *Conquerors and Rulers. Social Forces in Medieval China*, pp. 100–103.

199 Philip A. Kuhn, *Rebellion and Its Enemies in Late Imperial China. Militarization and Social Structure, 1796–1864*.

200 James Bunyan Parsons, *Peasant Rebellions of the Late Ming Dynasty*, pp. 192–193.

201 During the eighteenth and nineteenth centuries, secret societies or Triads directed against the Manchu regime also figured predominantly in the organization of South China's rural movements, but they do not seem to have done so in the Ommelanden of the early eighteenth century.

202 Remmelink, *Babad Tanah Jawi*, p. 308.

203 The following is a collage of Governor-General Adriaan Valckenier's report: 'Account of the Rebellion of the Chinese beginning on Monday 25 July and ending on Monday 10 October 1740' (NA 1.11.01.01, inv. 173) and the following anonymous broadsheets: (A) Kort dagverhaal van het gepasseerde in de Generale Revolte en verraad door de Chinesen; (B) Kort Relaas van het gepasseerde in de Chineese Revolte; (C) Nader en omstandig Dagverhaal wegens het gepasseerde omtrent den opstant en conspiratie der Chineesen; (D) Omstandig en allernaeuwkeurigst verhaal van den oorsprong, begin, voortgang en gelukkige ontdekkinge van het vervloekt en schelms verraadt; (E) Relaas van het voorgevallene met de rebelleerende Chineesen; (F) Verhaal van het verraad of opstand der Chinesen; (G) Chineezenmoord te Batavia, 1740; (H) Batavia's beroerte ofte oorlog der Chineezen, met de Europeezen; (I) Verzameling van verscheide echte stukken van Batavia herwaards gezonden; DROOM; waar in veele aanmerkelijke zaaken voorkomen; (J) Korte schets wegens het vervloekt verraat gesmeet door den Cinees luytenant genaamt Niloko in 't jaar 1737.

204 Vermeulen, *De Chineezen te Batavia*, p. 56.

205 NA 1.11.01.01, inv. 113, 'Taij Oeywansoeij zend desen brieff met groetenisse aan den Edelen Capitein Toalang'.

206 The contents of this letter were a matter of disagreement. In an alternative version of the letter, 'Translation of a Chinese letter written in the name of the field commander Tay Wansoey of the house of Oeij, who intends to attack Batavia with the use of arms, addressed to the Captain of the Chinese here', the Chinese commander insists that 'a country, however large, must be lost if it is not properly governed'. He states: 'The present Chinese Emperor, with a small and almost unremarkable force of sixty thousand men, overcame the great Chinese Empire, since there was

then a bad and foolish government in China' and then goes on to argue that in comparison with China, 'Batavia is small and impotent, and I can no longer bear the thought of so few Dutchmen oppressing so many Chinese so heartlessly and so unjustly, that the Chinese nation feels compelled to unite and declare war on the Dutch.' NA 1.11.01.01, inv. 113,33.

207 Pamphlet (A), p. 13.

208 Blussé and Nie, *Chinese Annals*, p. 132.

209 NA VOC 2486, Attachment to Adriaan Valckenier's secret letter to the Gentlemen XVII dd October 31, 3774–80. De Jonge, *Opkomst* IX, pp. 325–328.

210 NA 1.11.01.01, inv.174 c.

211 Testimony on November 4, 1740. NA 1.11.01.01, 10.

212 'Dagregister van het gepasseerde in den Optocht van de Compagnies Krijgsmacht, onder Kapitein Crummel' in *Verzameling van Verscheide echte stukken van Batavia herwaards gezonden.*

213 Here the insurgents followed the strategy of the renowned Chinese general, Tian Dan, who defended the city of Jimo against an attack by the army of Yan. He gathered all the city's cattle, attached sharp knives to
their horns, poured fat over their tails, and lit them on fire. He chased them all at once at the besiegers who fled in panic. Harro von Senger: *36 Strategeme: Lebens- und Überlebenslisten aus drei Jahrtausenden*, vol. 2, p. 176.

214 Leiden University Library, Manuscript collection. BPL 969, letter of Th. Reverhorst to family members and friends, January 10, 1741.

215 The pamphlets and broadsheets referred to in note 188 of chapter 13.

216 He referred to the decision to order the indiscriminate arrest of suspected Chinese in the Ommelanden.

217 Pamphlet (D) 'Omstandig en allernaeuwkeurigst verhaal', pp. 8–9.

218 Small indigenous boat.

219 Thedens and Van Imhoff watched over Diestpoort at the bend of the Great River on the southwest side where many Chinese lived in the adjacent southern suburb. Guillot and Van Berendrecht were given supervision of the nearby Nieuwpoort. Van Schinne and Lakeman kept watch over the surroundings of the Utrechtpoort on the west side. Van Suchtelen and Chavonnes controlled the Rotterdampoort on the east side, and Crul and Maccaré kept an eye on the Waterpoort on the north side. Nolthenius and Van Aerden were stationed with Valckenier and Schaghen in the Castle.

220 Leiden University Library, Manuscript Department. BPL 969 letter of January 10, 1741, p. 13.

221 Pamphlet (A), 'Kort dagverhaal', p. 14.

222 This is not true. Valckenier remained at the Castle.

223 Schwarz, *Reise in Ost-Indien*, p. 110.

224 Pamphlet (C), Nader en Omstandig Dagverhaal, p. 6.

225 Nolthenius, *Het geslacht Nolthenius*, p. 514.

226 Pamflet (E), Relaas van het voorgevallene, p. 12

227 According to local tradition, the Angke-river derives its name from the bloodbath. In China's Minnan dialect, Angke indeed reads as 'Red stream'. The name is, however, of Malay origin.

228 Leiden University Library, Manuscript Department. BPL 969 brief January 10, 1741, p.5.

229 Vermeulen, *De Chineezen te Batavia*, p. 103.

230 See Hans Gooszen, *Population Census in VOC-Batavia 1673–1792.* Intercontinenta series No. 25, Leiden: CNWS 2002.

231 Letter by Daniël Nolthenius (Batavia, November, 10 1740) to his brother Balthazar (Amsterdam). In Nolthenius, *Het geslacht Nolthenius*, p. 514

232 Before the rebellion 4954 males, 2540 females and 3273 minors. In 1741 707 males, 549 females and 570 minors.

233 NA 1. 10.01.01, inv. 113, cc t/m ff. 'Artikelen en vraagpoincten'. See the interrogations held on October 1, 1742, figuring Henry Abbis, Elisabeth Anna van Driel, widow of the supervisor of the Chinese hospital, Fortuijn van Boegies (manumitted slave), November van Bengalen, slave of Anna van Driel. Livinus de Heere, warden of the municipal jail, Paulus van den Boogaart, town surgeon, Andries Retting, warden of the Company's jail and others.

234 NA 1.11.01.01, inv. 113, rr, 'Artikelen en vraagpoincten, Abraham Abeleven, coopman en groot cassier'.

235 See, for instance, Timothy Snyder, *Bloodlands. Europe Between Hitler and Stalin*; John Roosa, *Pretext for Mass Murder. The September 30th Movement and Suharto's Coup d'État in Indonesia.*

236 'Akte van amnestie voor de Chinezen', in *Plakaatboek* IV, pp. 510–515.

237 Pamphlet (A) 'Kort dagverhaal van het gepasseerde in de Generale Revolte en verraad door de Chinesen aangevangen om de Stadt Batavia te overrompelen en al hetgeen Christen was te vermoorden. Beginnende met den 6en October 1740 tot den 11en derselver Maand'. Manuscript Westfries Archief.

238 NA VOC 767, *Resolutions Governor General and Council of the Indies*, f. 1530.

239 Remmelink, *Babad Tanah Jawi*, p. 309.

240 Vermeulen devotes a full chapter to this subject and concludes that there is no evidence that Valckenier ordered the massacre. Vermeulen, *De Chineezen te Batavia*, pp. 93–106.

241 *Plakaatboek* IV, p. 513. Letter Gentlemen XVII, dd November 16, 1742, see Vermeulen, *De Chineezen te Batavia*, p. 105.

242 Amnesty act in *DROOM*, p. 68.

243 Leiden University Library, Manuscript Department, BPL 969. Tweede brief van Reverhorst.

244 Westfries Archief, OAE 1533, January 10, 1741, J. de Roode to Jan van Minne.

245 NA Archief Valckenier 1.10.05.05, inv. 37.

246 The following paragraphs are based on the 'Precise Account of the violent arrest of three ordinary councilors of the Indies' (Naukeurig Verhaal van het gepasseerde bij de Geweldadige Arresteering der drie Ordinaire Raaden van India); see Pamphlet (I), 'Verzameling van verscheide echte stukken', pp. 73–104.

247 Leiden University Library, Manuscript Department, UB Leiden, BPL 969. 'Brieven Reverhorst'. January 10, 1741.

248 NA VOC 329, ; Patriase Missive', December 2, 1740.

249 Letter by Daniël Nolthenius to the Amsterdam Company director Dirck Trip, December 6, 1741 in Nolthenius, *Het geslacht Nolthenius*, p. 1021

250 He had succeeded his father Johannes Swellengrebel.

251 Placard March 14/16, 1741, *Plakaatboek* IV, p. 525; March 25, 1741. Van Goor, *Generale Missiven* X, p. 627.

252 NA 1.10.05.05, inv. 97 en 98.

253 NA 1.10.05.05, inv. 97 en 98.

254 In his biography of Ni Hoekong, Hoetink has described the following proceedings in great detail: 'Ni Hoekong. Kapitein der Chinezen te Batavia in 1740', pp. 447–518.

255 During the Republic, torture was a widely used means of bringing a suspect to a confession. It was not until 1798 that these torture practices were abolished.

256 Blussé and Nie, *Chinese Annals*, pp. 123–124.

257 NA 1.11.01.01, inv. 175, 'Relaas gedaan aan de oud schepen Augustinus Thornton door de Radens Badjo en Soera Ringga mitsgaders Sandi, lijfeigene van den Panembahan Bantam, 6 maart 1741'.

258 Vermeulen, *De Chineezen te Batavia*, p. 86.

259 W.G.J. Remmelink, *The Chinese War and the Collapse of the Javanese State, 1725–1743*, p. 12

260 Blussé and Nie, *The Chinese Annals*, p. 137.

261 March 3, 1741, 'Aanwijzing van de zuider-voorstad, blok O, te Batavia voor de Chinesche kamp aldaar', *Plakaatboek* IV, p. 522.

262 January 10, 1745, Van Goor, *Generale Missiven* X, p. 564.

263 Vermeulen, *De Chineezen te Batavia*, pp. 133–134.

264 'Brief aan den keizer van China, geschreeven binnen het Kasteel van de Stad Batavia op den 30 dag van de Maand April, in het Jaar 1741', in: S. Kalff, *OostIndisch Landjuweel*, pp. 180–183.

265 NA 1.11.01.01 Aanwinsten 165.

266 For translations of four different reports to the crown, i.e., one from Cai Xin, a high mandarin from Fujian, two sent by military officers from Fujian, and one from the censor, Li Qingfang, who had been asked to investigate "why trade with the southern seas should not be prohibited", see Blussé and Nie, *The Chinese Annals*, pp. 215–228. For the discussion at the court, see Jennifer Cushman, 'Duke Ch'ing-fu deliberates: a mid-eighteenth century reassessment of Sino-Nanyang commercial relations'.

267 For a biography of Cai Xin (Ts'ai Hsin), see Arthur W. Hummel (red.), *Eminent Chinese of the Ch'ing Period (1644–1912)*, p. 734.

268 Fu Lo-shu, *A Documentary Chronicle of Sino-Western Relations (1644–1820)*, p. 174

269 The following is based on P.A. Leupe, 'De raden van Indië Van Imhoff, De Hase en Van Schinne in Holland, 1741–1742', pp. 361–370.

270 The original charter was granted in 1602. It was renewed every 21 years until the Company was dissolved in 1799.

271 *Extract uyt het Register der Resolutien van de Hoog Mogende Heeren Staten Generaal der Verenigde Nederlanden*, October 30, 1741.

272 'Consideratiën over de tegenwoordigen staat van de Nederlandsche Oost-Indische Maatschappij met relatie voornamentlijk tot haar bestier, handel, scheepvaart en huishoudinge in Indiën, vervat in eenige poincten meer dan andere van opmerkinge ter aantoninge van het algemeen verval harer zaken en op wat wijse men deselve veel ligt zou kunnen redresseeren. See J.E. Heeres, 'De "Consideratiën" van Van Imhoff', pp. 441–621.

273 E.M. Jacobs, Merchant in Asia, pp. 400–404.

274 March 25, 1741. NA 1.10.05.05, inv. 38.

275 Second Letter written to his friends in Leiden, Leiden University Library, Manuscript department, BPL 617, p. 5.

276 Letter of Hackenberg to Cornelis Hop. NA 2.21.041, Collection G.M. van der Linden, inv. 95, Cape of Good Hope, March 14, 1742,

277 Van Malsem, *Waterland*, p. 103. Valckenier was invoking Solon of Athens (636–558 v.Chr.) the famous legislator.

278 Jan Minne to Nicolaas van Berendregt, April 30, 1742. See Herman de Vos, *Met sneejagt en kake van wint*, p. 110. Letter T 54.

279 Van Imhoff is here referring to the famous Thermopylae pass, where the Spartan hero, Leonidas, with a hundred warriors was able to block the advancing Persian army for three days.

280 *Plakaatboek* V, pp. 4–7.

281 Blussé and Nie, *The Chinese Annals*, pp. 139–140.

282 Krom, *Van Imhoff*, p. 145.

283 NA VOC 11149. 'Stukken betreffende verkoop in Batavia van de lading van de Hercules, Jason en Dauphin 1745–1753.

284 M.C. Ricklefs, *Jogjakarta under Sultan Mangkubumi 1749–1792, A History of the Division of Java.*

285 Johan Talens, *Een feodale samenleving in koloniaal vaarwater. Staatsvorming, koloniale expansie en economische onderontwikkeling in Banten, West-Java (1600–1750).*

286 May 21, 1745, *Plakaatboek* V, pp. 257–258.

287 Ng Chin-keong, 'The Case of Ch'en I-lao: Maritime Trade and Overseas Chinese in Ch'ing Policies, 1717–1754', in: Roderich Ptak en Dietmar Rothermund (eds.), *Emporia, Commodities and Entrepreneurs in Asian Maritime Trade, c. 1400–1750*, pp. 373–400.

288 Comment by Lin Cuipu at the occasion of Van Imhoff's death in 1750. Blussé and Nie, *Chinese Annals*, p. 138.

289 Nowhere in the archives of the Court of Holland have I been able to find traces of this civil case.

290 1.Kings 2:41–46. King Solomon ordered Simei to remain in Jerusalem on penalty of death. Several years later, when Simei left the city gate to seize a fled slave, he was arrested and executed by order of the king.

291 For the following, I have made use of the records of the trial in the Valckenier Archives NA 1,10.01.01 and other acquisitions in the National Archives at The Hague, the Van de Poll family archive, J.K.J. De Jonge's observations in his magnum opus *Opkomst van het Nederlandsch gezag over Java*, Vol. X: pp. xciii-ci, and the interesting article by the nineteenth-century jurist, A.G.M. Krabbe, "Overzigt der criminele procedures voor den Raad van Justitie te Batavia" (Survey of the criminal procedures of the Council of Justice at Batavia).

292 NA 1.10.01.01, inv. 11, June 29, 1743.

293 NA 1.10.01.01, inv. 12, October 30, 1743.

294 In the aftermath, the public prosecutor, Rosenboom, waived his demand for the death penalty because it was not clear to what extent Phillips had in fact carried out orders from higher up. We need pay no further attention to his case because the man died on August 4, 1745 before he was sentenced.

295 NA1.10.75.01, family archive Van Schinne, inv. 15, March 31, 1748.

296 Willem Fockens to A.A. van Iddekinge, September 28, 1751. In: G.J. Schutte, *Seer teder beminde heer vader*, p. 151.

297 September 9, 1749, NA 1.01.50, inv. 1158, *Stadhouderlijke Secretarie.*

298 Fred Jagtenberg, *Willem IV, Stadhouder in roerige tijden*, p. 786.

299 Krom, *Van Imhoff*, p. 150.

300 A fine copy of his will is preserved in the manuscript collection of the Leiden University library, BPL 617, first portfolio, inv. 4.

301 N. MacLeod, 'Uit de geschiedenis', II, *Indische Gids* (1909), p. 1750.

302 Letter by R. de Laver in Van de Poll archive.

303 NA 1.04.02 VOC 56, Resolutions of the Gentlemen XVII.

304 The majestic house at Herengracht 479.

305 Norbert Middelkoop, 'Faits divers, enkele illustraties bij de Kroniek van Jacob Bicker Raye (1703–1777)', in: *Jaarboek Amstelodamum* 104 (2012), pp. 8–34.

306 J.K. Galbraith, *Name-Dropping*, p. 194.

Acknowledgements

The Dutch version of this book was published in the spring of 2023. In addition to Madelon de Keizer, Arend de Roever, Willem Remmelink, Lodewijk Wagenaar and Ellen Kramer, to whom I owe a special debt of gratitude, I would like to thank Felipe Fernandez Armesto, Lincoln Paine and Manjusha Kuruppath, who critically read and commented on the first version of my translation. Thanks to them, the original text has been revised and adapted for English readers.

This book was conceived during the Covid period, when I had to work with material collected over time, and sources in the Dutch National Archives that were available on the Internet. In addition, a tin box containing a batch of personal papers of Governor-General Valckenier and his son was placed at my disposal by their heirs, Willem van de Poll and Henrick van Lennep. These papers have since been added to the Valckenier family collection at the National Archives in The Hague.

For this publication, Arman Haye kindly came out of retirement to prepare helpful maps. Saskia Gieling and her able staff at Leiden University Press ensured the speedy and efficient production of the manuscript after the project had lain dormant for a year.

Finally, over the past two years, enormous progress has been made in the exploration of the VOC archives by the GLOBALISE team at the Huygens Research Institute in Amsterdam. Thanks to their work, and thanks to the increased access to serious archival research at the National Archives of the Republic of Indonesia (ANRI) as a result of the TANAP project, a rich variety of data on the history of Batavia will become available. I am confident that hitherto largely untapped sources such as the notarial archives and the so-called *verzoekschriften* (petitions) will make it possible to closely examine various aspects of the 'Batavian Fury' and its impact on those involved.

Bibliography

Anonymous Pamplets

A) *Kort dagverhaal van het gepasseerde in de Generale Revolte en verraad door de Chinesen aangevangen om de Stadt Batavia te overrompelen en al hetgeen Christen was te vermoorden Beginnende met den 6en October 1740 tot den 11en derselver Maand.* Manuscript Westfries Archief.

B) *Kort Relaas van het gepasseerde in de Chineese Revolte in de Maand van October Anno 1740.* ANRI Jakarta Batavia 246: 99-119.

C) *Nader en omstandig Dagverhaal wegens het gepasseerde omtrent den opstant en conspiratie der Chineesen te Batavia in den jaare 1740* . Amsterdam: Jan van Houten 1741.

D) *Omstandig en allernaeuwkeurigst verhaal van den oorsprong, begin, voortgang en gelukkige ontdekkinge van het vervloekt en schelms verraadt, ... behelzende een dagverhaal van omtrent twee maenden tyts, beginnende met den 26. september 1740, en vervolgens door een zeer aenzienlyk Heer met de laetste retour-schepen overgezonden.* Utrecht: Johannes Evelt z.d.

E) *Relaas van het voorgevallene met de rebelleerende Chineesen op Batavia in den jaar 1740.* Manuscript. Westfries Archief.

F) *Verhaal van het verraad of opstand der Chinesen soo binnen als buijten de Stadt Batavia.* ANRI, Jakarta, nr. 246, pp. 35-45.

G) *Chineezenmoord te Batavia,* 'Suringar manuscript', Kongkoan archief, Universiteitsbibliotheek Leiden.

H) *Batavia's beroerte ofte oorlog der Chineezen, met de Europeezen, waarin vertoond wordt, hoe d'Hollanders als op het point stonden om gedestrueerd te worden. Alles naar het origineele gecopieert door N.N.*, in: *Lamsrust* 1741.

I) *VERZAMELING van verscheide echte STUKKEN van BATAVIA herwaards gezonden: Concerneerende den OPSTAND der CHINEEZEN buiten, en de daar op gevolgde gruwelijke MASSACRE binnen gemelde stad bestaande in I. KORT RELAAS van den OPSTAND en 't geen grootdeels binnen de stad is voorgevallen. II. DAGREGISTER van het gepasseerde in den optocht van de Compagnies Krijgsmacht, onder Kapitein Jan George Crummel. III ACTE VAN AMNESTIE. IV Naukeurig verhaal van de geweldadige ARRESTEERING der drie Ordinaire Raaden van lndie enz. v. DROOM; waar in veele aanmerkelijke zaaken voorkomen, tot opheldering van de voorgaande stukken enz.* Dordt: Van Braam z.d.

J) *Korte schets wegens het vervloekt verraat gesmeet door den Cinees luytenant genaamt Niloko in't jaar 1737 ...* Manuscript in possesion of C.A. Valenbreder.

Books and articles

Susan Abeyasekere, 'Slaves in Batavia: Insights from a Slave Register' in: Anthony Reid (ed.), *Slavery, Bondage & Dependency in Southeast Asia.* St Lucia: University of Queensland Press 1983, pp. 286-314.

Julia Adams, *The Familial State, Ruling Families and Merchant Capitalism in Early Modem Europe.* lthaca: Cornell University Press 2005.

Aad van Amstel, *Barbaren, rebellen en mandarijnen. De VOC in de slag met China in de Gouden eeuw.* Amsterdam: Thoeris 2011.

S. Arasaratnam, 'Baron van lmhoff and Dutch Policy in Ceylon 1736-1740', in: *Bijdragen Koninklijk Instituut (BKI)* (1962)118-4: pp. 454-468.

Reggie Baay, *Daar werd wat gruwelijks verricht. Slavernij in Nederlands-Indië.* Amsterdam: Athenaeum-Polak & Van Gennep 2015.

J.F.L. de Balbian Verster, *Burgemeesters van Amsterdam in de 17e en 18e eeuw.* Zutphen: Thieme 1931.

G.L. Balk. F. van Dijk, D.J. Kortlang (eds.), *The Archives of the Dutch East India Company (VOC) and the Local Institutions* in *Batavia. Arsip Nasional Republik lndonesia.* Leiden: Brill 2007.

N.P. van den Berg, *Uit de dagen der Compagnie, geschiedkundige schetsen.* Haarlem: Tjeenk Willink & Zoon 1904.

Ray Allen Billington, *The Genesis of the Frontier Thesis. A Study in Historical Creativity.* San Marino: The Huntington Library 1971.

Leonard Blussé, *Strange Company, Chinese Settlers, Mestizo Women and the Dutch in VOC Batavia.* Verhandelingen KITLV 122, Dordrecht 1986.

Leonard Blussé, 'Doctor at Sea: Chou Mei-yeh's voyage to the West (1710-17II)' in Erica de Poorter (ed.), As *the Twig* is *Bent ... Essays in Honour of Frits Vos,* Amsterdam 1990, pp. 7-30.

Leonard Blussé, 'No boats to China. The Dutch East India Company and the changing pattern of the China Sea trade, 1635-1690', *Modern Asian Studies* 30-1 (1996), pp. 51-76.

Leonard Blussé, 'Amongst Feigned Friends and Declared Enemies' in: Solvi Sogner (ed.), *Making Sense of Global History.* Oslo: Universitetsforlaget 2002. pp. 154-168,

Leonard Blussé and Chen Menghong (ed.), *The Archives of the Kong Kaan of Batavia.* Leiden: Brill 2003.

Leonard Blussé, 'Junks to Java: Chinese shipping to the Nanyang in the second half of the Eighteenth Century', in: Eric Tagliacozzo en Chang Wen-Chin (ed.), *Chinese Circulations, Capital. Commodities and Networks in Southeast Asia.* Durham: Duke UP 2011. pp. 221-258.

Leonard Blussé, 'Jakarta: Erberveld-monument, de nieuwe kleren van de koningin van het oosten', in: Maarten Prak (ed.), *Plaatsen van herinnering, Nederland in de zeventiende en achttiende eeuw.* Amsterdam: Bert Bakker 2006: 390-399.

Leonard Blussé, 'Nevenactiviteiten overzee, Valckenier en Van lmhoff en de Chinezenmoord van 1740', in: Anita van Dissel, Maurits Ebben en Karwan Fatah-Black (eds.), *Reizen door het maritieme verleden van Nederland.* Zutphen: Walburg Pers2015, pp. 273-292.

Leonard Blussé and Nie Dening, *The Chinese Annals of Batavia, The Kai Ba Lidai Shiji* (开吧历代史纪) *and Other Stories (1610-1795),* Leiden: Brill Publishers 2018.

Leonard Blussé en Jaap de Moor, *Een Zwitsers leven in de tropen. De lotgevallen van kapitein Elie Ripon in dienst van de VOC (1616-1626).* Amsterdam: Prometheus 2016.

Leonard Blussé, 'On the Waterfront: Life and Labour around the Batavian Roadstead', in: Haneda Masashi (ed.), *Asian Port Cities 1600-1800, Local and Foreign Cultural Interactions.* Kyoto University Press 2009, 119-138.

Michèle Boin, 'The Kai Ba Lidai Shiji chronicle of the Chinese community in Batavia' in *Papers from the Third European Colloquium on Malay and Indonesian Studies* (Naples, 2-4 juni, 1981). Napoli: lnstituto Universitario Orientale 1988, pp. 29-41.

Bondan Kanumoyoso, *Beyond the City Wall. Society and Economic Development in the Ommelanden of Batavia 1684-1740.* Leiden: proefschrift 2011.

Machiel Bosman, *De polsslag van de stad. De Amsterdamse stadskroniek van Jacob Bicker Raije (1732-1772),* Amsterdam: Athenaeum-Polak & Van Gennep 2009.

S. van Brakel, 'Het Plattelandsbestuur Der Bataviaasche Ommelanden', in: G.W. Eysbers (ed.), *Bepalingen en instructiën voor het bestuur van de Buitendistricten van de Kaap de Goede Hoop.* Amsterdam: Johannes Müller 1922.

H.A. Breuning, *Het voormalige Batavia.* Amsterdam: Allert en de Lange 1954.

Bea Brommer, *To My Dear Pieternelletje. Grandfather and Granddaughter in VOC Time, 710-1720.* Leiden: Brill 2015.

Peter H. van der Brug, *Malaria en Malaise: de VOC in Batavia in de achttiende eeuw.* Amsterdam: De Bataafse Leeuw 1994.

Iris Bruijn, *Ship's Surgeons of the Dutch East India Company. Commerce and the Progress of Medicine in the Eighteenth Century.* Leiden: Leiden University Press 2009.

J.R. Bruijn, 'De personeelsbehoefte van de VOC overzee en aan boord, bezien in Aziatisch en Nederlands perspectief', in: *Bijdragen en Mededelingen betreffende de Geschiedenis der Nederlanden* (1976) 91: pp. 218-248.

J.R. Bruijn, F.S. Gaastra, l. Schöffer (eds.), *Dutch-Asiatic Shipping in the 17th and 18th Centuries.* 's-Gravenhage: Marinus Nijhoff 1979-87, 3 volumes.

J.R. Bruijn en J. Lucassen (eds.), *Op de schepen der Oost-Indische Compagnie. Vijf artikelen vanJ. de Hullu.* Groningen: Wolters-Noordhoff 1980.

P. van der Burg, *Curieuse beschrijving van de gelegenheid, zeden, godsdienst en ommegang van verscheijden Oost-Indische gewesten en machtige landschappen.* Rotterdam 1677.

Elias Canetti, *Masse und Macht.* Hamburg: Claassen 1960.

Peter Carey, 'Changing Javanese Perceptions of the Chinese Communities in Centra! Java, 1755-1825', in: *Indonesia,* 37 (1984): pp. 1-47.

Chen, Boyi, *Beyond the Land and Sea: Diasporic South Fujianese in Hội An, Batavia, and Manila, 1550-1850.* Unpublished PhD-thesis, St Louis: Washington University 2019.

Chen Menghong, *De Chinese gemeenschap van Batavia, 1843-1865. Een onderzoek naar het Kong Koan-archief.* Leiden: Leiden University Press 2011.

Jean Chesneaux, *Le mouvement paysan chinois: 1840-1949.* Paris: Editions du Seuil 1976.

J.A. van der Chijs, *Nederlandsch-Jndisch Plakaatboek 1602-1816.* Batavia: Landsdrukkerij 1885-1900, 17 volumes.

J.A. van der Chijs et al. (eds.), *Dagh-Register gehouden int Casteel Batavia vant passerende daer ter plaetse als over geheel Nederlandts-India.* 's-Gravenhage: Martinus Nijhoff 1887-1928, 21 volumes.

H.T. Colenbrander, *Koloniale geschiedenis.* 's-Gravenhage: Martinus Nijhoff 1925, 3 volumes.

H.T. Colenbrander, *Jan Pietersz. Coen, Levensbeschrijving.* 's-Gravenhage: Martinus Nijhoff 1934.

H.T. Colenbrander (ed.), *Jan Pietersz. Coen, Bescheiden omtrent zijn bedrijf in Indië.* 's-Gravenhage: Martinus Nijhoff 1919-34, 5 volumes.

W.Ph. Coolhaas, 'Zijn de Gouverneurs-Generaal Van lmhoff en Mossel juist beoordeeld?' in: *BKI* (1958) 114-1/2: pp. 29-54.

W.Ph. Coolhaas, J. van Goor et al. (eds.), *Generale Missiven van Gouverneurs-Generaal en Raden aan Heren XVII der Verenigde Oostindische Compagnie.* 's-Gravenhage 1960-2017, 14 volumes.

Jennifer Cushman, 'Duke Ch'ing-fu Deliberates: a mid-eighteenth-century reassessment of Sino-Nanyang commercial relations'. *Papers on Far Eastern History* 17. Canberra: ANU, 1978.

Pieter van Dam (F.W. Stapel [ed.]), *Beschryvinge van de Oostindische Compagnie.* (RGP Grote Serie No. 63, 68, 74, 75, 76, 83, 87, 96) 's-Gravenhage: RGP 1927-1954, 7 volumes.

Olfert Dapper, *Gedenkwaerdig Bedryf der Nederlandsche Oost-Indische Maetschappye op de Kuste en in het Keizerrijk van Taising of Sina: Behelzende het tweede en derde Gesandschap.* Amsterdam: Jacob van Meurs 1670.

Daradjadi, *Geger Pacinan 1740-1743: Persekutuan Tionghoa-Jawa melawan VOC.* Jakarta: Penerbit Buku Kompas 2013.

M.L. van Deventer, *Geschiedenis der Nederlanders op Java.* Haarlem: H.D. Tjeenk Willink n.d.

T. Dijkstra en T. Weststeijn, 'Constructing Confucius in the Low Countries', in: *De Zeventiende Eeuw. Cultuur in de Nederlanden in interdisciplinair perspectief* (2017) 32-2: pp. 137-164.

Hoesein Djajadiningrat, *Critische beschouwing van de Sadjarah-Banten, Bijdrage ter kenschetsing van de Javaansche geschiedschrijving.* Haarlem 1913.

Wolfram Eberhard, *Conquerors and Rulers. Social Forces in Medieval China.* Leiden: Brill 1965.

Isabella van Eeghen, "T dompelen van de lijcken', in: *Maandblad Amstelodamum* 1954, pp. 52-54.

Johan E. Elias, *Geschiedenis van het Amsterdamsche Regentenpatriciaat.* 's-Gravenhage: Martinus Nijhoff 1923.

Monique Erkelens, *The Decline of the Chinese Council of Batavia: The Loss of Prestige and Authority of the Traditional Elites amongst Chinese Community between 1900-42.* Unpublished PhD thesis, Leiden University 2013.

J. Faes, *Geschiedenis van het particulier landbezit op Java.* Batavia: Ogilvie 1893.

Carl Fredrik Feddersen, *Principled Pragmatism. VOC Interaction with Makassar 1637-68, and the Nature of Company Diplomacy.* Cappelen Damm Akademisk 2017.

J. Fox, '"For Good and Sufficient Reasons": An Examination of Early Dutch East India Company Ordinances on Slaves and Slavery' in: Anthony Reid (ed.), *Slavery, Bondage & Dependency in Southeast Asia.* St Lucia: University of Queensland Press 1983, pp.246-262.

Fu Lo-shu, *A Documentary Chronicle of Sino-Western Relations (1644-1820).* Tucson: University of Arizona Press 1966.

Fokky Fuad, 'Peristiwa *Chinese troubelen* di Batavia: Sebuah Tinjauan Sejarah Hukum', *Jurnal Ilmiah Mimbar Demokrasi,* vol. 12, nr. 2, April 2013.

J.S. Furnivall, *Netherlands India, a Study of Plural Economy.* Cambridge: Cambridge University Press 1939.

F.S. Gaastra, *Bewind en beleid bij de VOC, 1672-1702.* Zutphen: Walburg Pers 1989.

F.S. Gaastra, *The Dutch East-India Company.* Zutphen: Walburg Pers 2007.

F.S. Gaastra, 'De Amfioen Sociëteit. Een geprivilegieerde handelsmaatschappij onder de vleugels van de VOC, 1745-1794', in: M. Ebben en P. Wagenaar (eds.), *De cirkel doorbroken, opstellen over de Republiek,* Leidse historische studiën 10 (Leiden 2006): pp. 101-115.

J.F. Gebhard, *Het leven van Nicolaas Witsen (1641-1717).* Utrecht: J.W. Leeflang 1881-1882, 2 volumes.

Roelof van Gelder, *Het Oost-Indisch avontuur. Duitsers in dienst van de VOC.* Nijmegen: Sun 1997.

Kristof Glamann, *Dutch-Asiatic Trade 1620-1740.* 's-Gravenhage 1981.

E.C. Godée-Molsbergen, *De geschiedenis van Nederlandsch-Indië* (deel IV). Amsterdam: Uitgeverij Joost van den Vondel 1939.

W.J. Van Gorkom, 'Ongezond Batavia, vroeger en nu', in: *Geneeskundig Tijdschrift van Nederlandsch lndië"* (1913) 53, 177-227.

H.J. de Graaf, 'Gouverneur-generaal van lmhoff's broeder en de Académie de Marine', in: *BKI* (1951), pp. 369-378.

H.J. de Graaf, 'De gezichten van Oud-Batavia vanuit Zee', in: *Tijdschrift Bataviaasch Genootschap* LXIX (1929), pp. 237-53.

H.J. de Graaf (ed.), *De vijf gezantschapsreizen van Rijklof van Goens naar het hof van Mataram (1646-1654)*, werken Linschoten Vereeniging LIX 's-Gravenhage: Martinus Nijhoff 1956.

H.J. de Graaf, *De regering van Sunan Mangkurat 1 Tegal-Wangi, vorst van Mataram 1646-1677*. 's-Gravenhage: Martinus Nijhoff 1961-1962, 2 volumes.

W.P. Groeneveldt, *De Nederlanders in China. De eerste bemoeiingen om den handel in China en de vestiging in de Pescadores (1601-1624)*. 's-Gravenhage: Martinus Nijhoff 1898.

Hugo de Groot, (P.C. Molhuysen et al. [eds.]), *Briefwisseling van Hugo Grotius*. 's-Gravenhage: Martinus Nijhoff 1928-2001.

Claude Guillot, 'Urban patterns and polities in Malay trading cities, fifteenth through seventeenth centuries', *Indonesia* 80 (2005), pp. 39-51.

André Gunder Frank, *Reorient*. Berkeley: University of California Press 1988.

A.K.A. Gijsberti Hodenpijl, 'Het ontslag en het opontbod van den gouverneur-generaal Mr. Diederik Durven op 9 october 1731', in: *BKI* 73 (1917), pp. 178-218.

A.K.A. Gijsberti Hodenpijl, 'Gustaaf Willem Baron van lmhoff als Gouverneur van Ceylon, 1736-1740', *BKI* 75 (1919), pp. 481-625.

A.K.A. Gijsberti Hodenpijl, 'De overgang van het bestuur op Ceylon van gouverneur Steven Versluys in handen van Mr. Diederik van Domburgh 1732-1733', in: *Bijdragen voor Vaderlandsche Geschiedenis en Oudheidkunde* (1919), 297-329.

A.K.A. Gijsberti Hodenpijl, 'Govert Cnoll', in: *Tijdschrift voor geschiedenis* (1918) 33: 129-142, 161-182, 225-247.

F. de Haan, *Oud Batavia*. Bandoeng: A.C. Nix & Co. 1935. 2 volumes.

F. de Haan, *Priangan. De Preanger-Regentschappen onder het Nederlandsch Bestuur tot 1811*. Batavia: Bataviaasch Genootschap van Kunsten en Wetenschappen 1910.

C.J.J. van Hall, *Insulinde, de inheemse landbouw*. Deventer: Van Hoeve 1939.

A. Hallema. 'Een vergeten Kaapsche Gouverneur Hendrik Swellengrebel 1739-1751', in: *De Indische Gids* (1932), pp. 5-23.

Onno Zwier van Haren (G.C. de Waard [ed.]), *Agon Sulthan van Bantam (1769)*, 's-Gravenhage: Martinus Nijhoff 1979.

J.E. Heeres, 'De "Consideratiën" van Van lmhoff', in: *BKI* (1912) 66-4: pp. 441-621.

Johann Wolfgang Heydt, *Allerneuester Geographisch- und Topografischer Schau Platz van Africa und Ost-Indien oder Ausfürhrliche and Wahrhafte Vorstellung und Beschreibung, van den Wichtigsten der Holländisch-Ost-Indischen Compagnie in Africa und Asia zugehörigen Ländere, Küsten und lnsulen*. Wilhermsdorff 1744.

B. Hoetink, 'So Bing Kong. Het eerste hoofd der Chinezen te Batavia', in: *Bijdragen tot de Taal-, Land- en Volkenkunde van Nederlandsch lndië*, in: *BKI* (1917) 73: pp. 344-415.

B. Hoetink, 'Chineesche Officieren te Batavia onder de Compagnie', in: *BKI* (1918) 78: 1-136.

B. Hoetink, 'Een Nalezing', in: *BKI* (1923) 79, pp. 1-44.

B. Hoetink, 'De weduwe van Kapitein Siqua – Djanda Kapitein Siqua', in: *Chung Hwa Hui Tsa chih*, vol. 2/1-2, pp. 16-25 en 98-107.

B. Hoetink, 'Ni Hoekong. Kapitein der Chinezen te Batavia in 1740', in: *BKI* (1918) 74: pp. 447-518.

W.R. van Höevell and Pieter Meijer (eds.), 'Chronologische geschiedenis van Batavia, geschreven door een Chinees, uit het Chineesch vertaald door W.H. Medhurst', in: *Tijdschrift voor Nederlandsch-lndië"* (1840) 3-2, 1-145.

W.R. van Höevell, 'Batavia in 1740', *Tijdschrift voor Nederlandsch-lndië"* (1840) 3-1, pp. 447-556.

W.R. van Hoëvell, 'De moord der Chinezen in Batavia', een woord aan den heer A.J. van der Aa', in: *Tijdschrift voor Nederlandsch-Indië"* (1846) 8-3: pp. 113-126.

Hong Dayong, (洪大勇), 后月港时代华商郭商其人其事考 The Chinese merchant Guo Qiao of the late Yuegang-period. An investigation into the man and his work), via: linnazhong.blog.163.com (site discontinued).

Joan van Hoorn, 'Corte Beschryvinge van het Noord-Oostelijckste gedeelte van Java's opkomst ende voortgangh', manuscript KITLV 73. KITLV Collection, Leiden University.

P. van Hoorn, *Eenige voorname eygenschappen van de ware deugdt, voorsichtigheydt, wysheydt en volmaecktheydt. Getrocken uyt den Chineschen Confucius,* Batavia: Johannes van den Eede 1675.

Johannes Huber, 'Chinese settlers against the Dutch East India Company: the rebellion led by Kuo Huai-i on Taiwan in 1652', in: E.B. Vermeer (ed.), *Development and Decline of Fukien Province in the 17th and 18th Centuries.* Leiden: E.J. Brill 1990, pp. 265-296.

J. de Hullu, 'Over den Chinaschen handel der Oost-Indische Compagnie in de eerste dertig jaar van de 18e eeuw', in: *BKI* (1917) 73: pp. 30-151.

J. de Hullu, 'De instelling van de Commissie voor den handel der Oost-Indische Compagnie op China in 1756', in: *Bijdragen tot de Taal-, Land-, en Volkenkunde van Nederlands lndië" BKI* (1923) 79: pp. 523-545.

Arthur W. Hummel (ed.), *Eminent Chinese of the Ch'ing Period (1644-1912).* Washington: US Government Printing Office 1943.

Huddy Husin, 'Ujung Senja Pabrik-Pabrik Gula di Batavia Awal Abad Ke-18', in: *Journal Sosio-E-Kons,* vol. 8, nr. 2 augustus 2016, pp. 139-147.

Ary Huysers, *Beknopte Beschrijving der Oost Indische etablissementen.* Utrecht 1789.

W. ldema, 'Confucius Batavus. Het eerste Nederlandse dichtstuk naar het Chinees', in: *Literatuur* 16 (1999), pp. 85-89.

Fred Jagtenberg, *Willem IV, Stadhouder in roerige tijden 1711-1751.* Nijmegen: Van Tilt 2018.

Els M. Jacobs, *Merchant in Asia, The Trade of the Dutch East India Company during the Eighteenth Century,* Leiden: CNWS Publishers 2006.

Jin Xianlin (transl. Jeff Crosby), *A History of Sugar.* Beijing: New Star Press 2013.

J.K.J. de Jonge, *De Opkomst van het Nederlandsch gezag over Java.* 's-Gravenhage: Martinus Nijhoff, 1862-1909. 13 volumes.

C.J.A. Jörg, *Porselein als handelswaar. De porseleinhandel als onderdeel van de Chinahandel van de VOC, 1729-1794.* Leiden: proefschrift, 1978.

S. Kalff, 'Een koloniaal hervormer', in: *De Indische Gids.* (1894) 1-16, pp. 946-968.

A.R.T. Kemasang, The Chinese Massacre of Chinese in Java: Curtain Raiser for the Dutch Plantation Economy', in: *Bulletin of Concerned Asian Scholars,* vol. 14, 1, 1982, pp. 61-71.

A.R.T. Kemasang. 'How Dutch colonialism foreclosed a domestic bourgeoisie: the 1740 Chinese massacres reappraised' in: *Review* IX-1, 1985, 57-80.

W.M. Keuchenius, *Over de oorzaken der sedert 60 jaren, toegenomen ongezondheid van Batavia en over de middelen van herstel.* Batavia: Bruining en Wijt 1812.

J.W. de Klein, *Het Préangerstelsel (1677-1871) en zijn nawerking.* Delft: Drukkerij J. Waltman 1931.

Gerrit Knaap, Henk den Heijer and Michiel de Jong, *Oorlogen overzee. Militair optreden door Compagnie en staat buiten Europa 1595-1814.* Amsterdam: Boom 2015.

W.P.C. Knuttel, *Catalogus van de pamfletten-verzameling berustende in de Koninklijke Bibliotheek.* Utrecht 1978. (reprint of the original edition of 1889-1920).

A.G.M. Krabbe, 'Overzigt der criminele procedures voor den Raad van Justitie te Batavia, gevoerd tegen den gewezen Gouverneur-generaal A. Valckenier cum suis', in: *Tijdschrift voor Nederlandsch-Indië,* 8 (1846), pp. 1-29.

Jochem Kroes, *Chinese Armorial Porcelain for the Dutch Market*. Zwolle: Waanders Publishers 2007.

H. Kroeskamp, 'De Chinezen te Batavia (1700) als exempel voor de Christenen van West-Europa', in: *Indonesië* (1953) 6: pp. 346-371.

N.J. Krom, *Gouverneur Generaal Gustaaf Willem van Imhoff*. Amsterdam: P.N. van Kampen & zoon 1941.

P.N. Kuiper, *The Early Dutch Sinologists (1854-1900), Training in Holland and China, Functions in the Netherlands Indies*. Leiden: Brill 2017, 2 volumes.

Philip A. Kuhn, *Rebellion and Its Enemies in Late Imperial China. Militarization and Social Structure, 1796-1864*. Cambridge: Harvard University Press 1980.

An Kumar, *Surapati, Man and Legend: A Study of Three Babad Traditions*. Leiden: 1976.

Manjusha Kuruppath, *Dutch Drama and the Company's Orient. A Study of Representation and its Information Circuits, c. 1650-1780*. Unpublished PhD thesis Leiden University 2014.

François Leguat, *De gevaarlijke en zeldzame Reyzen van den Heere F. Leguat met zijn bijhebbend Gezelschap naar twee Onbewoonde Oostindische Eylanden*. Utrecht: Willem Broedelet 1708.

H.S. van Lennep, *Genealogie van het geslacht Valckenier 1512-1934*, Naarden 1983.

Frank Lequin, *Het personeel van de Verenigde Oost-Indische Compagnie te Azië in de achttiende eeuw, meer in het bijzonder in de vestiging Bengalen*. Alphen aan de Rijn: Canaletto/Repro-Holland 2005. 2 volumes.

P.A. Leupe, 'De raden van Indië Van Imhoff, De Hase en Van Schinne in Holland, 1741-1742', in: *BKI* (1859) 6: pp. 361-370.

J.C. van Leur, *Indonesian Trade and Society*. The Hague: W. van Hoeve Publishers 1967.

J.C. van Leur, 'Boekbespreking J.Th. Vermeulen, *De Chineezen te Batavia*' in *Tijdschrift voor Indische Taal-, Land- en Volkenkunde van het het Bataviaasch Genootschap*, deel LXXIX (1939), pp. 147-149.

Claudine en Denys Lombard-Salmon, 'Paysage et exotisme à Batavia, la villa du gouverneur général Valckenier (1737-1741)', in: *Arts Asiatiques* 28-1 (1978), pp. 103-117.

J. de Loos-Haaxman, *Verlaat Rapport Indië, drie eeuwen westerse schilders, tekenaars, grafici, zilversmeden en kunstnijveren in Nederlands-Indië*. 's-Gravenhage: Mouton 1968.

N. MacLeod, 'Uit de geschiedenis der Oost-Indische Compagnie in de 18e eeuw', *Indische Gids* 1908- II: 1291-1300; 1447-1458. 1909 – I: 126-135; 851-860. 1909 – II: 995-1003.

H. van Malsen, *Waterland. Schetsen uit de koloniale en maritieme geschiedenis van het Nederlandsche volk*. Leiden: Sijthoff 1929.

H. van Malsen, *Vederwolken, Historische opstellen*. Leiden: Sijthoff no date.

H. van Malsen, 'Briefwisseling van den Gouverneur-generaal Gustaaf Willem baron van Imhoff met den advocaat-fiscaal der Amsterdamsche Admiraliteit enz.

Jacob Boreel Janszoon (1738-1750)', in: *Bijdragen Mededelingen van het Historisch Genootschap* 50 (1929), pp. 321-426.

H. van Malsen, 'Cultuurstrijd', in: *Algemeen Handelsblad*, 18 november 1930, p. 5.

Jan de Marre, *Batavia, begrepen in zes boeken*. Amsterdam: G. onder de Linden 1740.

Martinus Martini, *De Bello Tartarico Historia, in qua ...* Amsterdam: Johannes Janssonius 1654.

Martinus Martini, *Novus Atlas Sinensis*. Amsterdam: Joan Blaeu 1655.

W.E. van Mastenbroek, *De historische ontwikkeling van de staatsrechtelijke indeeling der bevolking van Nederlandsch-Indië*. Wageningen 1934.

Sucheta Mazumdar, *Sugar and Society in China. Peasants, Technology, and the World Market*. Cambridge, Harvard University Press 1998.

M.A.P. Meilink-Roelofsz, *Asian Trade and European Influence in the Indonesian Archipelago between 1500 and about 1630*. 's-Gravenhage: Martinus Nijhoff 1962.

M.A.P. Meilink-Roelofsz, R. Raben, H. Spijkerman (ed.), *De archieven van de Verenigde Oostindische Compagnie (1602-1795)*. 's-Gravenhage: Sdu Uitgeverij 1992.

P. Meijer, *Verzameling van Jnstructiën, Ordonnanciën en Reglementen voor de Regering van Nederlandsch lndië.* Batavia: Landsdrukkerij 1848.

Norbert Middelkoop, 'Faits divers, enkele illustraties bij de Kroniek van Jacob Bicker Raye (1703-1777)', in: *Jaarboek Amstelodamum* 104 (2012): pp. 8-34.

G.C. Molenwijk (ed.), C.E.S., *'t Verwaerloosde Formosa, of waerachtig verhael, hoedanigh door verwaerloosinge der Nederlanders in Oost-Indien, het eylant Formosa,*

van den Chinesen Mandarijn, ende zeeroover Coxinja, overrompelt, vermeestert, ende ontweldight is geworden. (Linschoten Vereeniging XC), Zutphen: Walburg Pers 1991.

Jacob Mossel, *Aanmerkingen over de zuykermolens rondom Batavia, in 't Bantamse, Ceribonse, en langs Java.* 31 SDecember 1750. Printed essay, NA Archief, Alting 1.10.03, inv. 39.

Jacob Mossel, *Aanmerkingen over Batavia's gesteldheit, in voldoening van de vrage der Heeren Meesters na de oorzake der grote sterfte aldaar, en wat tot redresse en afwending dier plaage zoude konnen dienen.* Printed essay. Batavia 24 June 1753.

Norman M. Naimark, *Genocide: A World History.* Oxford: Oxford University Press 2017.

Luc Nagtegaal, *Riding the Dutch Tiger, The Dutch East India Company and the northeast coast of Java, 1680-1743.* Leiden: KITLV Press 1996.

Ng Chin-keong, 'The case of Ch'en l lao: Maritime trade and overseas Chinese in Ch'ing policies, 1717-1754', in: Roderich Ptak and Dietmar Rothermund (eds.), *Emporia, Commodities and Entrepreneurs in Asian Maritime Trade, c. 1400-1750.* Stuttgart: Franz Steiner Verlag 1991, pp. 373-400.

Hendrik E. Niemeijer, *Batavia. Een koloniale samenleving in de 17de eeuw.* Amsterdam: Uitgeverij Balans 2005.

Hendrik E. Niemeijer, 'The closure of the Bindungan. The Colonial Port City of Batavia and the Contra! over its Primary Hinterland in the Seventeenth Century', unpublished article.

Johan Nieuhof, *Gezandtschap der Neêrlandtsche Oost-Indische Compagnie, aan den grooten Tartarischen Cham, den tegenwoordigen Keizer van China: Waarin de gedenkwaerdigste Geschiedenissen, die onder het reizen door de Sineesche landtschappen, Quantung, Kiangsi, Nanking, Xantung en Peking, en aan het Keizerlijke Hof te Peking, sedert den jaren r655 tot 1657 zijn voorgevallen, op het bondigste verhandelt worden. Beneffens een Naukeurige Beschrijvinge der Sineesche Steden, Dorpen, Regeering, Weetenschappen, Hantwerken, Zeden, Godsdiensten, Gebouwen, Drachten, Schepen, Bergen, Gewassen, Dieren, et cetera en oorlogen tegen de Tartar: verçiert met over de 150 afbeeltsels, na 't leven in Sina getekent.* Amsterdam: Jacob van Meurs 1665.

Erik Odegaard, *Colonial Careers. Johan Maurits van Nassau-Siegen, Rijcklof Volkertsz. Van Goens and Career-Making in the Seventeenth-Century Dutch Empire.* Unpublished PhD-thesis, Leiden 2018 (DISL 2018 404).

W.M. Ottow, *Rijcklof Volckertsz van Goens. De carrière van een diplomaat 16199-1655.* Utrecht: Pressa Trajectina 1954.

James Bunyan Parsons, *Peasant Rebellions of the Late Ming Dynasty.* The Association for Asian Studies: Monographs and Papers, nr. XXIV 1970.

E. du Perron, *De muze van Jan Compagnie.* Bandoeng: A.C. Nix 1948. M. Peters, *De wijze koopman. Het wereldwijde onderzoek van Nicolaes Witsen (1641-1717), burgemeester en VOC-bewindhebber van Amsterdam,* Amsterdam 2010.

Nonja Peters, *The Christian Slaves of Depok. A Colonial Tale Unravels.* Newcastle: Cambridge Scholars Publishing 2021.

Bauke van der Pol *(ed.), Mallabaarse Brieven. De brieven van de Friese predikant Jacobus Canter Visscher 1717-1725.* Zutphen: Walburg Pers 2008.

Wibowo Priyanto, *‚Struktur Sosial dan Aktivitas Ekonomi Politik Etnis Cina di Jawa Sesudah Kerusuhan Batavia 1740‘*, in: The 5th International Conference on Jndonesian Studies: Ethnicity and Globalization, diadakan oleh FIB UI di Yogyakarta 13-14 juni 2013.

Remco Raben, *Batavia and Colombo. The Ethnic and Social Spatial Order of Two Colonial Cities 1600-1800.* Unpublished PhD thesis Leiden University 1996.

Remco Raben, 'De Chinese Oorlog in Batavia in 1740', in: J.Th. Lindblad and A. Schrikker (eds.), *Het verre gezicht. Politieke en culturele relaties tussen Nederland en Azië, Afrika en Amerika.* Franeker: Van Wijnen 2011, pp. 106-123.

Remco Raben, 'Colonial shorthand and historical knowledge: Segregation in a Dutch colonial society', in: *Journal of Modern European History (2020)*, pp. 177-193.

Realia, Register op de Generale Resolutiën van het Kasteel Batavia 1632-1805. Leiden: Kolff 1882, 3 volumes.

J.J. Reese, *De suikerhandel van Amsterdam van het begin der 17e eeuw tot 1813.* Haarlem: J.L.E.L Kleynenberg 1908.

Anthony Reid (ed.), *Slavery, Bondage and Dependency in Southeast Asia.* St Lucia: University of Queensland Press 1983.

Anthony Reid, *Southeast Asia in the Age of Commerce 1450-1680.* New Haven: Yale University Press 1988,1993, 2 volumes.

W.G.J. Remmelink, *The Chinese War and the Collapse of the Javanese State, 1725-1743.* Leiden: KITLV Press 1994.

W.G.J. Remmelink, 'De worsteling om Java', in: Gerrit Knaap and Ger Teitler (eds.), *De Verenigde Oost-Indische Compagnie tussen oorlog en diplomatie.* Leiden: KITLV 2002, pp. 337-354.

W.G.J. Remmelink, *Babad Tanah Jawi. The Chronicle of Java. The revised Prose Version of C.F. Winter* Sr. Leiden: Leiden University Press 2022.

M.A. van Rhede van der Kloot, *De Gouverneurs-Generaal en Commissarissen-Generaal van Nederlandsch-Indië 1610-1888.* 's-Gravenhage: Van Stockum 1891.

M.C. Ricklefs, *War, Culture and Economy in Java 1677-1726. Asian and European Imperialism in the early Kartasura period.* Sydney: Allen and Unwin 1993.

M.C. Ricklefs, *The Seen and Unseen Worlds in Java 1726-1749. History, Literature and Islam in the Court of Pakubuwana 11.* Honolulu: University of Hawaii Press 1998.

M.C. Ricklefs, 'De Verenigde Oost-Indische Compagnie en de gewelddadige wereld van het vroegmoderne Azië', in: Gerrit Knaap and Ger Teitler (eds.), *De Verenigde Oost-Indische Compagnie tussen oorlog en diplomatie.* Leiden: KITLV 2002, 355-378.

Ronald Robinson, 'Non-European foundations of European imperialism: Sketch for a theory of collaboration', in: Roger Owen and Bob Sutcliffe (eds.), *Studies in the Theory of Imperialism,* Londen: Longman 1972, 117-140.

Vibeke Roeper en Roelof van Gelder, *In dienst van de Compagnie. Leven bij de VOC in honderd getuigenissen [1602-1799].* Amsterdam: Athenaeum-Polak & Van Gennep 2002.

P. de Roo de la Faille, 'De Chineesche Raad te Batavia en het door dit college beheerde fonds', in: *BKI* (1924) 80: pp. 302-324.

John Roosa, *Pretext for Mass Murder. The September 30th Movement and Suharto's Coup d'État in Indonesia.* Madison: University of Wisconsin Press 2006.

Matthias van Rossum, *Kleurrijk tragiek. De geschiedenis van slavernij in Azië onder de VOC.* Hilversum: Verloren 2015.

J. Rusconi, *Sjaír Kompeni welanda berberang dengan Tjina.* Wageningen: Veenman & Zonen 1935.

Claudine Salmon en Denys Lombard, *Les Chinois de Jakarta. Temples et vie collective.* Paris: Editions de la Maison des Sciences de l'homme 1980.

Claudine Salmon, 'Un Chinois à Java (1729-1736)', in: *Bulletin de l'école française d'extrême-Orient,* volume 59 (1972), pp. 279-318.

Georg Bernhardt Schwarz von Beutelspach, *Reise in Ost-Indien, worinnen mancherlei Merkwürdigkeiten, besonders aber die Anno 1740 in seiner Anwesenheit zu Batavia fürgefallene Rebellion der Chinesen, und derselben darauf erfolgte grosse Massacre umständlich und aufrichtig beschrieben worden.* Frankfurt and Leipzig 1748.

G.J. Schutte (ed.), *Seer teder beminde heer vader en vrouw moeder! Brieven van de Groninger familie Fockens in de Oost, 1748-1783.* Hilversum: Uitgeverij Verloren 2014.

J. Semmelink, *Geschiedenis der cholera in Oost-Indië voor 1817.* Utrecht: C.H.E. Breijer 1885.

Henry Sidney, *Diary of the Times of Charles the Second by the honourable Henry Sidney, Envoy to the States of Holland.* Londen 1843.

Timothy Snyder, *Bloedlanden. Europa tussen Hitler en Stalin.* Amsterdam: Ambo/Anthos 2011.

R. Soesilo, 'Malariabestrijding in den Oost-Indischen Archipel', *Feestbundel 1936. Geneeskundig Tijdschrift voor Nederlandsch-Indië.* Batavia: Kolff 1936, 45-72.

F.W. Stapel, *Geschiedenis van Nederlandsch-Indië.* Amsterdam: Meulenhoff 1930.

F.W. Stapel, *De Gouverneurs-generaal van Nederlandsch-Indië in beeld en woord.* 's-Gravenhage: W.P. van Stockum 1941.

F.W. Stapel (ed.), *Pieter van Dam. Beschryvinge van de Oostindische Compagnie,* RGP Grote Serie No. 63, 68, 74, 75, 76, 83, 87, 96, 's-Gravenhage: Martinus Nijhoff 1927-1954, 8 volumes.

F.W. Stapel, Hans Martin and H. Hoohenberk (eds.), *Indië schrijft zijn eigen geschiedenis.* Amsterdam: Elsevier 1945. 76-77, 90-91, 94-95.

A.W. Stellwagen, 'Gustaaf Willem Baron van Imhoff's Plakkaatboek 28 mei 1743-1 november 1750', in: *Indische Gids* II (1889), pp. 1384-1404.

Guillermo Ruiz Stovel, 'A Bloody Prelude: Chinese Uprisings in Spanish Manila, 1603-1689'. Master thesis History Department, Harvard University 2007.

Lilie Suratminto, 'Pembantaian Etnis Cina di Batavia 1740: Dampak Konflik Golongan "Prinsgezinden" dan "Staatsgezinden" di Belanda', *Wacana* vol. 6, nr. 1. april 2004, pp. 1-26.

Johan Talens, *Een feodale samenleving in koloniaal vaarwater. Staatsvorming, koloniale expansie en economische onderontwikkeling in Banten, West-Java* (1600-1750). Hilversum: Verloren 1999.

Tan Yeok Seong, *The Chinese in Batavia and the Troubles of* r740. Singapore: South Seas Society 1953.

Stephen F. Teiser, *The Ghost Festival in Medieval China.* Princeton: Princeton University Press 1988.

Patricia Tjiook-Liem, *De rechtspositie der Chinezen in Nederlands-Indië 1848-1942,* Leiden: Leiden University Press 2009.

Frederick Jackson Turner, 'The significance of the Frontier in American history', in: *The Annual Report of the American Historical Association for the Year* 1893, pp. 199-207.

R.P.J. Tutein Nolthenius, *Het geslacht Nolthenius.* Haarlem: Johan Enschedé 1930.

Adriaan Valckenier, 'Brief aan den keizer van China, geschreeven binnen het Kasteel van de Stad Batavia op den 30 dag van de Maand April, in het Jaar 1741', in: S. Kalff (ed.), *Oost-Indisch Landjuweel.* Haarlem: H.D. Tjeenk Willink 1902, pp. 180-183.

Hester J.E.M.C. Valckenier Kips, 'Valckenieren, fonteinen en forten, het Valckenier wapenporselein en grisaille', in: *Vormen uit Vuur* 244 (October 2020), pp. 9-15.

François Valentijn, *Oud en Nieuw Oost-Indiën.* Dordrecht: Joannes van Braam 1724-1727, 5 volumes.

W. de Veer, *Particuliere landerijen en de openbare veiligheid in de residentie Batavia.* Batavia: Javasche Boekhandel 1904.

Gerret Vermeulen, *Gedenkwaardige Voyagie naar Oost-Indiën 1668-1674.* Hoorn: Jan Claesz. 1677.

J.Th. Vermeulen, *De Chineezen te Batavia en de troebelen van 1740.* Leiden: Eduard IJdo 1938.

Bernard H.M. Vlekke, *Nusantara. A History of Indonesia.* Bruxelles: Les Editions A. Manteau 1961.

Joost van den Vondel, *Zunchin of de ondergang van de Sineesche Maatschappye.* Amsterdam 1667.

J.W. de Vries, 'De Depokkers: geschiedenis, sociale structuur en taalgebruik van een geïsoleerde gemeenschap', in: *BKI* 132, pp. 228-248.

Willem Vrijhoff, 'Traumatische herinnering. Bij wijze van inleiding', in: *Leidschrift* 3, 28 (December 2013), pp. 7-24.

Lodewijk Wagenaar, Anke Galjaard, Marianne Nierop, Marleen Speelman (eds.), *Gouverneur Van lmhoff op dienstreis in 1739. Naar Cochin, Travancore en Tuticorin, en terug over Jaffna en Mannar naar Colombo (zondag 25 januari tot zaterdag 18 april).* Zutphen: Walburg Pers 2007.

V.I. van de Wall, *Vrouwen uit den Compagnie's tijd.* Weltevreden 1928.

V.I. van de Wall, *Figuren en feiten uit den Compagniestijd.* Bandoeng: A.C. Nix 1932.

J.C.M. Warnsinck (ed.), *Reisen van Nicolaus de Graaff. Gedaan naar alle gewesten des Werelds. Beginnende van 1639 rot 1687 incluis, Oost Indise Spiegel.* Linschoten Vereeniging, nr. xxxiii, 's-Gravenhage: Martinus Nijboff 1930.

W. Wijnaendts van Resandt, *De Gezaghebbers der Oost-lndische Compagnie op hare Buiten-Comptoiren in Azië.* Amsterdam: Uitgeverij Liebaert 1944.

Arthur Westeijn. 'The VOC as a company-state, debating seventeenth-century Dutch colonial expansion' in *Itinerario,* XXXVIII, nr. I, 2014, 13-34.

Bodo Wiethoff, *Die Chinesische Seeverbotspolitik und der private Überseehandel von 1368 bis 1567.* Wiesbaden: Otto Harrassowitz 1963.

John E. Wills, Jr., *Pepper, Guns, & Parleys. The Dutch East India Company and China, 1662-1681.* Cambridge: Harvard University Press 1974.

John E. Wills, *Embassies and Illusions. Dutch and Portuguese Envoys to K'anghsi, 1666-1687.* Cambridge: Harvard University Press 1984.

Eric Wolf, *Peasant Wars of the Twentieth Century.* New York: Harper Torch Books 1961.

Xu Guanmian, *Pepper to Sea Cucumbers. Chinese Gustatory Revolution in Global History, 900-1840.* Unpublished PhD thesis Leiden University 2021

Xu Guanmian, 'The "Perfect Map" of widow Hiamtse: A Micro-spatial history of Sugar Plantations in Early Modem Southeast Asia, 1685-1710', in: *International Review of Social History,* vol. 67, nr. 1 April 2022 pp. 97-126.

Ardhi Yudhistira, Amsia Tontowi and M. Syaiful, 'Pengaruh Terjadinya Tragedi Angke Tahun 1740 Terhadap Bidang Sosial Ekonomi di Batavia', in: *Journal of Pesagi,* Vol. 1, nr. 6, 2013.

Kees Zandvliet, *De 500 Rijksten van de Republiek. Rijkdom, geloof, macht & cultuur.* Zutphen: Walburg Pers 2018.

Zhangzhou fuzhi (漳州府志, Zhangzhou Gazetteer), 1878.

Zhang Xie, *Dong-Xiyang kao* (张燮, 东西洋考, A Treatise of the Eastern and Western Oceans). Beijing: Zhonghua Shuju 1981.

Suze Zijlstra, 'Het vervloekt en schelms verraadt, beeldvorming en schuld in de berichtgeving over de Chinezenmoord van 1740 in Batavia', in: *Skript: historisch tijdschrift,* 31-2: 83-95.

Zhou Kai, *Xiamen zhi* (周凯 厦门志, Amoy Gazetteer, 1839) 5 volumes, Taibei: Qinghua Shuju 1961.

Illustration Credits

Foto section 1

Page 81: Map c. 1725–1751, unknown artist. Rijksmuseum nr. RP-P-OB-75-359,03

Page 82: above: date and artist unknown, collection Matsura Historical Museum; below: private collection author

Page 83: print c. 1160, made by Wouter Schouten, collection Rijksmuseum, nr. RP-T-1964-354 (V)

Page 84: print c. 1160, made by Wouter Schouten, collection Rijksmuseum, nr. RP-T-1964-351 (R)

Page 85: above: made by Auguste van Pers, Collection University Library Leiden, nr. KITLV37A22; below: painting c. 1640–1660, made by Andries Beeckman, collection Rijksmuseum, nr. SK-A-4070

Page 86: Map c. 1744, made by Johann Wolfgang Heydt, collection Wikimedia Commons, Koninklijke Bibliotheek, Atlas van der Hagen Part 4, nr. 1049B13_020

Page 87: above: collection and photo Hendrik E. Niemeijer; below: private collection author

Page 88: above and below: drawings made by Johannes Rach (1720–1783), from Johannes Rach and his work (Batavia: Kolff, 1928), collection Koninklijke Bibliotheek/Delpher

Foto section 2

Page 161: above: painting 1737, made by Theodorus Justinus Rheen, collection Rijksmuseum, nr. SK-A-3778; below: private collection

Page 162–163: Map dated 1754, after a drawing by I. van Ryne, collection Rijksmuseum, nr. RP-P-1921-693

Page 164: above and below: drawings made by Johannes Rach (1720–1783), from Johannes Rach and his work (Batavia: Kolff, 1928), collection Koninklijke Bibliotheek/Delpher

Page 165: drawing c. 1779–1785, made by Jan Brandes, collection Rijksmuseum nr. NG-1985-7-2-5

Page 166–167: drawing c. 1740–1784, unknown artist, collection Atlas van Stolk, inv.nr. 17290

Page 167: drawing c. 1740–1784, made by Simon Fokke, collection Rijksmuseum, nr. RP-T-00-3253

Page 168: above: Painting c. 1745, unknown artist, collection Rijksmuseum, nr. SK-A-3780; below: private collection author

Index of Names

Printed in the United States
by Baker & Taylor Publisher Services